The
Song
Of
Solomon

The
Song
Of
Solomon

George Burrowes

Sovereign Grace Publishers, Inc.
P.O. Box 4998
Lafayette, IN 47903

Printed In the United States of America
By Lightning Source, Inc.

The
Song
Of
Solomon

George Burrowes

Sovereign Grace Publishers, Inc.
P.O. Box 4998
Lafayette, IN 47903

Printed In the United States of America
By Lightning Source, Inc.

TO THE

Rev. JOHN C. BACKUS, D. D.,

PASTOR OF THE FIRST PRESBYTERIAN CHURCH OF BALTIMORE,

THIS VOLUME IS INSCRIBED

WITH EVERY FEELING OF REGARD.

CONTENTS

PAGE

FOREWORD 7

GEORGE BURROWES, D.D. . . . 9

PREFACE 11

SUMMARY OF THE SONG 13

TRANSLATION.

    CHAPTER I. 17

    CHAPTER II. 18

    CHAPTER III. 20

    CHAPTER IV. 21

    CHAPTER V. 23

    CHAPTER VI. 25

    CHAPTER VII. 26

    CHAPTER VIII. 28

ANALYSIS OF THE SONG.

    CHAPTER I. 31

    CHAPTER II. 36

    CHAPTER III. 42

    CHAPTER IV. 46

    CHAPTER V. 51

    CHAPTER VI. 55

    CHAPTER VII. 59

    CHAPTER VIII. 61

CONTENTS

COMMENTARY ON THE SONG.

CHAPTER I. 67

CHAPTER II. 180

CHAPTER III. 244

CHAPTER IV. 273

CHAPTER V. 324

CHAPTER VI. 371

CHAPTER VII. 392

CHAPTER VIII. 419

PUBLISHERS' NOTE

It has been decided to omit the long introduction, in order to reduce the cost of the volume.

FOREWORD

There is probably no book in the Bible which is so neglected as The Song of Solomon. There are many reasons for this.

The "higher" critics regard it as but the love song or poem of a king, written to one of his loves when he was probably under the influence of wine. They feel that it should not be in the Bible at all, that it has no spiritual value whatsoever, and that it is scarcely a fit book for good and moral people to read. It is not surprising therefore that they should neglect it.

But there are many who, while totally rejecting such a view, nevertheless neglect this book because they find it difficult to understand. They cannot see the meaning of the imagery and often find themselves in difficulties as to the exact speaker. They feel that it has a message but they cannot find it.

Contrasted with these there are those who regard this book as a mine of spiritual treasure and as one of the most exquisite expositions of the relationship between the believer and his Lord to be found anywhere in the Bible. Such, for instance, was the view taken of it by J. Hudson Taylor, the founder of the China Inland Mission, and his little book expounding it called "Union and Communion" is of great value.

Clearly, therefore, the average Christian needs help in order to be able to enter into this rich enjoyment.

It is because I know of nothing which in any way approaches this commentary in that respect that I am glad that it is being re-printed and made available.

It has everything that should characterize a good commentary—learning and scholarship, accuracy and carefulness, but, above all, and more important than all else, true spiritual insight and understanding. It provides a key to the understanding of the whole and of every verse which the humblest Christian can easily follow.

I predict that all who read it and study it will agree with me in saying that they have never read anything more uplifting and heart-warming. It will lead them to their Lord and enable them to know and to realize His love as they have never done before.

D. M. LLOYD-JONES

WESTMINSTER CHAPEL,
    LONDON.

GEORGE BURROWES, D.D.

George Burrowes, an eminent American divine of the last century, was born at Trenton, New Jersey, on April 3rd, 1811. He was educated at Princeton College where he graduated in 1832. Like so many others who became leaders in the North American churches he took his ministerial training at Princeton Theological Seminary, under the supervision of such distinguished teachers as Archibald Alexander and Charles Hodge. After leaving the Seminary in 1835 he entered his first pastorate at West Nottingham, Md., where he remained till 1850. In that year he was appointed professor of Latin and Greek at Lafayette College, Easton, Penn., and three years later he received his doctorate of divinity from Washington College. From 1857 to 1859 Burrowes was pastor of Newtown Presbyterian Church, Penn. In 1859 he was called to the west coast of America, and there he appears to have spent the remainder of his life being principally concerned in preparing men for the ministry. He built up the City College, San Francisco, during the years 1859-1865; was principal of the University Mound boarding-school near San Francisco, 1870-73; and finally became the first professor of Hebrew and Greek at the Presbyterian Theological Seminary, which was founded at San Francisco in 1872.

Such are all the facts we have been able to obtain. The time and manner of Burrowes' conversion, his spiritual experiences, his family, his closing years and date of death, these are all matters of which we have found no record. If any reader can provide the Publishers with such information they would be glad to include it in any future edition of this re-print.

Happily Burrowes' once famous commentary is now being retrieved from the oblivion in which it has long lain, and it will, after all, prove to be his best epitaph. This work was first published in Philadelphia in 1853 and by 1861 a third edition was called for. Although it was highly spoken of in this country by C. H. Spurgeon, Dr. Moody Stuart and others, it appears that this is the first British edition. This no doubt accounts for the extreme rarity of the book. Burrowes' other writings consisted of a selection of poems, published in 1856, and a treatise entitled "Advanced Growth in Grace", published in 1885 at San Francisco.

PREFACE.

THE notes which have grown into the following pages were begun amid the pious exercises and duties connected with the pastoral charge of a retired congregation, and without any idea of making a volume for the press. They have gradually taken their present form. The Analysis now stands, with no material alteration, as it was written some years ago; and subsequent research has brought to light no reason for changing the views then adopted concerning the general meaning of this portion of Scripture. To those who consider the misapprehension that has prevailed in reference to the Song, the Introduction may not seem unnecessarily long, inasmuch as an answer to objections, an argument in defence of the allegorical meaning, and a statement of the principles of interpretation, are required before proceeding to the exposition. The Summary and Analysis give the writer's idea of the meaning of the Song. In the exposition, the aim has been to unfold the truth, in the way supposed the most desirable to a soul animated with fervent love for the Lord Jesus, and craving the hidden manna which the Holy Spirit has lodged in this precious portion of the Scriptures. The heart hungering and thirsting for righteousness, does not rest satisfied with the stalk and husks, but is anxious for the luscious kernel, of these fruits of eternal life. As here viewed, the Song is a continuous and coherent whole, illustrating some of the most exalted and delightful exercises of the believing heart. According to our exposition, there will not be found in the book a single passage to which the most fastidious taste can take the least exception. A correct interpretation of the book is its only proper vindication. Those who engage in the work of Scripture exposition, become best aware of the difficulties of the undertaking; and while the writer is sensible of the difficulty attending a Commentary on the Song, and submits this volume with diffidence to those who love the adorable Redeemer, he shall be happy if any thing has been done, in however humble a degree, for enabling them to value this book, and draw herefrom truth for nourishing a more vigorous affection for their Beloved and their Friend.

EASTON, *May* 1, 1853.

SUMMARY OF THE SONG.

THIS Book consists of three parts: The first includes chapter i. verse 1; chapter ii. verse 7. The second extends from chapter ii. verse 8, to chapter vii. verse 9. The third includes the remainder of the book, chapter vii. verse 10, to chapter viii. verse 14.

I. The way in which the soul longing for the manifestation of the love of Christ is led along in the gratification of that desire, from one degree to another of pious enjoyment, until attaining the greatest delight possible for the saint in the present world. Chap. i. 1; chap. ii. 7.

These periods of enjoyment are separated by vicissitudes of fortune and diversity of feeling, through which the believer is brought to those more cheering scenes in his progress to heaven. These seasons may be repeated in our experience, some of them more than once, before we attain those which succeed. 1. We enjoy the love of Jesus, as manifested in pri-

vate communion, in "his chambers." Chap. i. 4.
2. In the way of duty and self-denial. Chap. i. 7—11.
3. In sitting with the King in the circle of his friends,
and enjoying, as one of them, the delights of social
communion with him. Chap. i. 12—14. 4. In delightful repose with him amid enlarged prospects of
spiritual beauty. Chap. i. 15—17. 5. In the protection and delights set forth in chap. ii. 1—3. 6. And
in enjoying, at last, the pleasures mentioned in chap.
ii. 4—7, the greatest possible on earth.

II. An exhibition of motives by which the Lord
Jesus would allure such soul away from the present
world, for being with him in glory. Chap. ii. 8; chap.
vii. 9.

As we are treated throughout our redemption and
discipline here, like beings possessing a will, the spiritual decays and sluggishness into which we are liable
to fall, must be counteracted by the presentation of
powerful motives to the mind; and our faith can be
best matured by strengthening the soul, as is done in
these periods of great enjoyment, and then leaving us
in that strength, without such sensible pleasures, to
manifest our steadfastness by struggling against difficulty and the absence of Jesus, by dependence on his
word and promises and love. Hence our Lord allures
us—

1. By the beauty of heaven, as a place he has prepared for us, and where he is awaiting us. Chap. ii.
8—17.

2. By the splendour of the reception awaiting us

there, no less than by the security and grandeur of our conveyance towards glory. Chap. iii. 1—11.

3. By his great love for us—an affection so intense as to be incapable of being fully expressed by the strongest illustrations, and so strong as to remain constant even amid our neglect. Chap. iv. 1; chap. vii. 9.

III. The effect produced on the heart of the saint by these manifestations of love, and by these motives. Chap. vii. 10; chap. viii. 14. 1. Assurance of hope. Chap. vii. 10. 2. Desire to be much alone in communion with Christ. Chap. vii. 11. 3. Willingness to engage in labours of holiness and love. Verse 12. 4. Consecration to him of our best and most valued gifts and possessions. Verse 13. 5. Desire that every thing hindering the full interchange of affection between Jesus and our soul may be removed. Chap. viii. 1—2. 6. The desire to guard against every sin and every act at all likely to cause the withdrawal of Jesus's love. Verse 3—4. 7. The pleasing consciousness of leaning on Jesus, and of being upheld by his everlasting arms. Verse 5. 8. Desire to lie continually near the heart of Jesus, and to be sustained by his power. Verse 6. 9. Willingness to sacrifice every thing coming between us and Christ. Verse 6. 10. A conviction of the meanness of every thing the world could offer for bribing us to renounce Christ. Verse 7. 11. An interest for the salvation of the impenitent. Verse 8—10. 12. A sense of our accountability as stewards of God, holding our property and our all in trust. Verse 12. 13. The privilege of access continually to the throne of grace, with full encouragement from our Lord for addressing to him our voices in prayer and praise. Verse 13. 14. The desire for the completion of our redemption, and for the perfecting of his love to us and of our love to him, by the second coming of our Lord. Verse 14.

TRANSLATION.

CHAPTER I.

Ver. 1. The Song of songs which is Solomon's.

Spouse.

2. O that he would give me kisses of his love:
  For thy love is more delicious than wine.
3. Thy perfumes are rich in fragrance;
  Thy name is perfume poured forth;
  Therefore the virgins love thee.
4. Draw me; we will run after thee:
  The king hath brought me into his apartments:
  We will be glad and rejoice in thee;
  We will cherish a more pleasing remembrance of thy
    love than of wine;
  They love thee sincerely.
5. Dark am I but lovely, O ye daughters of Jerusalem,
  As the tents of Kedar, as the pavilions of Solomon.
6. Look not on me, I am dark,
  Because the sun hath browned me;
  My mother's children were ill-disposed towards me;
  They made me the keeper of the vineyards;
  My own vineyard have I not kept.
7. Tell me, O thou whom my soul loveth,
  Where thou feedest? where thou makest thy flock to
    rest at noon?
  For why should I be as one veiled,*
  Among the flocks of thy companions?

* Regarded as a harlot.

BELOVED.

8. If thou know not, O thou fairest among women,
   Go forth in the footsteps of the flock,
   And feed thy kids beside the shepherds' tents.
9. I compare thee, O my love,
   To my chariot-steed from Pharaoh.
10. Thy cheeks are beautiful with rows of jewels:
    Thy neck with strings of pearls,.
11. Gold chains will we make for thee,
    Adorned with studs of silver.

SPOUSE.

12. While the king sitteth in the circle of his friends,
    My spikenard diffuses its fragrance.
13. An amulet of myrrh is my beloved to me,
    Which shall continually abide in my bosom.
14. A bouquet of cypress flowers is my beloved to me,
    From the garden fields of Engedi.

BELOVED.

15. Behold, thou art beautiful, my love,
    Behold, thou art beautiful; thine eyes are doves.

SPOUSE.

16. Behold, thou art beautiful, my beloved, yea attractive;
    And the green, flowery turf is our place of repose.
17. The roof of our summer-house is cedars,
    Our carved ceiling firs.

CHAPTER II.

1. I am the rose of Sharon,
   A lily of the valleys.

BELOVED.

2. As a lily among the thorns,
   So is my love among the daughters.

SPOUSE.

3. As a citron tree among trees of the forest,
   So is my beloved among the sons.
   In his shade I delight to sit,
   And his fruit is sweet to my taste.
4. He brings me into the banqueting-house,
   And his banner over me is love.
5. Revive me with cordials,
   Refresh me with citrons,
   For I am sick of love.
6. His left hand is under my head,
   And his right hand doth embrace me:
7. I charge you, O ye daughters of Jerusalem,
   By the gazelles and by the hinds of the field,
   That ye rouse not and disturb not
   My love, till he please.
8. Hark! my beloved: behold, there he comes
   Leaping over the mountains, bounding over the hills.
9. My beloved is like a gazelle, or a beauteous fawn.
   See! he is standing behind our wall;
   He is looking in through the window;
   He is throwing sparkling glances from behind the lattice.
10. My beloved begins to speak, and says to me;
    Arise, my companion, my beautiful one, and come away.
11. For, lo, the winter is past,
    The rain is over and gone.
12. The flowers appear on the earth,
    The time of singing of birds has come,
    And the voice of the turtle-dove is heard in our land.
13. The fig-tree is distilling aromatic juice into its green figs;
    And the vines in blossom are sending forth fragrance:
    Arise, come, my companion, my beautiful one, come
        away.
14. O my dove, in refuges of the rock,
    In a hiding-place of the precipice,
    Let me see thy countenance,
    Let me hear thy voice;
    For sweet is thy voice, and thy countenance lovely.

9

15. Take for us the foxes,
    The little foxes which destroy the vines;
    For our vineyard is in bloom.
16. My beloved is mine, and I am his;
    He feeds among the lilies.
17. Until the day break, and the shadows flee away,
    Return my beloved,
    Like a gazelle, or a beauteous fawn,
    Over the craggy mountains.

CHAPTER III.

1. On my couch, in the night,
   I seek him whom my soul loveth,
   I seek him but find him not.
2. I will arise now, and I will go about in the city;
   In the streets and in the public squares,
   I will seek him whom my soul loveth:
   I seek him and I find him not.
3. The watchmen who go around in the city found me;
   "Saw ye him whom my soul loveth?"
4. Hardly had I passed them,
   When I found him whom my soul loveth.
   I laid hold on him and would not let him go,
   Till I had brought him to the house of my mother,
   Into the apartment of her that bore me.
5. I charge you, O ye daughters of Jerusalem,
   By the gazelles and by the hinds of the field,
   That ye rouse not and disturb not
   My love, till he please.

Daughters of Jerusalem.

6. Who is this coming up from the wilderness,
   Like pillars of smoke,

Surrounded with the perfume of myrrh, and frankincense,
And all kinds of aromatic dust from the perfumer?

7. Lo, it is the palanquin of Solomon:
Around it are threescore valiant men,
The most valiant of Israel;

8. All of them with sword in hand, experienced in war,
Each with his sword girded on, against peril in the night.

9. A palanquin Solomon the king made for himself
Of the wood of Lebanon:

10. Its pillars he made of silver,
Its railing of gold, its seat purple,
The midst of it being tesselated with love,
For the daughters of Jerusalem.

11. Go forth, ye daughters of Zion,
And behold king Solomon,
With the crown with which his mother crowned him
On the day of his espousals,
On the day of gladness of his heart.

CHAPTER IV.

BELOVED.

1. Behold thou art beautiful, my companion, thou art
beautiful:
Doves are thine eyes within thy locks;
Thy hair is as a flock of goats
Which lie along downwards from mount Gilead.

2. Thy teeth as a flock of the same size,
Which come up from the washing-pool,
All of them bearing twins,
And none of them without its young.

3. Thy lips are like a thread of scarlet;
And thy mouth beautiful.
Like a piece of pomegranate,
Are thy cheeks within thy tresses.

4. Thy neck is like the tower of David
Built for an armory;
A thousand shields are hanging on it,
All bucklers of the mighty.

5. Thy two breasts are like two fawns,
Twins of a gazelle, feeding among the lilies.

6. Until the day break and the shadows flee away,
I will betake me to the mountain of myrrh and to the
hill of frankincense.

7. Thou art all beautiful, my companion;
And no spot is there in thee.

8. Come with me from Lebanon, my spouse,
With me from Lebanon;
Look from the top of Amana,
From the top of Shenir and Hermon,
From the dens of lions, from the mountains of leopards.

9. Thou hast ravished my heart, my sister-spouse,
Thou hast ravished my heart with one of thine eyes,
With one fold of thy necklace.

10. How beautifully delightful is thy love, my sister-spouse;
How much more delicious is thy love than wine,
And the fragrance of thy perfumes than all spices.

11. Thy lips drop as the honey-comb, my spouse:
Honey and milk are under thy tongue;
And the fragrance of thy garments is as the fragrance
of Lebanon.

12. A garden enclosed is my sister-spouse;
A spring shut up, a fountain sealed.

13. Thy productions are a paradise of pomegranates,
With delicious fruits, cypresses with spikenards,

14. Spikenard and crocus, calamus and cinnamon,
With all trees of frankincense;
Myrrh and aloes with all chief spices;

15. A fountain of gardens, a well of living waters,
And streams from Lebanon.

SPOUSE.

16. Arise, O north wind; and come thou south;
    Blow upon my garden that its perfumes may flow forth.
    Let my beloved come into his garden,
    And enjoy its delicious fruits.

---◇---

CHAPTER V.

BELOVED.

1. I have come into my garden, my sister-spouse;
   I am gathering my myrrh with my spice;
   I am eating my honey-comb with my honey;
   I am drinking my wine with my milk:
   Eat, O friends, drink,
   Yea, beloved companions, drink abundantly.

SPOUSE.

2. I was sleeping, but my heart was awake:
   Hark! the voice of my beloved! he is knocking:
   "Open to me, my sister, my companion,
   My dove, my perfect one;*
   For my head is filled with dew,—
   My locks with drops of the night."
3. I have put off my dress,
   How shall I put it on?
   I have washed my feet,
   How shall I soil them?
4. My beloved withdrew his hand from the aperture in the
        door;
   And my heart was moved towards him.

* Equivalent to our expression, "My angel."
        9*

5. I arose for opening to my beloved,
   And my hands dropped myrrh,
   And my fingers liquid myrrh,
   On the handles of the bolt.
6. I opened to my beloved;
   But my beloved had turned and gone away.
   My heart sunk in consequence of what he had said:
   I sought him, and found him not:
   I called him, and he answered me not.
7. The watchmen who go around in the city found me,
   They smote me, they wounded me;
   The guards of the walls stripped my veil from me.
8. I charge you, O ye daughters of Jerusalem,
   If ye shall find my beloved—
   What shall ye tell him?
   That I am sick of love.

DAUGHTERS OF JERUSALEM.

9. What is thy beloved more than another beloved,
   Thou most beautiful of women?
   What is thy beloved more than another beloved,
   That thou dost thus charge us?

SPOUSE.

10. My beloved is white and ruddy,
    Conspicuous among a host.
11. His head is finest choice gold;
    His locks young waving palm branches, black as the
       raven:
12. His eyes as doves by valley rills of water,
    Washed in milk, reposing by the full water springs:
13. His cheeks as banks of fragrant flowers,
    As towering trellises covered with aromatic blooms;
    His lips lilies distilling liquid myrrh:
14. His hands rollers of gold, set with the beryl;
    His body wrought ivory overlaid with sapphires.
15. His legs pillars of white marble
    Fixed on pedestals of fine gold;

His appearance is as Lebanon,
Pre-eminently noble as the cedars:
16. His voice is exquisitely sweet;
His whole being is constituted of delightful **attractions**:
This is my beloved, and this is my friend,
O daughters of Jeru alem.

CHAPTER VI.

DAUGHTERS OF JERUSALEM.

1. Whither has thy beloved gone, thou most beautiful of
women?
Whither has thy beloved turned away?
Tell, that we may seek him with thee.

SPOUSE.

2. My beloved has gone down to his garden,
To the banks of fragrant flowers,
To feed in the gardens, and to gather lilies.
3. I am my beloved's, and my beloved is mine,
Who feeds among the lilies.

BELOVED.

4. Beautiful as Tirzah art thou, my companion;
Elegant as Jerusalem;
Imposing as a military host with banners.
5. Turn away thine eyes from me,
For they are taking me by storm.
Thy hair is as a flock of goats
Which lie along downwards from mount Gilead.
6. Thy teeth as a flock of sheep,
Which come up from the washing-pool,

All of them bearing twins,
And none of them without its young.
7. As a piece of pomegranate,
   Are thy cheeks within thy tresses.
8. There are threescore queens,
   And fourscore concubines,
   And virgins without number:
9. My dove, my perfect one, she is the favourite;
   The darling is she of her mother,
   The delight of her who bore her.
   The virgins beheld her, and called her blessed;
   The queens and concubines also praised her.
10. Who is this that looks forth as the dawn,
    Beautiful as the moon, of purest brightness as the sun,
    Imposing as bannered hosts?
11. I went down to the fruit garden,
    To behold the green growths of the valley,
    To see whether the vine was putting forth buds,
    Whether the pomegranates were in bloom:
12. E'er I was aware, my soul made me
    As the chariots of Amminadib.
13. Return, return, O Shulamith;
    Return, return, that we may behold in thee,—
    What shall you behold in the Shulamith?
    As it were a festive choir of rejoicing hosts.

CHAPTER VII.

1. How beautiful are thy feet in sandals,
   O noble woman.
   The contour of thy person
   Is like the rounding of a necklace
   Wrought by the hands of a finished artist:
2. Thy waist is a round goblet
   Full of the rich spiced wine:

Thy body is a heap of wheat
Enclosed with lilies:
Thy two breasts as two fawns,
Twins of a gazelle.
4. Thy neck as a tower of ivory;
Thine eyes pools in Heshbon,
By the gate of Bath-rabbim;
Thy nose as a tower on Lebanon,
Looking towards Damascus.
5. Thy head crowning thee is as Carmel,
And the full flowing hair of thy head rich as purple:
The king is captivated by the tresses.
6. How beautiful and how charming,
O my love, art thou in fascinating graces.
7. Thy stature is like a palm-tree;
And thy breasts to its clusters.
8. I said I will go to the palm-tree;
I will clasp its waving branches;
And thy bosom shall now be as clusters of the vine;
And thy breath sweet as citrons;
9. And thy voice as the delicious wine
Which flows pure to my best loved friend,
Which makes the lips of the slumbering move gently.

Spouse.

10. I am my beloved's,
And his ardent affection is towards me.
11. Come, my beloved, let us go forth into the country;
Let us abide in the villages;
12. Let us be early in the morning in the vineyards;
Let us see whether the vine is budding, its blossom un-
folding;
Whether the pomegranates are in bloom:
There will I give thee my loves.
13. The choicest flowers are giving forth their fragrance,
And at the entrance of our summer-houses are all kinds
of delicious fruits,
Both new and old, which I have treasured up, my beloved, for thee.

CHAPTER VIII.

1. O that thou wert as a brother to me,
   Nourished in the bosom of my mother!
   Should I find thee abroad, then would I kiss thee,
   Nor should it be imputed to me as an impropriety.
2. I would lead thee, I would bring thee to the house of
       my mother;
   Thou shalt teach me how to gratify thy wishes;
   I will make thee drink of the spiced wine,
   Of my fresh juice of the pomegranate.
3. His left hand shall be under my head,
   And his right hand shall embrace me.
4. I charge you, O ye daughters of Jerusalem,
   That ye rouse not and disturb not
       My love, till he please.

DAUGHTERS OF JERUSALEM.

5. Who is this coming up from the wilderness,
   Leaning on the beloved.

BELOVED.

Under the citron tree I gained thine affection;
There thy mother pledged thee;
There she that bore thee betrothed thee.

SPOUSE.

6. Set me as a seal on thine heart;
   As a seal on thine arm:
   For love is strong as death;
   Devoted affection is unrelaxing as the realms of the dead:
   Its flames have the energy of lightning,
   Which have the fiercest blaze.
7. Many waters cannot quench love,
   And floods cannot overwhelm it:
   Should a man give all the wealth of his house for this
       love,
   It would be utterly despised.

8. We have a young sister,
   And she has not yet reached womanhood:
   What shall we do for our sister,
   With reference to the day when she shall be spoken for
      in marriage?

BELOVED.

9. If she be a wall, we will build on it a turret of silver;
   And if she be a door, we will enclose it with boards of
      cedar.

SPOUSE.

10. I am a wall and my breasts as towers;
    Then am I in his eyes as one finding favour.
11. A vineyard has Solomon in Baal-hamon;
    He has let out the vineyard to keepers;
    Each shall yield him for its fruit
    A thousand pieces of silver.
12. My vineyard which belongs to me, is under my own
       supervision;
    Thou, O Solomon, shalt have the thousand pieces of
       silver from it;
    And the keepers of its fruit two hundred.

BELOVED.

13. O thou who dwellest in the gardens,
    The companions hearken to thy voice;
    Cause me to hear it.

SPOUSE.

14. Make haste, my beloved,
    And be thou like a gazelle, or a beauteous fawn,
    Over the mountains of spices.

ANALYSIS OF THE SONG.

CHAPTER I.

THE desire which in the heart of the saint absorbs every other, is for the manifestation of the love of the Lord Jesus, through the influences of the Holy Spirit; and this love is thus ardently desired, because its effect is more reviving and exhilarating than any of the pleasures of sense, even of wine, the most refreshing of them all. Verse 2.

This desire is not a blind instinct or a fanatical impulse, but springs from an intelligent apprehension of the excellency of the nature of Christ, as transcending every thing known to man, more than the holy anointing oil of the sanctuary surpassed any other perfume;—an excellence so rich, that the pure in heart, and they only, love him, and they cannot do otherwise than love him. Ver. 3.

The thought of the excellency of the character of Christ and of the influences of the Holy Spirit shedding abroad his love in the heart, creates the desire of coming as near to him as possible, without any delay —of running to him; and as our own insufficiency and

10

weakness are felt sensibly at such times, we pray for
the attracting power of his grace and for the strength
of his Spirit.   This desire is never expressed in vain;
with kingly majesty and condescension, he brings us
into confidential communion with him apart from the
world; this communion is attended with fulness of joy
and a holy exultation in his superior grace; and these
manifestations of his love thus made, only to the
upright or pure, and by such sincerely appreciated,
are followed by remembrances, not painful, like the
pleasures of sense, but always refreshing and delightful.   Ver. 4.

This love is a perfect regulator of the powers of the
soul; and carrying with it true wisdom, gives us a
correct knowledge of ourselves, as the offspring of the
humility to which this divine love leads, and which
consists in thinking of ourselves according to the
whole truth, nothing more, nothing less, realizing that
while, black like the tents of Kedar, we are darkened
by native depravity, grace is working in us virtues
more beautiful than the curtains of Solomon.   Ver. 5.

The humility inseparable from this love makes us
modest and retiring, and prompts us to shrink from
courting admiration; because we are conscious of unworthiness; have been stripped of our spiritual beauty
by sin; have suffered many evils and afflictions; have
received ill treatment, not only from the ungodly
world, but from brethren of the same household of
faith; and have failed in many duties.   Ver. 6.

This love so captivates the heart with the Lord
Jesus, while keeping it thus humble, that we are

anxious, not only to enjoy his society in the blessedness of private communion, his chambers, ver. 4; but to follow the Lamb whithersoever he goeth, Rev. xiv. 4; to be with him in labours, fatigues, and dangers, no less than in the delights of his service—in the weariness of toil in the wilderness, no less than in the pleasures of the palace. It prompts us to inquire and seek, without waiting for commands, where we may labour with this gracious king as a shepherd, and enjoy his society;—where, in the discharge of duty, find his guidance and defence during the noon-tide heat of temptation, affliction, and sorrow; and makes us unwilling to be satisfied with any inferior love, or the company and teaching of any but Christ— unwilling to have any person or thing coming between us and Jesus.   Ver. 7.

Such inquiries he answers, by assuring the soul thus humble in its own esteem, that while conscious of unworthiness, and misused by men, we are held by him in the highest admiration—"fairest among women;"—and that he may be always found by our following in the footsteps of those who through faith and patience have inherited the promises; and by activity in his service, by ministering to the saints, and by labouring to train up the young of the flock, "feed the kids," in co-operation with the ministers of the gospel—"beside the shepherds' tents."   Ver. 8.

Having received these instructions, and going forth to carry them into practice, our soul is viewed with great interest by the Saviour, in our approaches to him. Seeing us, as it were, afar, he sets forth, by comparison to the horse, his impression of that character which is so despised by the world. In reference to its inherent vital energy, or principle imparted by the Holy Spirit, it is a character noble, adapted to impress us with respect and command admiration—possesses great energy and vigour, and inexhaustible powers of endurance—running without growing weary. Isa. xl. 31. Ver. 9.

Moreover, Jesus looks on those virtues which are superadded as ornaments to our character by grace, with a pleasure akin to what we feel in contemplating cheeks comely with rows of jewels, &c., viz. that golden chain with the pearls "love, joy, peace, meekness, &c." Gal. v. 22. Ver. 10.

The principle is, "to him that hath shall be given," Matt. xxv. 29; and though so beautiful are these ornamental graces now overlaying the soul by the Holy Ghost, Christ will add unto these, others wrought by his own hands, too exquisite to be made even by angels, a spiritual body, &c. He will adorn us to the utmost possible that such wisdom and power as his can confer. Ver. 11.

Thus, following Jesus in the way of duty, under the impulse of this love, we are received by him with kingly majesty, and as beloved friends, are entertained with princely magnificence at his table, spread with delicacies for the soul. This near approach to him, combined with his affectionate tenderness and great goodness, kindles the affections into a fervid glow, and draws from us the fragrance of the odoriferous graces—the spiritual spikenard—poured by the

Holy Ghost into the alabaster of the pure heart. Ver.
12.

At such times, in near communion with Jesus, and
with the affections in vigorous exercise, we feel our
Lord amazingly precious. If asked, How precious is
your Saviour? Tell me the impression thus made on
your spiritual apprehensions? We can do no better
than reply, Can you tell what is the sweet and
refreshing influence of a bundle of myrrh in the
bosom, or of a cluster of camphire in bloom, such as
is in the vineyards of Engedi? Ver. 14. The presence of Jesus produces an impression on my spiritual
faculties, far more delightful than the effect of these
perfumes on the bodily senses. Ver. 13.

Thus received by this friend and king, our beloved, and entertained by him, at the table of his
confidential companions, with the marrow and fatness of his grace—while, under these manifestations
of love, our heart is burning with affection, what is
the nature of the language interchanged between him
and us?—"We love him because he first loved us;"
we presume to address to him the language of affection,
because he first addresses us. He speaks to us in
terms of the strongest and most tender affection—assures us that whatever may be thought of us by the
world, we are beautiful in his eyes, and that love is the
expression of soul which draws his admiration. Ver. 15.

The heart is glad to reciprocate this feeling;
and calling him our beloved, the dearest object of our
affection, we rejoice to give utterance to our sense of
the beauty of his character, and the pleasantness of
10*

his society—together with the delightfulness of the
repose he grants to those whom he so loves as thus to
address—a peace sweet as repose on a bed of full
blown flowers of spring amid green pastures beside
still waters, and at the same time, while open to all
the fresh airs and balmy influences of the season, protected from the sun by day, the chill dews by night,
and from the rain, by a richly wrought ceiling of
cedar and cypress, shadowing forth the permanency
and excellence of the defence from evil afforded by
the divine righteousness of Christ, in a manner
stronger, if possible, than the shadow of a rock, or
than the pillar of cloud and of fire over the camp of
Israel.   Ver. 16.

CHAPTER II.

In verses 1—3, the spouse sets forth by beautiful
comparisons, the character of herself and of the
beloved, for putting before us the contrast between
her humility and loveliness, and his majesty and
beauty.   The believer is as the rose of Sharon and
the lily of the valleys;—Jesus is as the citron-tree
among all other trees.   The rose and the lily illustrate the Christian character, as possessing purity,
beauty, loveliness; as being like the lily among
thorns, in contrast with the general tone of character and feeling in the world.   The words, "As the
lily among thorns, &c.," ver. 2, are with propriety
put into the mouth of Jesus, as a suggestion made

immediately on mention of the features represented in ver. 1st, for reminding us that, as his people, our character must be the opposite of what it was by nature, and of what yet prevails among the ungodly, —as he also teaches in John xvi. 33; 2 Tim. iii. 12. He says that between earthly loveliness and the loveliness of the saint, there is as much contrast as between the lily and the surrounding thorns.

While, like the rose and the lily, the believer—the same who was seen in the foregoing chapter admitted to such delightful communion with the king at his table—is thus meek and lowly, beautiful in the modesty of humility;—Jesus towers on high in majesty and grandeur; the citron-tree is his emblem, and illustrates his character as combining majesty with beauty, as affording shelter and protection to his people, as capable of satisfying the wants of the soul. Ver. 3.

Such being the characteristics of Jesus and of the redeemed soul, the coming of such soul into fellowship with him, must yield it great pleasure. Hence, when we come under the shadow of Christ, we have great delight, and find food for the hungering heart; his ways are ways of pleasantness and all his paths are peace. Though addressed by him in language of such endearment and equality, and permitted to tell him our love, we are not the less sensible that he towers above us in the majesty of his divinity, far more than the citron-tree above the humble rose; that this majesty is our protection; and that the surpassing greatness of our joy springs

from the union in his character of such gracious condescension and such divine grandeur.

The Lord Jesus leads his people along to greater displays of the riches of his grace and of holy joy—as pleasures were found in the banqueting-house, richer and more varied than under the apple-tree. In chap. i., ver. 4, he is represented as bringing us into "his chambers," the place of his intimate friends;—in chap. i. ver. 12, as feasting us at his table, with a repast of holy joys; here, he is set forth as bringing us into the midst of means for securing the most abundant exhilaration and gladness of heart, where, like a person in the king's house of wine, we may be abundantly satisfied with the fatness of his house and may drink of the river of his pleasures. The foregoing passages show different stages of spiritual enjoyment, increasing in degree till they are the greatest possible. Ver. 4.

In all these manifestations to us, his banner over us is love. As the banner rallies for the defence of even the weakest citizen all the strength of the state —is his protection—so, the divine love is our defence against all evils, and secures for us all the aid that may be drawn from all the other attributes of God. As the banner shows the country of the soldier, it is by possessing love that we are seen to be citizens of heaven. As the soldier exults in the flag of his country, the saint glories in the consciousness of the divine love, and in having love shed abroad in the heart.

In the three following verses, viz. 5, 6, 7, is a

representation of the state of the believer, when, thus overshadowed by divine love, he is in the banqueting-house, in the full enjoyment of these overflowing riches of heavenly grace, to the greatest degree possible for man. 1. The state of the soul at times of the greatest spiritual enjoyment, "sick of love," ver. 5—filled with communications of love almost beyond its power to bear. 2. The feelings had at such seasons, ver. 6; great contrition and humility—the head was sinking; the consciousness of being sweetly and powerfully sustained by the Lord Jesus, through his imputed righteousness and by his inward grace, " His left hand is under my head;" we feel ourselves drawn very near to Jesus, " His right hand doth embrace me." 3. The desires then had, are—to be stayed or sustained by the fruits of the tree, the doctrines and promises of the gospel, " Stay me with flagons, comfort me with apples," ver. 5, and—to guard against any thing likely to make our beloved withdraw, " I charge you, O ye daughters of Jerusalem, &c." ver. 7.

As these overpowering manifestations of love cannot be expected to continue without interruption, and Jesus will for wise purposes withdraw from the soul, in verses 8 and 9 is set forth the way in which he returns and manifests himself after such withdrawal. In his approach, he makes us hear his voice, even when afar off, ver. 8. " The voice of my beloved, &c." He comes with perfect ease, over all obstacles intervening in consequence of sin, ver. 8; he comes unexpectedly, often surprising us by his grace, when we are looking not for it. Having thus returned, he cannot be enjoyed by us without much to hinder the full manifestations of his excellence and glory. Walls yet intervene between us and him; he is very near to us, but the vision of his glory is obscured, and the sound of his voice deadened by the barriers behind which he stands, the walls of the dungeon in which we are now confined, the walls of our earthly house of this tabernacle, of our present mortal state, ver. 8. At the utmost, we can now get nothing more than very partial glimpses of the glory of Christ, such as may be had of a person showing himself through the obscurity of a lattice. Ver. 9.

While in our present state, we are thus in the condition of persons in a dungeon with the doors thrown open, like Peter's, Acts xii. 7, and Jesus is standing without, in the invisible world, looking on us kindly through the lattice, and addressing us through the bars; he tries to allure us away from our darkness, loathsomeness, and chains, abroad into that bright and glorious world where he has gone to prepare a place for us—saying, " Rise up, my love, my fair one, and come away, &c." He addresses us in language of the tenderest love—" My love, my fair one." Loving us so strongly, he is even more desirous to have us with him where he is in glory, than we can be to depart and be with him. As motives for alluring us away from earth to heaven, he says that in the world to which he would draw us—" the winter is past;" there the curse, which has fallen so heavily even on the ground as to cause the desolations of winter, is for ever done away—all is fresh and uninterrupted spring. "The rain is over and gone;" afflictions and sorrows, all the former things are passed away. "The flowers appear on the earth;" every thing is there budding and bursting with beauty. "The time of the singing of birds is come;" there, all is vocal with enchanting melody, and even the inanimate creation are joining in the chorus. "And the voice of the turtle is heard in our land;" the burden of that music is love. "The fig-tree putteth forth her green figs;" there, every thing is found that can gratify our capabilities of enjoyment. Hence, he says, "Come away" from the sin and sorrows, &c. &c. of earth, come away to the skies, &c. Ver. 10—13.

The saint who is thus loved and allured by the Lord Jesus, is often found in the rough, afflictive scenes of this life, and in seclusion from the world, "in the clefts of the rock;" but he encourages us not to be disheartened by a sense of unworthiness, or cast down by sorrow, for the voice of such persons, however broken by contrition, is sweet to him, and their countenance, though marked with tears of penitence, is pleasant in his sight. Ver. 14.

Those who would be pleasant to Jesus, and enjoy frequent visits, such as mentioned in the foregoing verses, viz. 8—13, must be careful to guard against sin, and especially little sins; "the little foxes" will spoil the vines with tender grapes. Ver. 15.

Those who thus watch, and act, and love—who enjoy these manifestations of the beloved—may use the language of full assurance, and feel the amazing richness of the inheritance they have in Jesus. 1 Cor. iii. 22—23; John xvii. 10. The friendship and union existing between Jesus and his people, is of the most intimate and confidential kind; and as the feeding-place of the young hart is the place of his strongest desire, and though he may withdraw for a time from his pasture grounds, to them he must return; so, Jesus loves the dwelling-place among his saints, Ps. lxxvii. 2; lxxviii. 68; and though he seems to withdraw at seasons, he will not forsake us utterly, but will come back in his own good time, and make his abode with us. Ver. 16.

As these delightful visits of the beloved, the times when he comes over the hills and feeds among the lilies, must be interrupted, the saint here prays that he would repeat them as often as possible, until the day of eternal blessedness break, and the shadows now closing around us, for ever flee away. Ver. 17.

CHAPTER III.

This chapter consists of two parts, verses 1—5, show-ing the earnestness with which the believing soul seeks its absent Lord; and verses 6—11, illustrating the magnificence of the mode in which the saint is carried onward to glory.

The first verse, together with those following to the fifth, is connected with the last verse of the foregoing chapter. The prayer there offered for the repetition, as often as possible, of those precious interviews with Jesus, during the dark and lonely scenes of this life,

is a prayer which prompts to activity in seeking him.
This activity springs from a vehement desire kindled
in the heart by our experience of the excellence of
our Lord.   Having been overpowered with his loveliness, and feeling, by his withdrawal, how precious his
presence and how great the loss sustained by his absence, we have longings so intense for him as to be
unsatisfied with earnest prayers; as to rise above and
keep down the strongest cravings of our bodily nature.   Nothing is more importunate and necessary
than sleep; but the hungering and thirsting for righteousness, felt when the manifestations of Jesus are
withheld, are stronger than the claims of even sleep,
and cause us to seek him on our bed, during hours
belonging to repose.

But it does not stop in desires, however intense.
It incites to exertion for coming to him, though by
great efforts and self-denial, making us even leave our
bed and go out amid the chill dews and dangers of the
night.   Ver. 2.

Animated by the fervent emotion which makes us
feel Jesus to be him whom our soul loveth, we avail
ourselves of every aid in finding our Lord, and inquire
especially of those appointed as watchmen in Zion,
the ministers of the word, concerning our spiritual
state, and the means of being restored to the joy of
his salvation.   Ver. 3.

Under these circumstances, the promise is fulfilled,
"They that seek shall find;" and efforts showing such
earnestness and sincerity of purpose, are rewarded by
the return of Jesus to our longing hearts.   Ver. 4.

11

Having found him, we are anxious to enjoy the blessedness of his society, where there can be no restraint, and we may commune with him in secret, of all that is in our heart; we desire to be alone with Jesus, and the influences of his Spirit are laid hold of with the greatest eagerness.

The desire before expressed, is again felt, to avoid every thing at all likely to make him withdraw from us. Ver. 5.

These manifestations of the loveliness of Christ on earth, lead to the glorious displays of his love in heaven; and our finding him, as just noticed, is the preparatory step to finding him in the splendour of his throne at the right hand of God. She who was allured by the motives in chap. ii. 10—13, to arise and come away, having embraced the invitation, finds on coming out from the walls of her dungeon, the royal palanquin waiting for her, under escort of a powerful guard; and the angels who desire to look into these things, view with admiration this imposing procession, as coming up from the wilderness lying between this world and heaven, the cortege is overshadowed by the reality represented in the pillar of cloud and of fire, by the cloud and smoke by day, and the shining of a flaming fire by night; while around is ascending the perfume of those odoriferous graces which are fed by the oil of gladness, and kindled by the flame of the Holy Ghost. In this manner, is the soul of him who is so humble in his own eyes, and neglected by the world, carried by the angels to Jesus' bosom. Luke xvi. 22.

In this progress to glory, the soul is overshadowed

by the glorious covering or protection of the divine nature of Christ, our righteousness, like pillars of smoke or cloud, breaking the force of the rays of divine justice, and surrounded by the incense of prayer and all other graces, more pleasing than the perfumes burned in golden censers around the eastern bride. Ver. 6.

The soul is resting in a palanquin guarded by the angels who minister to the heirs of salvation; and who, in consequence of the dangers besetting us, are fully armed, and competent for every emergency. Ps. xxxiv. 7. Ver. 7, 8.

This conveyance is one of royal magnificence, belonging to Jesus, and made by the hands of him who did by himself purge our sins. Heb. i. 3. Ver. 9.

It has been built of the most precious and costly materials imaginable; materials so costly as to be obtainable not with corruptible things, as silver and gold, but with the precious blood of Christ. The conveyance in which we are borne onward to heaven, is so rich and precious that the lining of it is love; and however heavy the storms and rough the scenes around us, we are in a litter, or portable pavilion, where the soul is o'ercanopied with love, where it is reclining on love, where the head is pillowed on love, and where every thing its eyes rest on, is curiously wrought with the emblems of love. Ver. 10.

The meeting of Jesus with a redeemed soul clothed upon with a spiritual body, in the last day, at our entrance into heaven, is represented as the day of our espousals with him. He is waiting to receive us, in his kingly robes and crowned with many crowns; and those who have been on earth "a spectacle unto the world, and to angels, and to men," 1 Cor. iv. 9, shall then be viewed with admiration by all the holy angels and heavenly host. Ver. 11.

CHAPTER IV.

In this chapter, with verse 1 of chap. v., we have, 1. The estimation of the beauty of holiness in the saint, as it appears in the eyes of Jesus. Ver. 1—5. 2. His gracious designation of a place where he wishes such souls to meet with him even now, until the day of glory in heaven cause our shades to flee away. Ver. 6. 3. The reasons, nine in number, given by him for alluring us to meet with him where he has appointed. Ver. 7—15. 4. The effect of these truths and reasons on the heart, to make us seek in prayer those influences of the Holy Spirit, which alone can prepare the soul for these meetings with our Lord. Ver. 16. 5. The consequence of thus hearkening to his voice and seeking the Holy Spirit, is that Jesus comes into our souls, and, by his presence sensibly felt, manifests his acceptance of us, and with the light of his smiles, fosters our pious virtues, chap. v. 1;—while the angels who rejoice over the soul first repenting, gather around it with no less joy, when our Lord comes again to visit and revive his garden.

The soul thus on the road to this glorious destiny, is humbled with the growing sense of its unworthiness, and feels more deeply that in our flesh dwells no good thing—sees nothing in us that we can suppose Jesus will love. The growing conviction of our sinfulness, attending growth in grace, would create despondency, did not our Lord give us assurances of his esteem; and those who are thus humble may be safely entrusted with these assurances, without danger of being exalted above measure. We must observe how much of this book, especially henceforward, is occupied with these expressions of Jesus' love to the saint, and how small, in comparison, the space given, viz. chap. v. 9—16, to our expressions of the beauty of Christ.

The proper meaning of the words in verses 1—5, and indeed of the subsequent addresses of the same kind, must be got by gathering together all the different impressions of beauty felt when we gaze on the eyes of doves, the flock of goats feeding on mount Gilead, the flock of sheep coming up from the washing, the thread of scarlet, the tower of David, covered with its thousand shields, the two young roes feeding among the lilies; each one of these separately, is viewed with great pleasure, but when we sum up the feelings of satisfaction had in contemplating them all unitedly, then may we have a representation of the delight with which Jesus dwells on the soul of the believer in process of sanctification.

While in this world, and in preparation for the day of our espousals, we are not cut off from communication with Jesus. His love makes him wish to have us with him even now, though it must be in a different way from that in which we shall be with him hereafter.

11*

In this world, he comes and manifests himself to us. John xiv. 21, 23.

He has appointed a place for such interviews, where he may always be found. He appointed the mountain of the Lord's house of old, where the Shechinah dwelt, as the place where he would meet with his people, and dwell among them, and commune with them, obscurely indeed, but really;—the place where he has now recorded his name to dwell there, is the mountain of myrrh and the hill of frankincense; the hill where the mercy-seat is established; where the cloud of the Holy Spirit's influences abides in dews richer and more refreshing than the dews on the mountains of spices. Ver. 6.

That we may have no hesitation in coming to meet him on the hill of frankincense, till the day break and the shadows flee away, he gives us eight reasons for our encouragement:

1. Thou art to me all beautiful, without spot or any such blemish. Eph. v. 27. Ver. 7.

2. Here only canst thou be safe; the choicest spots of this world, though beautiful as the top of Amana, or Shenir, or Hermon, or that goodly mountain, even Lebanon, are full of peril—lions' dens and leopards; therefore come away with me from all these, however inviting; come away to the mount where I meet with my loved ones, under the bright cloud of the Holy Ghost, dropping on their souls the myrrh and frankincense of the heavenly world. Ver. 8.

3. Come away with me to this mount; because my heart is enraptured—is taken away—with only the

partial development of thy loveliness that as yet appears; with one of thine eyes unveiled to me, with one chain of thy neck: thy graces are not yet perfected, sanctification is not yet completed, nor thy spiritual body prepared; but even the little now seen in thee of the glory that shall be revealed, enraptures my heart. Ver. 9.

4. He wishes us with him there, because our love, wrought by the Spirit, is beautiful in his eyes; this is what is especially delightful to him, and in the absence of any other excellence, commends us; and this love is more pleasing to him than wine to our taste. Not only is the affection of love thus grateful to him, but equally so are all those graces of the heart which are the fruit of the Spirit, Gal. v. 22—23; Eph. v. 9, and are the perfume of the soul—better even than the holy oil shed over the head of Aaron. Ver. 10.

5. The language of the heart thus filled with love as the consequence of being anointed with our glorious Head, with the oil of gladness—distils in accents as pleasant to him as drops of the honey-comb to our tongues. He sees within the heart a fountain of this loveliness, not soon exhausted, because springing from a source no deeper than the lips, but springing up into everlasting life—"honey and milk are under thy tongue." Ver. 11.

6. The presence of the saint is altogether pleasant to our Lord, as much so as the fragrance of Lebanon to us. Ver. 11.

7. For showing why he wishes us to come away with him, he states that his delight in the soul of the

D

believer is as great and pleasing as what is felt by
us in enjoying the most beautiful garden.   Verses 12
—15.

This garden is enclosed, abounds in all pleasant
fruits, is full of trees of frankincense and all the chief
spices, and is watered, not only from an unfailing
spring in its midst, but also with cool, refreshing
streams from the snowy tops of Lebanon.   Thus precious in the eyes of our Lord is the soul which Jehovah has set apart for himself, Ps. iv. 3; which yields
the peaceable fruit of righteousness; which sends up
its desires as incense; which enjoys those copious
streams issuing from the fountain of the Holy Spirit
within the heart, and coming with the refreshing influence of waters from a more glorious than Lebanon
in the skies.

The effect of such impressions of Jesus' love, creates the desire that he may come into our hearts and
make his abode with us; that he may sup with us,
and we with him. Rev. iii. 20.   We wish, however,
to prepare the way of the Lord, and therefore address
ourselves to prayer for the influences of the Holy
Spirit to revive our graces; "Awake, O north wind!
and come, thou south," &c.   Then, when the soul has
been thus prepared by the Holy Ghost, we rejoice in
finding Jesus coming into our hearts and enjoying the
pleasant fruits of our sanctified graces.   Ver. 16.

8. And if we thus come to him with preparation of
heart, he will come down into our souls by his Spirit,
and spread around us a host of angels rejoicing to be
our guard. Chap. v. 1.   Prayers thus offered under
the intercession of the Spirit, are answered without

delay, by Jesus coming and dwelling in our hearts,
Eph. iii. 17; ii. 22, and manifesting his acceptance of
our services and graces; the great acceptableness of
which to him is illustrated by the combination of
gratifications had in a pleasant garden, where we are
regaled with pleasant odours, beautiful scenes and
flowers, and delightful fruits. Nor does Jesus enjoy
these by himself. He who is anointed with the oil of
gladness above his fellows, desires those associates—
anxious as they are to look into the mysteries of redemption—to come and enjoy with him the beauties
and delights of this new creation, over which, while
he rejoices as a bridegroom over his bride, they, the
sons of God, may sing together and shout for joy.

CHAPTER V.

In chapters v. vi. and vii. we have 1. The effect of
sluggishness and indifference when the Lord Jesus
draws near to the soul; viz. the loss of his presence
and favour: ver. 2—6. 2. The anxiety, labour, and
trouble to which this neglect gives rise, in our efforts
for seeking him: ver. 7, 8. 3. The answers given
to the questions put by those who witness our anxiety
and sorrow at such times—viz. What is the character of him who is so anxiously sought? ver. 9, and,
Where has he gone, where may he be found? chap.
vi. 1. 4. The willingness of Jesus, even when he
has been forced from us by our own sins, to receive
his people who seek him in sincerity and truth, as
shown by the address of the beloved to the spouse,

chap. vi. 4; vii. 9. 5. The feelings towards our Lord by the soul thus kindly received into his love, expressed in the wish to enjoy retirement with him, and to offer him our best gifts, chap. vii. 10—13 and to the end of chap. viii.

After the most glorious displays to us of the love of Jesus, we may soon sink into indifference, entangled and overcome through weakness of the flesh, Matt. xxvi. 41, by the necessary duties of life running out into temptations; our perceptions being allowed to close against these manifestations of grace, through our own apathy and sluggishness. But while at such time, the flesh may be weak, the spirit remains willing—we sleep but our heart waketh; though there is a law in our members, warring against the law of our mind and bringing us into captivity to the law of sin, we do yet delight in the law of God after the inward man, Rom. vii. 22: though the outward evidences of love to Christ have very much disappeared under the pressure of spiritual sloth and decay, grace is still in the heart with its glimmerings; the heart is awake, but not in sufficient strength to counteract the pressure of carnality and control the doings of the body. So far from fulfilling his wishes and coming away from Lebanon, &c., chap. iv. 8, to the mountain of myrrh, there to meet with him, we prefer the indulgence of our fleshly, carnal inclinations— sleep—to all the attractions of his loveliness and society. Ver. 2.

But so strong is his love, that when he does not find us meeting him at the appointed place, he gra-

ciously comes to seek us, even in our sloth, and tries
to allure us away, by considerations the most endearing and affecting: "Open to me, &c." Rev. iii. 20.
Unmoved by these, we content ourselves in our apathy, by excuses the most frivolous. The love of our
Lord does then prompt him to go further than en-
treaty, to use exertions, for finding his way into our
heart: "My beloved, &c." Ver. 4.

At length, moved by his tender addresses to us,
and by the measures of mercy used by him for reviving our love, the affections begin to move, and we
arise to meet him. Instead, however, of running at
once to meet him, and opening our soul to him, just
as it is, we delay in order to prepare ourselves to
see him; and the consequence of this delay is, that
although we bring with us the best of our acts and
endeavours, our hands dropping with myrrh, &c., he
is gone. Nothing of our own, however costly, as duty
and self-denial, and mortification, can excuse us for
hesitating to rush into his arms; and as many a repenting sinner loses all interest in him, and also the
soul, by delaying in order to make himself fit to come,
so does many a saint often lose precious interviews
with the Lord. Ver. 5—6.

Her soul had been deeply moved under the language of the beloved standing at the door; and thus
moved, does now impel her to seek him. While the
withdrawals of Jesus are a just recompense for our
sluggishness, they give occasion for calling into exercise our love, and for showing its strength. What
was lost by indifference, can now be got only by great

exertion; we seek him; we call on him without receiving an answer; we have to suffer reproach and ill-
treatment from the watchmen of Zion, who, instead of
helping us in our zeal, view our love and devotion as
fanaticism, and both misuse and expose us to shame;
"Took away my vail, &c." The sympathy that is
often denied to the devoted heart by those high in
office in the Church, may be found among our pious
equals; and seeking an interest in their prayers, Eph.
vi. 19; 2 Thess. iii. 1, we entreat their aid, serving,
seeking, and following our Lord. Ver. 7—8.

This earnestness and zeal is not without its effect
on others before whom the light of the believer is
thus made to shine. Seeing the manifestations in
various ways, of such intense love to Christ, a love
that will be satisfied with nothing short of himself,
and which is willing, for the enjoyment of his presence, to incur any self-denial and any humiliation,
they naturally inquire, What there is in Christ above
others, that so strongly affects us? The illustration
or setting forth of his beauty, that follows in verses
10—16, is unequalled for beauty and richness. It is
the Holy Spirit, by the mouth of an inspired saint,
illustrating the beauty of Christ by language, through
the same means used in creation, drawn from the
beauties of the world. The most fine gold, the raven's
blackness, the eyes of doves, the beds of spices, the
lilies dropping sweet-smelling myrrh, &c.; all these,
as works of Christ, show his excellence. But when
we would understand the loveliness of that human
person through which the Son of God, the eternal

Creator, manifests himself as our Redeemer, these separate clusters, radiant with his glory, and scattered at large in his works, must be gathered into a form of the man Christ Jesus; and we are told that, just as beautiful as a person must be, whose appearance would impress us with all the ideas of loveliness got from the most fine gold, the beds of spices, the majesty of Lebanon, &c. &c.; so beautiful is Christ. Yes, though even in a case like this, there would still be something wanting; in Jesus there is every thing that can be desired; he is altogether lovely. This person, combining beauties beyond what man may possess, or the mind of man, in the farthest stretch of his imagination, unaided by the Spirit of God, could conceive—"this is my beloved, and this is my friend." Ver. 9—16.

CHAPTER VI.

Such a representation of the excellence of our Lord, creates in those hearing it a desire to see him for themselves; and they inquire where he may be found, "Whither is thy beloved gone? that we may seek him with thee?" Ver. 1.

The reply is, that he may always be found and seen in "his garden," in his church, which is in the midst of this world, a sacred enclosure, beloved by him, Ps. lxxx. 12; Isa. v. 1—where is his strongest desire, Matt. xxviii. 20; there does he dwell among his people, to enjoy the fragrance of the beds of spices, the grateful incense of desires arising from sanctified hearts, and "to gather lilies,"—to take to his bosom,

12

transfer to heaven those ripe for the change. Though Jesus may be withdrawn from the heart of one and another of his saints, he is never absent from his Church; he is always in some part or another of it, among the beds of spices; and those who have estranged him from them by neglect, must seek for him there. Ver. 2.

The bright manifestations of Jesus' love may be withdrawn from us, without unsettling our hope; the absence of joy, and of such views as represented in chap. ii. 5, iv. 1—15, &c., does by no means imply the absence of piety or faith. Faith reposes on Jesus when the light of his countenance is withheld; and, as we follow him, though amid gloom and trial, makes us still feel and say, in the absence of all spiritual comforts—even in the deadly gloom of the greatest spiritual darkness—"I am my beloved's, and my beloved is mine;" though his presence is not manifested now to my soul, I know that "he feedeth among the lilies," that his nature constrains him to dwell among his saints; and there, by keeping within his garden, under the influence of the means of grace, I shall again soon find the joy of his salvation, in the fulness of his presence. Ps. xlii. 1, 5, 11. Ver. 3.

A faith thus steadfast is never disappointed. The soul, thus following hard after Christ, and seeking him, perhaps with tears, finds him. The gracious Friend who had been so misused, chap. v. 2—6, though he had forsaken the soul for a season, rejoices to receive us when we show our sorrow by seeking him, Ps. ciii. 9; Isa. lx. 10; lxiv. 5. He comes to meet us as he sees and hears us following him through the paths of his garden; and he assures us his love is unchanged; he encourages us to come to him, by such language as is used in verses 4—13, &c. This passage, down to chap. vii. 9, is the language of Jesus to the believing soul when restored from the estrangement caused by neglect of his love, as stated in chap. v. 2—6. At such times, humbled by our unworthy conduct towards such a friend, we hesitate until reassured of his unabated love. As Tirzah, situated on Judea's beautiful hills, and Jerusalem, "beautiful for situation," and a bannered host, were objects impressing the mind with sensations of beauty, and of commanding dignity and majesty; so appears the soul of the saint advancing towards Jesus awaiting us amid the beauties and fragrance of his garden. Ver. 4.

In accommodation to human modes of speaking, he says the impression is the greatest possible, is overpowering. Ver. 5.

Then, as though to reassure us that, after our unworthy conduct, his love is still the same, he uses the same language previously addressed to us, chap. iv. 1—3. Ver. 7.

Around the Lord Jesus, God the Son, there are innumerable lovely and glorious beings, "queens, and virgins without number," on whom he might bestow his love; but among these the soul of the believer stands pre-eminent; this is the *one* amid that host, whom he loves above all others, and loves as devotedly as though there were no other to love. Moreover, that soul thus sanctified, thus beautified with the beauty of holiness, is the object of universal admiration; all that saw her praised her; the redeemed, fully perfected are the admiration of the heavenly host. Ver. 8, 9.

And as he sees the estranged soul of his saint hastening towards him, impressed with her beauty and dignity of bearing, he exclaims, Who is this approaching, covered with the blush of beauty and glow of health, more pleasing than the dawn of the morning; beautiful as the moon in her silvery brightness; pure and impressive in loveliness as the brilliancy of the sun; grand and imposing in her demeanour as hosts with streaming banners? Num. xxiii. 21. This is even my ransomed one, new created through the Holy Spirit. Ver. 10.

Receiving the returning saint with this cordiality and love, our Lord proceeds to tell his feelings during his withdrawal. He withdraws not in anger, but in love; he feels, without ceasing, the strongest desire to return to us; he earnestly invites us to return; he continues still to view us with unabated love, with even greater pleasure than he views the angels, the hosts seen by Jacob at Mahanaim. Though leaving the individual soul, he went into other portions of his garden, God's husbandry, 1 Cor. iii. 9, the Church, for exercising over it his care. But the strength of his love towards us, unkind though we had been to him, would not allow him to forget us; his mind, his heart, was on us, even though he was withdrawn, and his countenance hid; and spontaneously, almost before he was aware, his nature being love, he found himself inclined to us with tender compassion, and returning to meet us, with the rapidity of the chariots of Amminadib.   Though we grieve Jesus by our neglect, and compel him to leave us, he departs in sorrow and in love, drawn towards us still by the strongest affection, and not only willing to receive us if we seek him again, but coming with the greatest rapidity to meet us, Song ii. 8; Luke xv. 20.   Ver. 11, 12.

With tenderness and emphasis, he encourages us not to hesitate, but to come on, "Return, return, &c.," assuring us that his heart had been with us, and that he is not only willing, but desirous, to look upon us.   And does any one ask, What he sees in this sanctified soul, that so captivates?   He replies by summing up the whole in one expression—the festive chorus of two hosts.   He has as much pleasure in contemplating this redeemed spirit, as we could have, were we permitted to gaze on hosts mingling in the festal dances and rejoicing of a day of triumph— such hosts as were seen by Jacob at Mahanaim, and exulting in such rejoicings as were seen when, over the first creation, "The morning stars sang together, and all the sons of God shouted for joy."   Job xxxviii. 7.   Ver. 13.

CHAPTER VII.

The commendation of the beauty of the pious soul, for the purpose of encouraging it to trust in Jesus, notwithstanding past neglect and estrangement, is

12*

continued without interruption to verse 9.   The same
principles of interpretation apply here that have been
used for interpreting the other similar passages, chap.
iv. 1—5; v. 10—16.   Having set forth this beauty,
he is represented as held enchained by it, ver. 5,
"the king is captivated by those locks;" and expresses that his most delicate and pleasing delight is
had in the company and contemplation of the new
creation going forward in the soul of the saint.   Ver.
1—6.

As a consequence, he wishes to gather us in his
arms, and carry us in his bosom, Isa. xl. 11, and to
hearken to our voices engaged in thankfulness and
praise; the agreeableness of which to our Lord is as
great as to ourselves would be such wine as mentioned
in verse 9.   Ver. 8, 9.

With the 10th verse, begins the third part of the
book, which contains a statement of the effects produced on the heart by the manifestations of love, and
by the motives before mentioned.

1. The effect is the full assurance of hope, "I am
my beloved's, and his desire is towards me."   Ver. 10.

2. We wish to be much alone with Jesus in retirement, "Let us go forth into the field, &c."   Ver. 11.

3. We engage spontaneously in labours of holiness
and love, such as enjoined by our Lord, "Let us get
up early to the vineyards, let us see if the vine
flourish, &c.," ver. 12.   In such ways and duties as
these do we give Jesus our love.

4. For him do we lay up, and to him do we conse-
crate our best gifts, as well as our diligent services,

under the influence of this love: "All manner of pleasant fruits, which I have laid up for thee, O my beloved." Ver. 13.

CHAPTER VIII.

5. The next effect mentioned, is a desire that every thing hindering the full and perfect interchange of affection between Jesus and our soul, might be removed, and that it were possible to enjoy his love to us, and express our love to him, as we shall be able to do in heaven. Much as we may now long for stronger displays of his love, and to give stronger evidence of our love to him, we acquiesce in the present state of things, because we feel there would be an impropriety, no less than impossibility, in those overpowering exhibitions of love that belong to heaven. But this does not preclude us from feeling that, were it seen best by him, we would rejoice, even now, in those raptures which belong to heaven, where we shall be able to speak of his love in the strongest language, and give expression to it in the most exalted praise, without danger of exposing ourselves to the contempt of the ungodly. Ver. 1. There shall our fellowship and communion with him be far more intimate and endearing than ever on earth. Ver. 2.

6. Yet though this desire, of ver. 1 and 2, cannot be granted, we wish to have as much as can now be enjoyed of Jesus, even such seasons as are here mentioned, and had been enjoyed in chap. ii. 6, 7, and with it, the desire, as there expressed, that nothing be done

to interrupt it. This seems mentioned as though it was viewed by the soul as a blessed and satisfying foretaste of what may be expected hereafter, and as much as is best or possible for us in this world. Ver. 3, 4.

7. But though we cannot now enjoy what we could desire, and what shall be enjoyed in heaven; though the delightful scenes now had must be interrupted, yet we are permitted to go up from this wilderness, leaning on the beloved; we feel that underneath us are the everlasting arms; in all circumstances he sustains us; and throughout our pilgrimage we are thus upheld by him who first found us, raised us up, and took us into covenant relation "under the apple-tree," as in chap. ii. 3, under the shadow of Christ. Ver. 5.

8. Another result of this love is the desire to be continually near to the heart of Jesus, to be perpetually in his remembrance, and sustained by his Almighty power; that like the stones engraved with the names of Israel on Aaron's breastplate, and like the stones on the shoulder of the High Priest, we may be set as a seal on his heart, as a seal on his arm. Ver. 6.

9. This love sacrifices every thing that would come between us and Christ. Death cannot arrest us—we love Jesus better than life, "for love is strong as death." Matt. xvi. 24, 25. The delights of it being such as have been represented in the foregoing verses, 1—4, and other parts of this book, we desire to abide on the heart of Jesus, and run to embrace even death, if necessary, sooner than lose his love. As there is

nothing which jealousy will not sacrifice, so there is
nothing which this love will not sacrifice for the full
enjoyment of Christ.

10. Every thing that the world can offer for bribing
or enticing us away from our Lord, is rejected; as
this love cannot be got from Jesus with silver and
gold, neither can the heart which feels it in the
fulness here described, be induced to part with it for
the world. Ver. 7. It is felt to be more precious
than rubies, and all the things thou canst desire
are not to be compared unto it. Ps. iii. 15; Phil.
iii. 8.

11. While thus enjoying the love of Christ in such
fulness and power, we are not unmindful of the impenitent among our friends, &c., feeling them a kindred to us by the flesh, Luke x. 29; Rom. ix. 3, and
anxious for them to obtain like precious faith. As
a younger sister not yet of marriageable age was
thought of by her who was exalted to be the queen
of even Solomon in all his glory, and had a care exercised over her for raising her in due time to an eligi-
ble position of dignity, wealth, and splendour—so
the impenitent are not forgotten by those who are
already enjoying the pledges of the love of Christ;
these watch for souls as those who must give account,
that we may present them with us in the day of the
Lord. Ver. 8.

The change that will be then wrought in the condition of souls thus brought from their estrangement,
nigh unto Christ, is illustrated in ver. 9. Though
in their natural condition they are like an ordinary

wall without ornamental work, they shall be made
beautiful as a palace of silver built on such a foundation, or as a door of ordinary materials encased in
cedar, the most polished, and costly, and beautiful, of
all wood. The Holy Spirit takes our nature, dark
and unseemly as a wall, and is raising thereon, and
from the midst of these dilapidated and ruined materials, that which shall be more beautiful than a palace
of silver, a spiritual temple, an habitation of God
through the Spirit. Eph. ii. 12. In this world we are
to glorify God, by seeking our own holiness, and the
salvation of others; to show forth his praise by being
a wall on which shall be built the silver palace of our
holiness, and by being a door, which, encased in the
most precious materials of its kind, shall stand in
beauty worthy of admiration while opening to others
the way of life.

Though, like the spouse's sister then unfitted for
her exalted destiny, the impenitent are in a state
giving no promise whatever of the glory just stated,
and attainable only by the workmanship of the same
Spirit who is the builder and maker of the heavenly
Jerusalem, Heb. xi. 10, the saint feels that by nature
such were we, 1 Cor. vi. 11—"I am a wall"—and
that the grace which so changed us, made us fit, gave
us power, John i. 12, to become the sons of God, to
find favour in his eyes—can, will change them from
sin to holiness, so that though they have lien among
the pots, they shall be as the wings of a dove covered
with silver, and her feathers with yellow gold. Ps.
lxviii. 13.   Ver. 10.

12. This love makes us feel and labour for the souls of the impenitent, by making us sensible of our accountability as the stewards of God, 1 Cor. iv. 1; Luke xii. 42; Matt. xxi. 33; xxv. 15; Luke xix. 13. All our property, gifts of intellect, influence, &c., are entrusted to us by God, are things held in trust from the Lord, who will require of us an account of our stewardship. Ver. 11.

This responsibility is felt by him whose heart is alive with love to Christ, while others refuse to acknowledge it; and in view of his obligations, the saint cheerfully consecrates to his Lord the due portion of his services, his income, his all. Ver. 12.

13. Thus constrained by the love of Christ in the way of duty, the soul enjoys the privilege continually of audience with the King of kings through Christ the Saviour, and is encouraged in the exercise of prayer and praise, not only by a sense of our need and by the delights of holy worship, but by the assurance that our voice thus heard is pleasant to Jesus, chap. ii. 14;—that these expressions of holy emotions so agreeable to our companions in the kingdom and patience of Jesus, Rev. i. 9, abiding with us here in the gardens of his grace, are heard with still greater pleasure by him who now dwells in these gardens by the Shechinah of the Holy Spirit, chap. v. 1, as he shall hereafter dwell among us in the paradise of God, its light and glory, Rev. vii. 15—17; Rev. xxi. 23. Ver. 13.

14. Thus encouraged to dwell at the mercy-seat in confidential and constant communion with our Lord

E

on earth, we are becoming fitted for being with him in heaven; and this fitness. combined with the displays of his love before mentioned, carries with it a stronger and stronger desire for the enjoyment of his glory as it shall be revealed when the Lord perfects that which concerneth us—at his second coming when the day breaks and the shadows flee away. To this, as the ultimate, absorbing desire of the soul, do all these assurances of the love of Jesus lead. As the book begins with a burst of desire for the love of Christ as that love can be enjoyed only by his intimate friends, chap. i. 2, it ends with a prayer for the hastening of the time when we shall no longer see him through a glass darkly, but face to face—when there shall be nothing to interfere with the manifestation of his love to us, and the expression of our love to him: this desire is expressed, and its intenseness shown by the prayer, that he would hasten that happy day, and come with the celerity of a roe or a young hart bounding over the mountains of spices, and at every step shaking fragrance from the dewy boughs. Rev. xxii. 7, 12, 20.   Ver. 14.

COMMENTARY

ON THE

SONG OF SOLOMON.

CHAPTER I.

Ver. 1.—The Song of songs, which is Solomon's.

These words are as unmistakenly given by inspiration as any succeeding portion of this book, and show the estimation in which the Song is held by the Holy Spirit. It is called the Song of songs, or the most excellent Song. For the purpose of meeting the numerous objections brought against this portion of Scripture, the divine wisdom writes on the front of it, an attestation of its superior excellence, not only to the thousand and five songs by Solomon, but to all the songs ever produced by all other poets. He who cannot err, tells us, in language of no doubtful meaning, that this Song is unrivalled.

Poetry is the expression of the best and most beautiful thoughts, of exalted emotions, in the best and the most beautiful language. The language of poetry is the language of excited feeling. The best poetry must have the noblest theme, deal with the purest emotions, and be adorned with the richest ideas. God has garnished his works of every kind with beauty, and formed us with a capability of receiving pleasure from that beauty. Hence, in conveying to us important truth, he does throughout the Scriptures make it attractive, by adapting it to this love within us of the beautiful. Now, love is the very excellence of God; for God is love. Love is the purest, deepest, and most powerful emotion known to man. Nothing can, therefore, be better or more beautiful than the subject of this Song; and being a song, a poetical composition, it must be in the best and most beautiful language. A translation gives no idea of the excellence of Homer; and beautiful as is this Song, in our English version, we must remember that it is the poetry of an age more remote than the earliest Greek poets, in a modern language of very different structure and idiom.

The fact that this Song is so much rejected, is a proof of its excellence. How many persons can see no excellence in the best productions of genius, even when there is about them no allegory, as is here the case, to be interpreted by the Holy Spirit. "A work of genius, designed in a lofty spirit, and executed with a fine sense of the noblest functions of poetry, is assuredly not worthily appreciated, unless by those who have in some measure apprehended that world of suggestive thought which the poet aims at embodying in his imaginative scenes and figures; and, if a series of poetic images suggest, to diverse minds, diversified trains of reflection and emotion, this is perhaps the clearest evidence of their poetical intensity and truth."* The better the

* Ed. Review, No. 181, Art. 7.

poetry, the more profound the ideas embodied in it, the farther is it above the range of the common mind, and the more likely to be appreciated only by the cultivated few whose taste has been carefully refined. This being the Song of songs, the same thing must be expected here, and to a much greater degree, because there is need of a taste which cannot be attained without the supernatural aid of divine grace. Even when the highest beauty and excellence was personified in Jesus Christ, how perfectly was all this above the comprehension of man. They saw in him no beauty that they should desire him. Isa. liii. 2. His beauty cannot be seen and understood without a taste imparted by the Holy Spirit. "No man can say that Jesus is the Lord, but by the Holy Ghost." 1 Cor. xii. 3. Much is said about the Beautiful, the Good, and the True. Jesus was the personification of them all. In him did God represent unto us these abstract, spiritual excellences, in a sensible, bodily form. In its loftiest flights, the imagination of man never had so glorious a conception as that which is given in the union of the divine and human natures in the person of Jesus Christ. The object of this Song is the celebration of the love which led to that union—its beauty, its attractiveness, and its glorious results. Others of the divine songs of Scripture celebrate some particular consequences flowing from this love; the song of Moses at the Red Sea, speaks the praise of Jehovah for their deliverance; the Psalms are utterances of pious feeling, for various mercies; this Song goes to the spring of all that is beautiful, good, and true, and celebrates the love which is the fountain of all blessedness. Ho-

mer, generally received as the prince of poets, sings of
the malignant passions, the wrath of his hero, the cause
of woes unnumbered; this book sings of the wondrous
love of God, which is the spring, not of desolation, misery, and tears, but of the new creation, the
deliverance from guilt, the consolation, the heavenly
anticipations that are abroad in our world of woe. It
sings of the same love which is the burden of the new
song in heaven. How glorious was the chorus when
at the completion of creation, "the morning stars sang
together, and all the sons of God shouted for joy."
Will not that be the Song of songs which shall be
heard amid the new heavens and the new earth wherein dwelleth righteousness, when the innumerable company of the redeemed and the angels join to celebrate
the love of the Lamb that was slain. The theme of
this Song is the same redeeming love; and those
whose hearts are here brought by grace to feel the
excellence of this portion of Scripture, are already
learning that Song which no man could learn but those
redeemed from the earth.

    God can express to us inward spiritual beauty, only
through the means of outward sensible beauty; and in
this Song he makes use of this outward beauty for impressing on us that which is inwardly beautiful, true,
and good. What beauty is comparable to the beauty
of holiness? This is the source of all other beauty.
All the deformity, ugliness, and filthiness in this world,
are owing to the want of holiness. In the sky or heavens, where no stain of sin has fallen, there is nothing
but beauty. This beauty of holiness is that which the
Psalmist so earnestly desired to behold. Ps. xxvii. 4.

And the celebration of that beauty in this divine poetry, renders it the Song of songs. A few years ago, on a clear winter's night, there burst forth a northern light that suffused the whole heavens with a rosy tinge, and threw over the snow and landscape the same unearthly hues, different from any thing previously seen, and causing emotions of inexpressible pleasure in those who beheld this transient burst of heavenly splendour: this Song, is, as it were, a rosy burst of the divine love, which, through the Lamb, is the Shechinah of heaven; and those whose souls have the spiritual perception for seeing the divine light here beaming, feel their hearts thrill with the beauty of the tinge it throws over our blighted and wintry world. Elsewhere there can be seen nothing of equal or like beauty.

It was proper that such a Song should be written by Solomon. Aaron having prefigured Christ as a priest, and Moses foreshadowing him as a prophet, Solomon prefigured him as a king. And while David represents Jesus as suffering persecution and subduing the enemies of his people, Solomon represents him as the triumphant Prince of peace. Under Solomon, the kingdom of Israel was perfectly established by the conquest of all their enemies, and by the building of the temple in Jerusalem; and as the camp in the wilderness may represent the Church in this world, the reign of Solomon may be a representation of the Church in heaven. While, therefore, David sung, in the Psalms, of the various conflicts of the Christian life, Solomon here sings of that which is the end of all our conflicts, the consummation of the love of Christ and his Church.

His mental endowments were as glorious as his position. Not only did he surpass all others in wealth and splendour, the most kingly of kings; before him there was none like him for wisdom, neither after him shall any arise like unto him, 1 Kings iii. 12; and he possessed noble poetic powers. A man combining these rare qualifications, was very properly selected by the Holy Spirit as the means for conveying to the saints this divine allegory, this unequalled Song of love.

VER. 2.—Let him kiss me with the kisses of his mouth: for thy love is better than wine.

In the opening scene of this poem, as in this verse, the king had probably gone forth, according to oriental customs, to meet the bride, and was awaiting her, with his princely retinue, in an encampment where his rich pavilion stood pre-eminent. The spouse, looking forward with great interest to this meeting, on coming in sight of those kingly tents, almost involuntarily, as it were, gives utterance to the strong emotions of her heart, in these words.* Kitto remarks: "There are few acts bearing more diversified and contrasted significations than the kiss. It denotes as well the tenderest affection, as the most profound and even adoring

---

* Reiske, as quoted by Dopke, says: "It is a fundamental principle of the Arabic language, without which we cannot understand their best writers, and by ignorance or neglect of which we get into inextricable perplexity, that very frequently poets do not name that which they designate, because the reader or hearer may easily gather the sense from the thread of the discourse and character of the epithets used."

reverence." The words "kisses of his mouth," are not merely a redundant expression, like "words of my mouth," Ps. xix. 14, and "with their mouth they speak," Ps. xvii. 10; but a mode of distinguishing the kiss which was evidence of the tenderest affection, from the kiss which was the expression of submission, reverence, and obedience. In the East the kiss was impressed on the mouth, the hands, the feet, the garments, and even the ground where the feet had trodden —the difference being caused by the greater or less intimacy between the individuals. Permission to kiss the hand of a sovereign is considered an honour; but for that sovereign to give another the kisses of his mouth, is evidence of the tenderest affection, and is the highest possible honour. This metaphor is common to all oriental poets: "O suffer me to quaff the liquid bliss of those lips! Restore thy slave with their water of life." Thus again: "Thou who sippest nectar from the radiant lips of Pedmá, as the flattering Chacóra drinks the moon-beams!"*

The language of the spouse is, therefore, a desire that the beloved would give her those evidences of affection which none but the most cherished friends can have right to receive. They express the desire of the pious heart, that the Lord Jesus would give us manifestations of the love which none but his dearest friends can receive, or have reason to expect. Jesus says to his people, " I have called you friends," John xv. 15; "He that loveth me, shall be loved of my

* From the Gitagovinda.

Father, and I will love him, and will manifest myself
to him." John xiv. 21. The persons to whom these
words were spoken, understood them as referring to
manifestations very different from any thing the world
could receive: "Lord, how is it that thou wilt manifest thyself unto us, and not unto the world?"

What are those manifestations of Jesus' love which
none but his friends can receive? He explains them
to consist in the influences of the Holy Spirit. As
the burst of feeling which in the bosom of the spouse
swallowed up all others, was for these expressions of
affection; so the predominating, absorbing desire of
the believer, is for the full communications of the
Holy Ghost. It is a point of the greatest importance
for a man to know, what is the one thing which should
be the leading principle of his life, to be pursued with
oneness of view and indivisibility of purpose. Every
person has some such aim; and if the object thus
selected be a wrong one, here is a radical error which
must throw every thing else astray. The influences
of the Holy Spirit are that primary, essential object.
It is much for the impenitent to know that his nature
can be renewed only by God's Spirit; and much has
been done towards making us Christians of more than
ordinary growth, when we feel more than ordinarily
the necessity of being filled with the Spirit according
to the full capacity of our souls. Great advances
in holiness must be made by seeking eminent measures of the Spirit. Those will be most holy, will
feel most deeply the love of Jesus, who seek the
greatest degrees of the communications of the Spirit.

Preparation for heaven does not consist in rising to any imaginary standard of piety, in being as holy as we may consider some illustrious saints, in rising to certain frames of which we have heard and which we have desired; but in being filled as full of the Holy Spirit as our capacities can bear. Do you ask, How can I attain eminent holiness? Seek with undeviating and self-sacrificing purpose, eminent measures of the Holy Ghost.

There are various ways in which God may show his love, even to the saints. The multiplied comforts of life, home, family, friends; the continuance of health, reason, eyesight; the exercise of our faculties of body; exemption from calamity; prosperity in ordinary duties; enjoyment of spiritual privileges; all these are ways in which God may manifest love to his people. But while thankful for these as tokens of divine love, the saint fixes his eye far above and beyond them--on the influences of the Holy Spirit. In his view of life, the principal thing is held to be not wealth, not honour, not popularity, not power, but the riches of this heavenly grace. His ruling passion is to amass the durable riches and righteousness of the Holy Ghost. He views the Spirit as the strongest pledge of the love of Jesus—a gift so important that God can now confer on us no other gift of equal value. Jesus did not promise his disciples crowns, or riches, or honour, or ease in this world; but he did promise them affliction, with the Holy Ghost. John xvi. 33; xiv. 16. And as the Spirit touches our soul in the communication of his grace, how delightful the sensations. When they told Jacob "all the words of Joseph which he had said unto them, and when he saw the wagons which Joseph had sent to carry him, the spirit of Jacob their father revived, Gen. xlv. 27: how much richer the feelings of the patriarch, when that long lost son presented himself unto him, and he fell on his neck, and wept on his neck a good while. Gen. xlvi. 29. The gift of the best robe and the costly ring was not to the prodigal so precious a proof of his father's love, as that given when the father fell on his neck and kissed him. Luke xv. 20. While the common gifts of Providence are received with thankfulness, as evidences of God's love, and our spirit may revive in meeting with the conveyances loaded with blessings, that have been sent to encourage and refresh us, by Jesus our Brother, exalted to more than a second place in the heavenly kingdom; no proof of his affection is so much coveted, is so delightful, as when, coming through the person of the Holy Spirit, he gathers us, the lambs of his fold, with his arms, and carries us in his bosom, Isa. xl. 11—manifests himself unto us not as unto the world. Refreshing as are good news from a far country; more pleasing is the letter written by the well known hand; more so the sight of the absent friend; best of all the return, when we press him again to the bosom: and refreshing as are the words of Jesus, written to us in the Scriptures; blessed as is the ministry of his angels, who like Jacob's sons with the wagons from Egypt, come to us laden with mercies ministered to the heirs of salvation; pleasing as are the daily gifts of his providence; our greatest happiness is enjoyed, when he impresses on our hearts his love through the Holy Spirit.

In the latter clause of this verse, the reason is given, why those influences of the Spirit are so ardently desired: "Thy love is better than wine;" that is, thy love is more reviving and exhilarating than the effects of wine, the most delightful of the pleasures of sense. In Eden, the most precious of the trees, even where was every thing that is pleasant to the sight and good for food, was the tree of life which stood in the midst of the garden. Jesus, the true wisdom, is the tree of life to them that lay hold on him, Psalm iii. 18; his love shed abroad in our hearts by the Holy Spirit, is the fruit of this tree of life; and who will tell how much better was the fruit of the tree of life in Paradise, than the fruit of Canaan's richest vines?

The love of Christ is reviving, and counteracts the debilitating effects of sin, felt so painfully through body and soul.

"The stream that feeds the well-spring of the heart,
    Not more invigorates life's noblest part,
    Than virtue quickens with a warmth divine
    The powers that sin has brought to a decline!"*

A more powerful stimulant than the love of kindred, the love of money, or the love of fame, it so revolutionizes the heart as to make the ambitious man

* Cowper's Table Talk.

sacrifice his vanity, the proud man his reputation, the
vindictive man his vengeance, the drunkard his drunkenness, the sensualist his lust, the miser his gold, for
the name of Jesus Christ. It changes the parched
ground of the selfish soul into a limpid pool of beneficence, and the thirsty land of the sensual heart into
water springs of holy affections. Unlike the pleasures
of sense, this love is more than a temporary stimulant.
As satisfying as it is pure, this is the antidote of
spiritual death, the principle of eternal life; and when
age enfeebles the body, palsies the hand, and makes
cold the heart, this love, so powerful, so reviving,
keeps the spirit vigorous, the mind active, the affections warm; renews our youth like the eagle's; until
at last, from the very ashes of this bodily frame, it
makes the spirit emerge, like the angels from the
tomb of Jesus, with the vigour of youth and immortality in its wings.*

* "There is this difference between my poetship and the
generality of them—they have been ignorant how much they
stood indebted to an Almighty power, for the exercise of those
talents they have supposed their own; whereas I know, and
know most perfectly, and am perhaps to be taught it to the
last, that my power to think, whatever it be, and consequently
my power to compose, is, as much as my outward form,
afforded to me by the same hand that makes me in any respect
to differ from a brute."—Cowper to the Rev. John Newton.—
Southey's Edition of Cowper's Works, vol. iv. 186.
Such was the experience of Madame Guyon: "When God
gave back to me that love which I had supposed to be lost, he
restored the powers of perception and thought also. That
intellect, which I once thought I had lost in a strange stupidity,
was restored to me with inconceivable advantages. I was

This love is exhilarating, raises the spirits, gives cheerfulness to the soul. "Wine maketh glad the heart of man." Ps. civ. 15. "Give wine unto those that be of heavy hearts." Prov. xxxi. 6. And religion maketh glad the heart of man; give the love of Jesus unto those that be of heavy hearts. Religion is not the gloomy thing so frequently supposed by the votaries of worldly pleasure. Purifying the heart for seeing God, it clarifies our enjoyments. The amusements of the irreligious world are inventions for recruiting the tone of the spirits, which impiety depresses and corrodes. The glitter and revelry of the ball-room, the excitement of the theatre, the ten thousand little trickeries of dress and artifices of manners for drawing applause, the empty novel, the table of hazard, all are efforts by man for doing what religion would do for him in a noble and effective mode; not by convulsions, but by opening in the heart a well of water springing up into everlasting life. Those who have never known the elation of soul springing from the love of Christ, have yet to learn what is meant by exhilaration of spirits. How much better than wine is the love of country? the love of family? the love of friends? How much better than all these is the love of Jesus? The joys of sight and sound, combine them all, and yet there is no comparison.

astonished at myself. The understanding, as well as the heart, seemed to have received an increased capacity from God; so much so, that others noticed it, and spoke of its greatly increased power."—*Life by Upham*, i. 258.

"Nor rural sights alone, but rural sounds,
　　Exhilarate the spirits and restore
　　The tone of languid nature:"

If these utterances, speaking of the divine wisdom and goodness through the heavy medium of material things, do, as we well know, thus enliven and recruit the soul, how delightful and life-giving must be those spiritual visions unfolded to our minds by grace, and those sounds conveyed directly to our heart by the Holy Spirit—expressions of power and goodness, but expressions of power and goodness as the means of filling our souls with emanations of mercy and love.

VER. 3.—Because of the savour of thy good ointments, thy name is as ointment poured forth, therefore do the virgins love thee.

This verse would be better translated, Thy perfumes are rich in fragrance; thy name is perfume poured forth, therefore the virgins love thee. The universal use of rich and costly oils and perfumes among the orientals, for health and beauty, and at public entertainments, especially on nuptial occasions, as well as in common domestic life,* renders this language ap-

* "The custom of anointing the body is usual in hot climates, and contributes greatly to comfort. Even the Greeks, Romans, and others, whose limbs were mostly protected by clothes from the dryness of the air, found the advantage of its use. In going to entertainments, it is probable, that like the Greeks, the Egyptians anointed themselves before they left home; but still it was customary for a servant to attend every guest, as he seated himself, and to anoint his head; and this was one of the principal tokens of welcome. The ointment was contained sometimes in an alabaster, sometimes in an

propriate, and made such a comparison not unusual;
as in Eccl. vii. 1, "A good name is better than
precious ointment."

"The name of God is used as a compendious
formula to denote his whole moral greatness, the sum
of his whole attributes and character. And it is in
Jesus that we have the full exhibition of this moral
and spiritual excellency."* The nature of Christ is

elegant porcelain vase; and so strong was the odour, and so
perfectly were the different component substances amalgama-
ted, that some of this ancient ointment in one of the alabaster
vases in the museum at Alnwick Castle, yet retains its scent,
though between two and three thousand years old."—Wilkinson's Ancient Egyptians, vol. iii. 379. "To what extent the
luxury of using fragrant oils and the like was carried on, may
be inferred from Seneca, Epist. 86, who says, that people
anointed themselves twice or even three times a day, in order
that the delicious fragrance might never diminish. The
wealthy Greeks and Romans carried their ointments and
perfumes with them, in small boxes of costly materials and
beautiful workmanship."—Smith's Dict. Antiquities.

* Russell on the Covenants, p. 310. "The name of the Lord
is the Lord in the richness of his deeds." Hengstenberg on
Ps. cxxiv. 8. "One name would serve as well as ten thousand,
if we had but one relation to, or one idea of God. For instance,
could we, being perfect creatures as angels, only depend on
him as our great Creator, that name would have been sufficient for us to declare him: but being sinful creatures, yet
creatures to be redeemed, our Creator stood immediately in
many relations to us, according to our several conditions of
sinfulness, recovery, redemption, and salvation, which it was
necessary for us to know, that we might apply to him under
these relations, and receive every benefit and blessing we need.
He hath, therefore, suited himself, as it were, to us, in the
revelation of his names."—Serle's Hor. Sol. 444.

here illustrated by the richness and pleasantness of the best perfume; and as the very best known to men was not good enough to represent the character of him who was fairer than the sons of men, God had a perfume compounded for the express purpose of showing the divine riches of our great High Priest, the holy anointing oil of the Jewish sanctuary. The whole nature of Christ is as this fragrant oil, so pure, so delightful, and so excellently divine. The loveliness of Jesus consists in this divinity, this fountain of liquid perfume which is continually pouring forth in deeds of kindness to his creatures; and these acts of goodness are the means of showing forth his glory, and developing his excellence. The comparison in the second verse sets forth the pleasantness of the love of Christ in its effects on our hearts, as there shed abroad by the Holy Ghost; the third verse exhibits the richness of that love in its own inherent nature, as it exists in the divine excellences of the man Christ Jesus.

The three chief means of purification under the law were blood, water, and oil: the last was the type of the Holy Spirit, as the source of healing and of life. Nothing capable of notice by the senses, could be more precious and fragrant than the holy oil; hence the Holy Spirit* is called "the oil of gladness," Heb. i. 9; and in the passages where mention is made of pouring out the Spirit, reference is had to this emblem. The

* See Serle's Essay on the Oil of Gladness, in his Horæ Solitariæ; Leighton's Sermons on this verse, and on 1 Pet. ii. 9.

pouring of the precious oil upon Aaron's head in such
profusion that it ran down even to the skirts of his
garments, had its fulfilment, when at his baptism
Jesus was anointed with the oil of gladness above his
fellows, by the Shechinah settling on him, even the
Holy Spirit, symbolized by the dove. Hence, the Redeemer never received any public official unction of
this priestly oil from the hand of man. "The Spirit
of the Lord God is upon me, because the Lord hath
anointed me." Isa. lxi. 1. When Jesus is said to be
anointed, more is meant than merely setting him apart
to office; the idea is that of his receiving the Holy
Ghost without measure, John iii. 34, as Aaron received
the holy oil without measure—a divine nature into
union with the human nature. The shedding of the
Spirit on our Lord constitutes his designation to office,
and his fitness for that office. A ody was prepared
for him, Heb. x. 5, that it might be the dwelling-place
of the Spirit, and the means of pouring this oil of
gladness forth among men for healing the soul from
the corruption of sin, and adorning it with the beauty
of holiness. In him dwelt all the fulness of the Godhead bodily, or really, and not merely symbolically,
as it dwelt in the cloud over the mercy-seat, Col. ii. 9.
This holy perfume of the divine nature, as exuberant
and infinite as it is excellent, fills the precious alabaster of his human nature full, and running over on
every side, like a golden vessel of the sanctuary overflowing with the fulness of the sea. In this immeasurable fulness of the Spirit of holiness, is the difference
between Jesus and his fellows. They are anointed as

the leper, when a drop of oil was put on his ear, and his hand, &c., Lev. xiv. 17: Jesus was anointed with the Holy Spirit as with an illimitable sea of liquid perfume. His superior excellency to his fellows, the angels, the prophets, and the saints, associated with him in the work of redemption, consists in his having all the infinite riches of the Godhead.

He has by inheritance, by partaking of the nature of God as a son partakes of the nature of a father, and by possessing a right in all things, not through donation or conquest, but through his right as a son, a more excellent name or cluster of perfections than the angels, thereby being made so much better than they. Heb. i. 4. The unfolding of these excellences to us, is as the pouring forth of the precious oil of the sanctuary. The precious oil of the heavenly sanctuary is the divine nature of Jesus Christ. All his garments smell of myrrh, aloes, and cassia, as he came out of the ivory palaces of the heavenly glory, Ps. xlv. 8; and this is because God has anointed him with the oil of gladness above his fellows. The object in filling his human nature to so overflowing a degree with the precious perfume of the Holy Spirit, was that this oil of gladness might be poured forth among men. There was no way of sending it down to us, but through this human nature of the Lord Jesus. Before this, the emblem of God towards us sinners was a consuming fire, such as was placed at the east of Eden, and was seen on the top of Sinai. How great the contrast between the fire which on the mountain burned into the midst of heaven, Deut. iv. 11, and the holy oil poured forth in rich perfume under the shadow of the peaceful cloud over the mercy-seat: the former consuming with terrible vigour, and shooting forth lightning and death, if even a beast, much less a sinful man, touch the mountain, represents God as he must ever be towards the guilty; the latter, delicious in its fragrance, soft in its richness, and healing in its efficacy, shows the loveliness and grace of God as reconciled through Christ. As the woman broke the alabaster box, and poured the pure spikenard, very precious, on the head of Jesus, and the house was filled with the odour of the perfume; so, through his broken body, are these excellences of the divine nature, mercy, love, grace, truth, forgiveness, and sanctification, unsealed to ruined man. And though his name was poured forth in so many ways, under the Old Testament, by prophecy, by providence, and by types; all these were through his broken body, and in connection with the shedding of his blood. His crucifixion was the breaking of the alabaster containing the precious oil; and then did the fragrance of his name begin to spread abroad for filling the world. Even as in the operations of nature, using means for sending the knowledge of his excellence into all the earth by the gospel preached to every creature, he who brought from heaven this sacred treasure of healing truth, deposited it not in vessels of gold, found in the palaces of Herod and Cæsar, but in men of humbler mould, in earthen vessels gathered at random on the shores of Galilee, that the excellency of the power might be of God.

His name is poured forth by the shedding abroad of the Holy Spirit in our hearts. The truth, the sacraments, the ordinances, are means subserving the end of the Spirit; and ministers of the gospel "are unto God a sweet savour of Christ, in them that are saved, and in them that perish," because they are vessels through which the Spirit pours out the holy oil on the perishing. 2 Cor. ii. 15. From Jesus as the head, the Holy Ghost is shed down on all the members of his spiritual body. As thus poured forth, how precious is his name, in the hour of repentance, in trouble, in affliction, in temptation, in sickness, in death! As the Holy Spirit pours the healing oil of grace into the heart, how can these truths be felt sinking down through the soul! There is something peculiar and inexplicable in the sweetness and attractiveness of the name of Jesus to the saint, soothing, delightful, refreshing, life-giving; and when we begin to open up any one of his perfections, there seems to rise around the soul something richer than "a steam of rich-distilled perfumes."

The persons that love him whose name is thus precious, are "the virgins," the pure in heart. As the purity of Jesus, or his holiness, is his great attractiveness, and as in love there must be an adaptation of our affections to the virtues of the loved one, those only can love Jesus, who purify themselves even as he is pure. 1 John iii. 3. Those by whom he is despised and rejected, are they to whose spiritual leprosy the oil of gladness has never been applied, and whose constitution is filled with all unrighteousness, as sadly pointed out in Rom. i. 29—31, and in Gal. v. 19—21. Those whose souls have been made pure by the fruit of the Spirit, as in Gal. v. 22, whose hearts have been fed by heavenly grace, like the candlestick all of gold, with the two olive trees by its side, which through the two golden pipes emptied the golden oil out of themselves, Zech. iv. 2, are continually ascending to Jesus in the purity of flames of love, nourished by the Holy Ghost. Their love is rendered thus ardent, not so much because he is the means of their escape from hell and suffering, as by their perception of his inherent purity, excellence, and loveliness.

While, therefore, the first desire of the saint, as here expressed, is for the influences of the Holy Spirit, we are led, in the next place, to the infinite excellence of Christ. These two grand truths are the proper introduction to such a book as the Song; like the two pillars at the entrance of the temple, Jachin and Boaz, firmness or foundation and strength, the doctrines of the righteousness of Christ as our corner-stone, and of the grace of the Spirit as our strength, are never lost sight of by the believer, and become more precious to us as we grow in holiness. We cannot behold the beauty of the Lord, and inquire in his temple for the utterances of his love, without having on our right hand and left, these grand and sustaining truths.

VER. 4.—Draw me, we will run after thee. The King hath brought me into his chambers: we will be glad and rejoice in thee; we will remember thy love more than wine: the upright love thee.

The imagery of the allegory in this verse, and

indeed in the greater part of the first chapter, seems based on the supposition that Solomon had, according to oriental custom, gone forth in kingly state to meet his bride on the road. Hence the tents of the king and of his attending nobles would be set up with royal magnificence, at the place where he was to meet the spouse. It is now customary in the east for persons of distinction to lodge in their own costly tents on a journey. Van Egmont and Heyman state that the festivities attending an occasion of great public rejoicing, when they were at Constantinople, were held in a camp pitched for that purpose in the neighbourhood of the city.* In this place, we may suppose

* "It must be owned, that the Turks spare for nothing in rendering their tents convenient and magnificent. Those belonging to the Grand Signior were exceeding splendid, and covered entirely with silk; and one of them lined with a rich silk stuff, the right side of which was the apartment for the eunuchs. But even this was exceeded by another, which I was informed cost twenty-five thousand piasters. It was made in Persia, and intended as a present to the Grand Signior, and was not finished in less than three or four years. The inside of this tent was lined with a single piece made of camel's hair, and beautifully decorated with festoons and sentences in the Turkish language."—*Van Egmont and Heyman*, vol. i. 212.

"Maillet states that the Beys of Egypt are wont to be attended by large bodies of servants, magnificently dressed; that one of them did, on days of ceremony, appear with a train of three hundred horsemen, all his slaves, mounted on horses of value, whose harness was of silver gilt, and with saddle cloths embroidered with gold and silver, hanging down to the ground. The sight of the different Beys, with their attendants, riding in troops in the neighbourhood of Cairo, had a very magnificent and imposing effect."—*Harmer*, 200.

that the bride, in her progress towards the royal city,
comes in sight of these tents of the kingly party awaiting her, and gives expression to her feeling in the
language of these verses. The conveyance seems
hardly swift enough for the ardour of her love, and
she gives utterance to her deep emotion in the words,
"Draw me," &c.

The perfections of Christ are transcendent in excellence, and infinite in variety and extent, for they are
nothing less than the excellences of the Godhead.
The glories and delights centring in Jehovah as the
fountain of life and beauty, are an illimitable treasury,
an ocean of light, resplendent with greater riches
than gold and gems, into which we are permitted to
gaze, through the person of the man Christ Jesus;
he is the door, John x. 7, Eph. ii. 18, the central
aperture of light, through which, during eternity, we
shall be seeing and hearing things impossible for man
to utter—so glorious as to have merely a foreshadowing in what was beheld by the apostle when a door
was opened in heaven, Rev. iv. 1, and he saw the
wonders and heard the chorus of the heavenly host.
Every glimpse of the beauty of Christ increases our
desire to know more of his loveliness, and strengthens
the ardour of our affections. Expanding and growing
more intense, through ages of ages, with the enlarge-
ment of our view of the perfections of God unfolded
to us through Christ, our love towards him will
increase with a progression, and to a degree, now
incomprehensible, and will draw us to him with a

gentle power and wondrous pleasantness, of which
the mind cannot now even remotely conceive.

As those precious perfumes or excellences of character were the cause of attraction or love, the first
words of this verse are a prayer that he would unfold
his loveliness, and thereby draw the soul to himself.
The character of Christ, as opened to the heart by
the Holy Spirit, is the corrective of our natural
sluggishness, and kindles within us the desire of following him with all our energy, of running after him;
but as our weakness is more sensibly felt as this
desire strengthens, we pray that his strength may be
made perfect in our weakness, and we may be constrained by the influence of his grace. "The love of
Christ constraineth us." 2 Cor. v. 14. "All my
springs are in thee." Ps. lxxxvii. 7. Nothing is
more attractive than a lovely character, to those
capable of relishing its beauties. The Creator has
made us susceptible of this attraction, as naturally as
matter is susceptible of attraction by gravitation.
When the Holy Spirit unfolds the loveliness of Christ,
and restores the perceptive powers of the heart, we
are spontaneously drawn towards Jesus.

When we are inclined towards our Lord with animated affections—running after him—he receives us,
and brings us into his apartments, the place into
which none are admitted but his confidential friends.
There was the court of the garden of the king's palace,
where the king made a feast unto all the people, Esth.
i. 5; and there was the inner court of the king's

house, where none were permitted to enter but invited guests, Esth. iv. 11, v. 2, and there were the apartments here called chambers, where he saw only those whom he intimately cherished and loved. These apartments are what is meant by the words, "In the secret of his tabernacle shall he hide me," Ps. xxvii. 5; "He that dwelleth in the secret place of the most High shall abide under the shadow of the Almighty." Ps. xci. 1. How beautiful was the holy of holies with its sides overlaid with gold, its veil of blue and purple and scarlet, and the mercy-seat of pure gold, overshadowed by the two cherubim of gold beaten out of one piece, while the cloud of glory was its only light; this was the representation of the spiritual chambers in which the king who dwelleth between the cherubim receives his faithful friends, and of those mansions prepared in heaven, where, when he comes again, he will receive us unto himself. The Psalmist says of one thus favoured, "His soul shall dwell at ease," or lodge in goodness, the divine goodness forming the walls of the dwelling in which he passes the night of his sojourn on earth. The secret of the Lord is with such, Ps. xxv. 14; he treats them as confidential friends. And as he revealed to Noah the secret of the flood, and to Abraham the secret of the destruction of Sodom, Gen. xviii. 17, and to Daniel the secret of the king's dream, Dan. ii. 19, so does he show unto us his covenant, speaking to our hearts in the still small voice of his Spirit; and, while giving unto us the white stone, in which is a new name written that no man knoweth saving he that receiveth it, feeding us on better than angel's food, even the hidden manna of the riches of his grace. How can we utter the blessedness of having such an intimate friend? Do we need wisdom? Our confidential friend is Christ, the wisdom of God. Do we need protection? Our dearest friend is Christ, the power of God, able to save to the uttermost, even from the grave, and from hell. His is a friendship that no change of circumstances can alienate. Unlike the heartless friends of the world, he does not forsake us when riches flee away; he gathers us more closely to him in the hour of sorrow. Touched with the feeling of our infirmities, he binds up the broken-hearted, and pouring the oil of gladness and the wine of grace into the bruised spirit, from which even the priest and Levite had turned away, he says, "I will never leave thee nor forsake thee." In him are hid all the treasures of wisdom and knowledge; with him are durable riches and righteousness; he holds for us, in his right hand, a crown of glory that fadeth not away. No friendship is so intimate, reliable, honourable, and confidential, as that existing between Jesus and the soul of the saint. No secret entrusted to him will ever be dishonourably divulged. When father and mother forsake, he remains faithful still. To him may we go with our secret griefs; to him may we unburden our heaviest sorrows, with the confidence of being never received with coldness, of being welcomed with the tenderest sympathy and most compassionate love. Though we have forsaken him like Peter, he remembers our iniquities no more, and receives us with no heavier rebuke than the look he turned upon that weeping disciple. Happy are they who know how to value such a friend.

The words, "We would be glad and rejoice in thee," show the results of this communion with Christ, great joy and exultation. The Psalmist sings, "How good and how pleasant it is for brethren to dwell together in unity;" much greater is the pleasure had in dwelling with Jesus as our confidential friend. In his presence is fulness of joy. With him is the fountain of life; and as our joy must increase in purity and intensity with every step of approach towards him, when we rest with him at the throne of grace, our joy must be full. Unlike the pleasures of the world, these gratifications are attended with no painful remembrances: "We will remember thy love more than wine." Here, with Jesus, we have great peace in present possession, glorious hopes for the future, sweet recollections of the past. What are the remembrances continually gathering around an irreligious life? Hopes blasted, expectations disappointed, a sense of having never realized what was anticipated from any source, the enfeebling effects of dissipation, apprehensiveness of detection and exposure in unrighteous gratifications, and forebodings uttered by conscience of judgment to come; these are the best fruits that memory can gather from the past, wherein there have been no visions of Jesus. How empty is the recollection of even the temperate and allowable enjoyments of the irreligious! But how sweet is the remembrance of God's grace! These memories are as a luminous stream of living waters,—unlike the seas whose waves follow the track of the ship with light at midnight,—winding amid the deepening gloom and ruins of the past. How tender the recollection of the times and places where first this precious Friend met us with the assurance of forgiveness, where his Spirit melted down the soul in deep contrition, where we had brightening views of heaven, where Jesus showed us his glory and gave us his love! Could any pleasures of wine, of sense, of the world, be remembered as fondly as the disciples cherished the recollection of the farewell words of their Lord, of the discourse on the road to Emmaus, of the scene at the transfiguration? And as the tide of time will not allow us to make tabernacles and dwell where thus our Lord met us, memory delights to build her shrines there, and linger fondly on those consecrated hills.

The last clause, we would read, They love thee sincerely, rather than, "The upright love thee."* In ver. 3, it is said, the virgins, or the pure in heart, love him for the excellences of his character. Here, the same

---

* Following the Latin Vulgate, the English translators have thus rendered this clause. The version here given is more correct. Something must be supplied in the Hebrew, in order to make out the sense in the English version. In Ps. lxxv. 3, the same word here translated "the upright," is rendered "uprightly." There is no reason why it should not be thus rendered here. With the Hebrew word used adverbially, rather than as a substantive, the connection of the clause with the foregoing part of the verse is obvious; and the meaning is, They, that is, the virgins, love thee sincerely. The import of the words then is, that they who love Jesus, love him sincerely, with an affection lawful, deep, and pure.

persons are said to love him with sincerity, with a love they have good reason to indulge—a love pure, deep, and intense, separated from all interested motives, and stronger from being thus pure. These words are the natural expression of a heart occupied with such love. And when our precious Lord has drawn us by his grace, so that the soul rises towards him with the energy of eagles' wings; when he has taken us apart into chambers filled with visions more glorious than those had by Moses in the mount; where he saw the God of Israel, and under his feet as it were a paved work of a sapphire stone, and as it were the body of heaven in its clearness; then, how deep, how reasonable, how sincere is felt our love! As Satan accused Job of serving God from selfish motives, and as a bad man will not admit that others can be actuated by pure, disinterested principle; we feel, on the other hand, that, like ourselves, our brethren are controlled by simplicity and godly sincerity in their devotion and love to Jesus.

VER. 5.—I am black, but comely, O ye daughters of Jerusalem, as the tents of Kedar, as the curtains of Solomon.

Received in these tents with royal magnificence, and seeing around her a company of female attendants on the king, here called the daughters of Jerusalem, the spouse notices the contrast between the freshness of their complexion, always shielded at home for exposure, and her own dusky hue, contracted from being abroad under the scorching sun; she accordingly expresses her feelings by saying that though dark, she was beautiful, and illustrates her meaning by a comparison drawn naturally from the surrounding encampment. Even now the Arabs generally make use of tents covered with black hair-cloth; those of Kedar especially are thus covered, and being generally low and of flat appearance, cause a camp of such tents at a distance, to look like a number of black spots. The curtains of Solomon are here most probably put for a splendid state-tent of that monarch, something like those even yet known among oriental monarchs. "History has recorded, that at the famous marriage feast held by Tamerlane at Ranighul, the royal tents were gilded, and adorned with precious stones. Each tent had twelve columns of silver, inlaid with gold; the outside was scarlet and seven other colours, and the inside was lined with satin of all colours. The curtains were of velvet and the ropes of silk. At the encampment of the same conqueror in the plain of Ourtaupa, the pavilions were richly ornamented, and hung with curtains of brocade covered with golden flowers. At other times, we read of tents 'covered with tartaries full nobly:' and at the great encampment at Minecgheul the tent of Timur himself was under a canopy supported by forty pillars, and was as spacious as a palace. In the middle of it was a throne, so ornamented with precious stones that it resembled a sun. The contrast between such glorious pavilions as these, and the sombre tents of the pastoral tribes, is great indeed."*

* Kitto's Daily Bible Readings, on the Song. See notes on ver. 4.

Love and communion with Jesus is the means of imparting to us a more correct knowledge of ourselves—"I am black, but comely, O ye daughters of Jerusalem." The daughters of Jerusalem mentioned in Luke xxiii. 28, were the native women of Jerusalem; and by these words are here meant those companions of the spouse, the saint, in the spiritual Jerusalem, with whom we, though strangers and foreigners, are brought into association by conversion. To these pious brethren are these words addressed, as those who love the Lord speak often to one another, and the Lord hearkens and hears. Mal. iii. 16. The spouse was aware of her deficiency in point of beauty, and was yet conscious of an excellence that had been imparted to her. There is no correct knowledge of our nature, without the prior knowledge of Christ, The maxim of the ancient sage, "Know thyself," was an impossibility without the gospel and the Holy Spirit. Man may feel the want of things, without being able to attain the knowledge for relieving such want. The unpretending disclosures in the Scriptures give a deeper view into the nature of man, than all the philosophy of all ages. They give us all the knowledge of our nature now necessary, and lead to the Holy Spirit as the means of enlightening the mind. Our condition by nature is one of atheism, Eph. ii. 12, without God as well as without Christ. Atheism is well defined, "an invincible ignorance, fancying itself the highest knowledge;"* it might be

---

* Plato against the Atheists. The Laws, book x. 1

G

added, an ignorance of self, originating in ignorance of God. The spring of our being is in God; in him is the source of our knowledge no less than our pleasures. In the study of every science or subject, there are elementary truths which cannot be disregarded without affecting all our subsequent investigations with more or less error. The first principles of the knowledge of ourselves, for which metaphysics is but another name, are found in the Scriptures, must be studied at the feet of Jesus, and can be read only in the light diffused by the Holy Spirit. Such branches as mathematics and physics may be pursued without any material tendency to error, arising from want of religious knowledge; the metaphysician must, however, begin by being a pious man. The fine theories woven by the most acute minds and dignified as transcendentalism, show the importance of building all such structures on the foundation of the apostles and prophets, with Jesus Christ as the corner-stone.

The Holy Spirit does not give us distorted views of our nature, but shows that nature as it is; its deficiencies and its virtues. Like the dark tents of Kedar, a wandering tribe of the desert descended from the second son of Ishmael, the spouse was of a swarthy colour; the original beauty of the human soul has been thus clouded and blackened by sin, yet through grace, there is gathering around it a drapery of holy virtues, beautiful as the curtains adorning the pavilion of Solomon. 1 Kings x. 28; Ezek. xxvii. 7. While our earthly house of this tabernacle is, without, black as the tents of Kedar, uncomely to mortal eyes; the redeemed soul, the king's daughter, is all glorious within, as there adorned with curtains of pious graces, wrought in heaven by a greater than Solomon, and hung around the sanctuary of this spiritual temple by the hands of angels under the eye of God the Spirit. The beauty and glory of the believer are now very much hidden from the world. Our life is a hidden life. There is a fulness of "glory which shall be revealed in us" at "the manifestation of the sons of God." Rom. viii. 19. When the apostle, speaking of heaven, says, "I saw no temple therein," Rev. xxi. 22, he would intimate that the outer covering of the tabernacle, with its golden walls and all its costly appendages, had fallen away, that nothing had been left but the holy of holies, with the cloud of glory, and this holy place had been expanded into the dimensions of the paradise of God: thus when Christ, who is our life, shall appear, we also shall appear with him in glory; the secrets of all hearts shall be revealed; the image of Christ within us the hope of glory, shall be manifested; our earthly house of this tabernacle shall be dissolved, and the soul emerge from it like the most holy place of the heavenly sanctuary, pure, spiritual, luminous with the divine glory. Of the existence of holy graces within us, we cannot be unconscious, if we are the sons of God; yet will we be painfully sensible of our depravity and corruption. Humility consists in a true knowledge of our character, without being insensible of what grace has done for us, while aware of our extreme unworthiness. How

useless and unnecessary would it have been to put
such fine and costly curtains on the outside for the
covering of a tent exposed to the sun, wind, and
rain. The tabernacle was covered with coarse skins;
the costly vail was within, screened from the eyes of
the multitude; so the beauteous, transparent drapery
of holiness, which the Spirit of God is hanging
around the soul, is within, concealed from the gaze
of the world, while the outer covering of this habitation of God through the Spirit, Eph. ii. 22, is the
coarse fabric of this dark and weather-beaten body.
The crystal palace reared in London has been justly
the admiration of the world; like it, there has been
nothing seen in any age; an unlettered savage could
hardly be made to understand how a building could
be formed so beautiful, so transparent, and how there
could be gathered in it such choice products of skill,
into the beauties of which even kings and nobles naturally desire to look. In the heavenly Jerusalem,
will be reared a spiritual palace which shall be the
admiration and ornament of that world of light and
glory; nothing will there be known more splendid;
it will rise on those heavenly hills a new and aston-
ishing creation, of materials clearer and more beautiful than a fabric of glass and gold, open on every
side to the rays of the Sun of Righteousness, stored
with those choice products of the Holy Spirit's wisdom and power, the graces of the sanctified heart—
into which things the angels desire to look. That
crystal palace is the redeemed Church; even a more
glorious temple is every sanctified soul.

VER. 6.—Look not upon me, because I am black, because the sun hath looked upon me: my mother's children were angry with me; they made me the keeper of the vineyards; but mine own vineyard have I not kept.

Having acknowledged the whole truth concerning herself, dark but comely, the spouse seems here to say, that she was not worthy of the high regard with which the daughters of Jerusalem beheld her; for she was of a tanned or swarthy colour, and this had been caused by exposure to the sun, in the discharge of menial services, to which she had been compelled by her kindred.* She shrinks from their admiration, by a consciousness of unworthiness. She had beauty, as travellers even now speak of Arab women met with in Syria, who, though swarthy, have good features. Zenobia, the celebrated queen of Palmyra, is described by historians as a woman of remarkable beauty, possessing a dark brown complexion, eyes black, sparkling, and of an uncommon fire, a countenance highly animated and sprightly, a person surpassingly graceful and genteel, with teeth white as pearl, and a voice strong and musical. But though thus beautiful, the spouse does not encourage

---

* D'Arvieux observes of the Arabs of the Holy Land, that though the ordinary women are extremely tawny, yet the princesses are not so, but of a very fair complexion, being always kept from the sun. Shaw made a like observation as to the women of Barbary. Thevenot states that when he travelled into Mesopotamia, though he wore on his head a great black handkerchief, like a woman's hood, which sort of handkerchiefs the Turks commonly use upon the road, yet his forehead was scorched many times, and his hands continually.

them to admire her for her beauty; she rather
entreats them to turn away from her their gaze,
because she felt that over her beauty had been
thrown a shade.

Communion with Jesus leads the soul enjoying it
to shrink from courting the attention and admiration
of men, even of our fellow Christians: "Look not
upon me, because I am black." The desire of applause is deeply rooted in the natural heart, and is
as universal and strong as the love of gold. Pursuit
of this seems the business for which many irreligious
persons are living. From the frail beauty flutter-
ing in the ball-room, to the politician with his wily
schemes, and the soldier seeking "the bubble reputation at the cannon's mouth"—all are trying to push
themselves into notoriety, and their feeling, though
policy keeps it unuttered, is, Look on me, see how
worthy I am of admiration.

> "Fame is the spur that the clear spirit doth raise,—
> That last infirmity of noble minds,—
> To scorn delights, and live laborious days."*

This principle, springing from vanity, is seen in weak
minds no less than in the highest genius, in poor as
well as in rich, in the obscure no less than in the
most exalted. Hard is it for the believer to get this
propensity eradicated; and often does it injure, even
destroy, the ambassador of Christ. Grace crucifies us
to the world, makes us see through the speciousness of
"the things of the world," abates our desire for them,

* Milton's Lycidas.

and absorbs the soul in a passion for the honour that
is from God. It makes us see our vileness and weakness, so as to feel unworthy of any commendation,
and realize how dangerous is praise to the good of
the soul. Hence those whom Jesus loves are often
subjected to humiliation and mortification from the
world, for training them to a renunciation of the
pride which is the root of ambition, and for obliging
them to cultivate lowliness of heart. So far from
seeking worldly honour and applause, he who is our
example, when he perceived that they would come
and take him by force to make him a king, departed
again into a mountain himself alone. John vi. 15.
In Ps. cxxi. 5, "The Lord is thy shade upon thy
right hand; the sun shall not smite thee by day, nor
the moon by night; the Lord shall preserve thee from
all evil, he shall preserve thy soul;" the sun is represented as the source of the evils from which we need
to be screened, and Jehovah as our protection and
shade. Thus the words "the sun hath looked upon
me," express the cause of this injury to the beauty
once natural to the soul, the withering and darkening
effects of sin, of the divine justice blazing forth towards
us as a consuming fire. This sense of inward depravity,
of the hateful effects of sin on the heart, better known
to ourselves than any others through the illumination
of the Spirit, makes us shrink from the applause of
men, and feel unworthy of the favour of God. Far
from the desire of climbing to the conspicuous eminence of worldly fame, we seek to withdraw in quietness to the calm retreats found in the "shadow of the

great Rock in a weary land." With Moses, **we** prefer the solitude of Horeb to the splendour of the court of Egypt. The cause of the comeliness **or** beauty of the soul is not noticed in this verse, as **it** springs so evidently from communion with our Lord, "in his chambers," at the throne of grace, where "we all with open face beholding as in a glass the glory of the Lord, are changed into the same image from glory to glory, even as by the Spirit of the Lord."

Love to the Lord Jesus, special tokens of his favour, meekness, and lowliness of heart, are no security against hatred and ill-treatment from the world, and even from followers of Christ. Such was the case of Jesus on earth; we must expect the same. "My mother's children were angry with me,* they made me the keeper of the vineyards."† This was a work laborious and menial. Those whom Nebuzaradan left for vine-dressers and husbandmen were the poor of

* "In the East, the husband is a stern and unfeeling despot; his harem, a group of trembling slaves. The children espouse with ardour, unknown to those who are placed in other circumstances, the cause of their own mother, while they regard their common father with indifference or terror. It greatly aggravated the affliction of David, that he had become an alien to his mother's children, Ps. lxix. 8; the enmity of his brethren, the relations of his father's other wives, or his more distant relatives, gave him less concern."—*Stackhouse's History of the Bible*, book viii. chap. 4.

† "Great care was taken to preserve the clusters of the vine from the intrusion of birds; and boys were constantly employed, about the season of the vintage, to frighten them with a sling and the sound of the voice."—*Wilkinson's Ancient Egyptians*, vol. ii. 149.

the land. 2 Kings xxv. 12. The blessings promised to his people by the coming of the Messiah, are represented by freedom from this service. "The sons of the alien shall be your ploughmen and your vine-dressers." Isa. lxi. 5. Well is it that the saints have been made to feel that the Saviour's kingdom is not of this world. Temporal power is as prone to ruin the Church, as riches and ease are to ruin individual Christians. Feeling the uncongenial and hostile spirit of the world, the young believer fondly trusts to find among his fellow Christians the sanctuary of a brotherhood, unclouded by envy, undisturbed by a jar. Experience shows how fallacious was his expectation. The remains of corruption in the hearts of good men prove elements of dissension, discord, and collision. The love of power, desire of prominence, jealousy of rivals in ability and influence, frequently excite to efforts for keeping down brethren whose offence is that they are apparently superior in learning, piety, or usefulness. "Whence come wars and fightings among you? come they not hence, even or your lusts?" Jas. iv. 1. While sanctification remains imperfect, these tendencies to discord will more or less frequently rise above the control of grace, as well as surmount the influence of natural affection. Members of irreligious families are yet exposed to persecution on becoming pious; and the believer often finds a man's foes are they of his own household of faith. The same unhallowed principle, not yet entirely uprooted by grace, is the cause of the ill treatment and ill feeling received by the humble saint from the wicked world, from other religious denominations, and from members of the same church. How common for different sects, even of evangelical Christians, to endeavour to injure, if not destroy, each other's influence, when their energies combined against the enemies of all religion, would produce little enough impression; when there is more than a sufficiency for them all to do in converting the world; and when each is designed by the Head of the Church to exert an influence, and occupy a position the other is not adapted to fill. The spirit of detraction and selfishness, so rife in the world, will never be entirely banished from the Church, till we reach the spirits of just men made perfect. Among those of the same sect, how common for such as live near to Christ to be envied, maligned, and ill treated by their brethren. Speaking to him that is poor and of a contrite spirit, and trembleth at his word, the Holy Spirit says: "Your brethren that hated you, that cast you out for my name's sake, said, Let the Lord be glorified: but he shall appear to your joy, and they shall be ashamed." Isa. lxvi. 5. In his last affecting address to them, Jesus insists strongly on his disciples loving one another, because, among other reasons therefor, they would be hated by the world, John xv. 17; and though the intolerance among rival sects, and the envy often apparent in Christian brethren, may be overruled for good, just as other sin may be, Ps. lxxvi. 10, those show themselves to have departed most from the temper of the world, and come nearest to Jesus, who strive not to pull down others, but cultivate love to Christ's people wherever found, manifesting kindness and forbearance towards the persecuting spirit yet hanging around them, as well as towards the malice of the impenitent.

The soul thus blest with Jesus' love, feels and confesses its omissions, short-comings, and neglect of duty; "my own vineyard have I not kept." A sense of unworthiness increases with growth in grace. As advancement in learning makes us more sensible how little we know, so the more we increase in Christian activity, the more active do we wish to be, and the more painfully are we conscious of deficiencies. No man feels so acutely how far he falls below the full measure of holy duties, pious zeal, and heavenly love, as he who is growing up nearest to the stature of a perfect one in Christ. He who has done most for the Redeemer feels himself to have done least. Our obligations to Jesus are seen to be so great, love to him would so constrain us, that after stretching our powers to the utmost, we are ready to weep that we do no more. Though the trust committed to us has been kept, we are humbled with the consciousness that in many respects it might have been kept with greater faithfulness. Duties have been neglected, opportunities of usefulness misimproved, watchfulness unheeded, prayer offered with coldness, temptation tampered with, self-denial too little exercised, every thing, indeed, however laborious our piety, bearing traces of the imperfection inseparable from earth,, and filling us with deep humiliation. With contrition and tears, we acquiesce in the words of Jesus, "When ye shall have done all those things which are commanded you, say, We are unprofitable servants." Luke xvii. 10. The moral man will look with complacency on some trifling deeds done for religion, thinking he is conferring an honour on Christ, and is showing a praiseworthy condescension in such a work of supererogation: our feeling is, "in many things we come short all." Many duties have been crowded out of place by selfish desires; and with those which have been done are mingled many imperfections, and much of an improper spirit. Sensible of these things, we feel the uprightness of God in his chastisements, even when from the ands of brethren, rather than of the wicked; and instead of fretting against our Father in heaven, or complaining of those who misuse and oppress, we find in our own unworthiness more than sufficient reason for all these ills, and are filled with wonder that our blessings are yet so numerous, and our sorrows so few, that while we deserve a sea of troubles, God has sent only a surge. Grace makes the believer feel painfully, how much more closely he might have walked with God, how much more his privileges might have been improved.

VER. 7.—Tell me, O thou whom my soul loveth, where thou feedest, where thou makest thy flock to rest at noon: for why should I be as one that turneth aside by the flocks of thy companions?

For carrying out the design of the allegory, this regal encampment is here represented as moving from place to place, in search of green pastures, cooling shades, and still waters, under the guidance of their shepherd-king. The spouse having been received so kindly and feeling increased ardour of affection, wishes to follow the beloved, not merely as one among the mixed multitude, but enjoying, as she had already, the pleasure of his pavilion and society.*

The first burst of desire from the pious heart is for the fulness of the Holy Spirit, as in verse 2; this

* "It would be difficult to describe the appearance of a large tribe, like that we now met, when migrating to new pastures. We found ourselves in the midst of wide-spreading flocks of sheep and camels. As far as the eye could reach, to the right, to the left, and in front, still the same moving crowd. Long lines of asses and bullocks laden with black tents and variegated carpets; boys driving flocks of lambs; horsemen armed with their long tufted spears, scouring the plain on their fleet mares; riders urging their dromedaries with their short hooked sticks, and leading their high-bred steeds by the halter; colts galloping among the throng; high-born ladies seated in the centre of huge wings, which extended like those of a butterfly from each side of the camel's hump, and are no less gaudy and variegated. Such was the motley crowd through which we had to wend our way for several hours. When we reached the encampment, our horses, as well as ourselves, were exhausted by the heat of the sun, and the length of the day's journey. The tents were pitched on a broad lawn in a deep ravine; they were scatered in every direction, and amongst them rose the white pavilions of the Turkish irregular cavalry."—*Layard's Nineveh*, vol i. 91. "Looking to the east, flocks and herds were seen spreading through the undulating valleys. In one place, we saw many of them gathered together under a shady tree, waiting till the excessive heat of noon should be abated. At other times, the shepherds gather the flocks beside a well, as we afterwards saw at Lebonah, where many hundreds were lying down around the well's mouth."— *Mission of Inquiry to the Jews*, p. 109.

creates the anxious wish to run after Jesus, ver. 4;
and this feeling receives its gratification in being
brought to intimate communion with our Lord, ver. 4.
The soul thus blessed desires to follow Jesus whithersoever he goeth, Rev. xiv. 4; John x. 27; and when
this Shepherd-king goes abroad to take charge of his
flock, we would go with him, anxious to be with him
in difficulty, fatigue, and danger, no less than amid
the luxuries of his palace. The formalist and luke-
warm have their view occupied with the difficulties
and self-denial likely to be encountered; the spiritual
Christian has his attention so engrossed with the loveliness of Christ, as to overlook, or encounter with
alacrity, all obstructions in reaching the presence of
his Lord.

This results from the intensity and energy of his
love—a love such that his whole soul seems melted
down into this one affection, and its delighted expression is, "O thou whom my soul loveth." When love
to Jesus is compared with love felt for any thing that
may be a man's ruling passion, such as the love of
fame, of power, of money, we are far from doing it
justice. These are strong; but far stronger is love
to Jesus. In these cases there is but one solitary
thing, and that an inferior one, to satisfy all the
cravings of all the powers of the soul; the one propensity is only partially satisfied, and the other affections are still more restless. But in Christ, love taking the lead, as its most exalted exercise is in cleaving to an object as far above every other as the
Creator is above the thing created, all the faculties

find in him the richest field for activity; and the
Holy Ghost does in the meantime, open to us his
loveliness, and brace up every fibre of the soul for
beholding, adoring, and loving him; so that all our
energies are concentrated on this one point of love to
Christ, and thus drawn to a focus, burn with a
heavenly radiance, a consuming fervour. Love to
Christ thus becomes the strongest passion which can
take possession of the soul of man. Husband, wife,
children, father, mother, life, however fondly cherished, are so much less loved, that in comparison with
Jesus they may be said to be hated. Matt. x. 37;
Luke xiv. 26. By the power of the Spirit, who
makes us partakers of the divine nature, we are
through this love so absorbed in Jesus as to be one
with him; so that as Christ thus dwells in our hearts,
and being thus rooted and grounded in love, we know
his love which passeth knowledge, we are filled with
all the fulness of God, and approximate to the feeling
enjoined in the command, "Thou shalt love the Lord
thy God, with all thy heart, and with all thy soul,
and with all thy strength, and with all thy mind."
Luke x. 27. With what depth of blessedness does
the soul then look earnestly towards Jesus, and say:
"O thou whom my soul loveth!"

"Tell me, where thou feedest;"—where thou dost
watch over thy flock as a shepherd;—where I may
be under thy care as my shepherd. The word "feed"
in this verse, as well as in Isa. xl. 11, Rev. vii. 17,
means to discharge the office of a shepherd. As in the
services of the law, a variety of sacrifices and purifica-

tions was necessary, because no one type could prefigure every thing necessary to be known about Jesus Christ in the work of purchasing redemption; so, various illustrations are used for showing the different relations he sustains to the saints, in applying the benefits of his purchase. The blessedness of the seasons when we are favoured with delightful communications of the Holy Spirit, is set forth by communion with the king in his chambers; but as our course is long and lies through difficulties, trials, and dangers, wherein we are of ourselves helpless and need the superintending care of an all-powerful hand, Jesus is represented as a shepherd; Ps. xxiii. 1, as the Shepherd and Bishop of souls, 1 Pet. ii. 25; as the chief Shepherd, 1 Pet. v. 4; as the great Shepherd of the sheep, Heb. xiii. 20. This includes protection, guidance, provision for the soul, pastures and waters, and company with our Lord. There are places where Jesus may be thus found; and as the sheep that wanders from the shepherd loses these benefits, we must be careful to keep near him, among his flock. He has a variety of pastures into which he leads his flock, all increasing in richness and luxuriance, as we draw nearer to the limits of this wilderness and the borders of the promised land in heaven. At first, under his pastoral care, these green pastures and still waters of the spiritual life are found at intervals, like the green spots in the desert, wells of water and palm-trees, with many a weary journey between; but as we draw nearer to heaven, more frequent evidences are met of our approaching a better country; the desert tracts are less desolate and less extensive; the verdure grows richer, as lying more nearly under the influence of a more refreshing than Hermon's dews; until at length we pass over into that good land, where the Lamb which is in the midst of the throne, shall feed us, and shall lead us into living fountains of waters. In the illimitable wilderness around us, how can we find these precious spots, without his guidance? If we rest in green pastures, it is he that makes us lie down there; if we repose beside the still waters, it is he that leads us thither. The world has many alluring scenes for drawing us away from Christ; but we wish to come away even from Lebanon and Hermon, Song iv. 8, to leave Egypt itself, and Goshen, for Horeb, desolate as it may seem, if there we may, like Moses, find the good Shepherd, in the attractive manifestations of his glory. Exod. iii. 2. Tell me—make me to know by the inward voice of thy Spirit, and by the outward guidings of thy providence, where and what are those situations and occupations in life, and those seasons pervaded by more than usual influences of the Holy Spirit, in which I may dwell, not by my own choice, but by thine appointment, and there enjoy unceasing thy gracious presence and thy shepherd-care.

"Where thou makest thy flock to rest at noon."*

* "'Tis raging noon; and, vertical, the sun
  Darts on the head direct his forceful rays.
  Welcome, ye shades! ye bowery thickets, hail!
  Around th' adjoining brook that purls along
  The vocal grove, now jutting o'er a rock,

H

At noon, they led their flocks aside into the shade, and by wells or streams, that they might be sheltered from the oppressive heat, and enjoy the refreshment of cool waters. Gen. xxix. 7. "They shall feed in the ways, and their pastures shall be in all high places. They shall not hunger nor thirst; neither shall the heat nor sun smite them: for he that hath mercy on them shall lead them, even by the springs of water shall he guide them." Isa. xlix. 10, Ezek. xxxiv. 13. The day has not more certainly its noon, a time when in the East all are glad to seek repose in the shade, by springs, to slake their consuming thirst, than has the life of the believer its period of trial and sorrow. In following our Lord, we must expect not only to enjoy seasons when every thing in the spiritual life is calm,

> Now scarcely moving through a reedy pool,
> Now starting to a sudden stream, and now
> Gently diffused into a limpid plain;
> A various group the herds and flocks compose."
>
> —*Thomson's Summer.*

We might further mention in illustration the Culex of Virgil, ver. 116.

> "Now at the shepherd's call, the kids once more
> Seek the deep shade, their devious rambles o'er,
> Where murmuring waters wash th' o'erhanging moss
> And limpid steal along the blue-tinged fosse.
> While from his mid-day course the sunbeams beat,
> To shades the shepherd and his flock retreat."

And again, Georg. iii. 331.

> "When noon-tide flames, down cool sequestered glades,
> Lead where some giant oak the dell o'ershades,
> Or where the gloom of many an ilex throws
> The sacred darkness that invites repose."

dewy, and refreshing, like the morning; but also to encounter times when all things conspire to weary, discourage, and exhaust the spirit with the withering power of an oriental noon. But there are at such times, wells and fountains in this wilderness, like these which were concealed in the desert, and to which the wearied hosts of Israel were led by "the Shepherd of his flock." They are known to our good Shepherd, and he will so guide us, that, like Jesus, wearied with his journey, and sitting on Jacob's well at noon, John iv. 6, we may, when worn with the difficulties of our pilgrimage, sit there, and drink, and with joy draw water out of the wells of salvation. There is an "hour of temptation," Rev. iii. 10, and an hour of affliction. These are sure to follow any remarkable communication of grace to us. It was directly after the baptism of the Holy Spirit, that Jesus was tempted by the devil. In all these times, when the soul is ready to wither under the power of trials and sorrows, Jesus has provided "a tabernacle for a shadow in the day-time from the heat." Isa. iv. 5. To this refuge will he lead his chosen ones; and there, in time of trouble, he will hide us in his pavilion, in the secret of his tabernacle will he hide us. Wearied with the assaults of Satan; worn with toil; oppressed with grief; with the cherished objects that requited our affection, gone by death; and those from whom we have a right to expect better things, treating us with neglect, ingratitude, and scorn, how anxiously does the soul, feeling there is but the one object, even Jesus, left for it to love, seek his hand to guide us where there is shelter from evil, and where on his bosom the weary are at rest. "And the sheep hear his voice, and he calleth his own sheep by name, and leadeth them out; and when he putteth forth his own sheep, he goeth before them, and the sheep follow him, for they know his voice." John x. 3, 4.

"For why should I be as one that turneth aside by the flocks of thy companions?"* The divine love

* Concerning the precise import of the word here rendered "turneth aside," interpreters are divided. It properly means "to cover;" and the feminine participle "covered, veiled;" that is, Why should I be as one veiled among the flocks of thy companions,—Why should I, as a faithless harlot, turn away from thee with an unsteady, erring love, and seek among those connected with the flocks of thy companions some new and improper object of affection. Thus, Gen. xxxviii. 15, "He thought her to be an harlot, because she had covered her face." Not only did she wish to seek no other love; she wished to avoid even a suspicion of not being entirely devoted to him; and consequently desired to know precisely where she might find him, without having to make the inquiries, and to incur the treatment afterwards met with from the watchmen. Chap. v. 7. Hence, Mercerus happily remarks, "The spouse wishes to create the impression of her devoted affection, as though there were danger while she wanders about inquiring for him, that she be taken for a harlot." According to Kitto, "it is customary for all the women inhabiting towns to go about closely veiled; while all the women of the different pastoral people who live in tents do not commonly wear veils, or at most only so far as to cover their foreheads and lower parts of the face, leaving the countenance exposed, from the eyebrows to below the nose. It is evident, that although the use of complete coverings was known, the women of the pastoral patriarchs did not conceal their faces completely, except on extraordinary occasions."—*Illustrated Commentary*, Gen. xx. 16.

which constrains us to follow Jesus with earnest self-denial wherever he may see best to lead, whether through dark and rough valleys, or into the most refreshing pastures; which makes us seek his direction in trouble, and rest in the covert in which he would then have us to abide, does equally incline us to dread any liability of being led astray from him, and to avoid following any but Jesus. Companions of Jesus are mentioned in Acts i. 21, John xv. 27, Luke i. 2; they were the Apostles. Sin consists in apostasy from God. It creates in the heart a repulsion to God, and a disposition to occupy the powers of the soul with any thing in preference to the Creator. Whatever the manifestations of God, however attractive and glorious, depravity so changes our constitution as to carry us away from Jehovah by its natural opposition to holiness. It is the nature of a sinful being to fall away from God. Such cannot be drawn and kept near the Fountain of light and life, the Sun of Righteousness, without the restraining influences of the Holy Spirit. From God, as manifested in Paradise, in the flood, on Sinai, sinful man turned spontaneously away; and when at last he disclosed himself to us in the fulness of grace and truth in the Lord Jesus, the same native propensity towards evil and darkness inclines us to adopt the teachings of others rather than of Christ; to worship and serve the creature more than the Creator thus incarnate; to turn aside from the Redeemer, even though no farther than after his companions. From the first there was a disposition to say, "I am of

Paul, and I of Apollos, and I of Cephas." 1 Cor. i. 12. And ever since, much of the divisions among Christians has sprung from the disposition to turn away from God even in Christ, and cleave to men, to church organizations or forms of doctrine, to any thing, indeed, though an idol or a crucifix, if thereby the Author of our being, the Spirit of holiness, may be displaced from the heart. Even when holding firmly to Christ, we find within us a propensity to model our religious life after the example of our pious associates, without thinking of rising above the general tone of feeling around us, and to take as the pattern to which our ambition and efforts for holiness aspire, the life of some eminent saint, rather than the glorious righteousness of Christ. This love, as here expressed, desires to follow Jesus only, to take his example. Unsatisfied with being led by any other, we feel with Bunyan's Pilgrim, "Wherever I have seen the print of his shoe in the earth, there I have coveted to set my foot too." Taking his truth as the first rule of duty, and his life as the only perfect representation of what ours should be, we study to be not so much like any development of piety in any saint however eminent, as to be like Christ. While valuing church organizations, this love puts them in their proper place, without letting them come between the soul and Christ, and rejoices in the prosperity of religion among undoubted Christians, even though not of its own sect. Phil. i. 18. While these means of grace, creeds, and denominations, are seen necessary in the present state of man, we are able to feel they are trivial things in comparison with Jesus, to be done away in heaven. 1 Cor. xiii. 10. Through this divine love absorbing the soul, we are able in a measure to rise in our desires, above every thing else, however closely allied to him, and feel Christ to be all in all. Like many things and associations viewed as very important during childhood, but lost sight of under weightier considerations in riper years, these earthly things, even those essentially connected with religion, will be seen in their true proportions, and sink down into their proper place, when that which is perfect shall come, and that which is in part shall be done away in heaven.

VER. 8.—If thou know not, O thou fairest among women, go thy way forth by the footsteps of the flock, and feed thy kids beside the shepherds' tents.

These words are an answer to the inquiry in the foregoing verse. It is necessary for the good of those having too high an opinion of themselves, that they be reproved and humbled: there are pious spirits so borne down by humbleness of heart, as to need encouragement. Some must be held in with bit and bridle; others are so lowly they may be guided by the good Shepherd's eye, Ps. xxxii. 9, and need encouragement by his speaking to their heart. Among the latter, are those having the state of mind expressed in verses 5 and 6, "I am black, but comely, &c." Jesus seeing the lowliness of such, and unwilling to break the bruised reed, comforts them, and says, "O thou fairest among women." While the pious are despised by the world, as pos-

sessing nothing of loveliness, Jesus looking on the
heart, beyond the mere accomplishments of person
and manners, beholds the saint as the fairest among
the sons of men.   Heart has very little if any thing
to do with beauty among the fashionable world.
The most accomplished there, is most heartless.
Speaking of the court of Louis XV. a writer observes, "Generations of luxury had given to the
manner of court-minions the polish of steel, and its
hardness to their hearts."   All is outward polish and
grace, while inward deformity and corruption.   The
devotee of fashion is at best but a whited sepulchre,
beautifully garnished to the eye, but full of all uncleanness; his courtly bearing an embroidered pall,
which it has been the whole business of his life to
weave, covering from the view of men, perhaps of
himself, spiritual loathsomeness and death.   God, who
is love, begins his estimate of beauty, by taking into
consideration, first of all the heart, and the heart
purified by love.   Whatever our outward circumstances, even though unfavourable in appearance as
those of Lazarus, we are beautiful in his eyes, if the
heart be filled with the limpid and life-giving influences of the Holy Spirit.

Having thus received encouragement, so that by
knowing the opinion had of her by the beloved, the
spouse might be cheered onward in following him,
she was prepared to hear the duty that is enjoined in
reply to her inquiry: If thou know not, if you are
at any time in doubt, go thy way forth by the
footsteps of the flock, follow the example of those

gone before you to glory. The same direction is given in Heb. vi. 10—12. They are exhorted to "be not slothful, but followers of them who through faith and patience inherit the promises." This is to be done with a diligence continued to full assurance of hope, and on to the end. The state of heart thus acceptable with God, and inclining us to those ways where are the footsteps of the flock, shows itself in works and labours of love, manifested towards the name of Jesus, by ministering to his saints. Christ is given as our example: "Leaving us an example that ye should follow his steps." 1 Pet. ii. 21. We are to follow the saints as they follow Christ. 1 Cor. xi. 1. It is necessary to have the examples of both constantly before us. If the Scriptures had given nothing but doctrines in a didactic form, we must have had difficulty in comprehending and obeying them. We require something sensible and tangible; we must see the thing not only described, but done before our eyes. There is in the mind a propensity to personify abstract things, arising from the extreme difficulty of making them otherwise intelligible to beings, who, like us, derive their knowledge mainly through the senses. When the poets would make their instructions attractive and impressive, they resort to personification; and try to represent abstract truths as nearly as they can be represented, by allegorical forms. With this, the ancient mythology abounds. The Jewish ritual was formed on this principle. In making to the Jews promises and threatenings, God often had them symbolized by both acts and things. Thus the truths of religion brought down from time to time into the darkness of our world, like rays of glory from heaven, were not left to shoot afar at random, but have been concentrated, embodied, clothed with a living form, in the person of Jesus Christ; and of him may be said with truth, what was said of a heathen god;

> "Each conception was a heavenly guest,
> A ray of immortality, and stood
> Star-like around until they gathered to a God."*

There is danger of overlooking Christ as our exemplar, while receiving him as our teacher. It is required in an instructor that himself should do what he teaches others. This was eminently done by Jesus when sojourning on earth. While receiving his teachings, we must study to find how he carried out the spirit of such instructions, in his actions. The artist who seeks perfection in painting or statuary, devotes himself to the study of the works of the best masters and the models of antiquity. God has set forth, in the incarnation of Christ, a perfect model for those who would attain moral perfection. As ancient temples were ornamented with statues and sculpture, so in the temple of our God in heaven, there will be pillars, Rev. iii. 12, living statues, wrought out from the living stones here found in the horrible pit, of which the cherubim and palm-trees carved in the golden walls of the earthly temple were the foreshadowing, 1 Kings vi. 29; Ezek. xli. 18; and

* Childe Harold, Canto 4, clxii.

those of us who are co-workers with God in forming
our souls for that position of glory, can accomplish
our trust, can, under the co-operating influences of
the Holy Spirit, have our whole man reduced to the
beauty of holiness, only by taking as our model, him
in whom, when on earth in human form, did all the
fulness of the Godhead dwell. It has ever been a
device of Satan, to draw attention away from Jesus
to his saints—first from his example, and then from
his instructions—to the lives of martyrs and the
teachings of the fathers, as they are called. When
he cannot succeed in doing both, he will be satisfied
in turning our view from the example of Christ, while
we retain our hold on his word. He knows that in
proportion to the degree, he can thus turn the eye
from Jesus, the only perfect teacher and perfect
model, will be his success in introducing error; because no man is infallible, either in doctrine or practice, and accordingly, those who are content with
human guides, may be more easily corrupted by
imbibing their errors. The coldness of many Protes-
tants springs from losing sight of the living example
of Christ, while his word may be retained and perhaps studied; the errors of Popery arise from dis-
placing both the word and the example of Jesus, and
giving the attention to the doctrines and lives of the
so-called saints.

But the example of the followers of Christ, is
nevertheless of great value. In many things, Jesus
cannot be imitated. While found in fashion as a
man, there are things which he could not have in

common with our nature. He was a man, but a man who did no evil, who was sinless. In devotion to the will of God, in bearing reproach, in all things pertaining to holy living, he is a perfect model. But there are spiritual exercises arising from our being fallen sinners, and in a course of sanctification, that Jesus could never know. Regeneration, repentance, contrition, conversion, temptations to sin caused by corruptions of the heart, are things he could not have personally experienced: these things modify the whole tenor of our spiritual exercises; and, consequently, if we are to enjoy on this ground, the advantage of any who has been before us, this must be found, not in the history of Jesus, but in the lives of his people. The fall of David, his recovery and the feeling attending this recovery, as given in the Scriptures, is necessary for the encouragement of the saint under discipline: the same is true of the exercises of Paul, mentioned in Rom. vii. 15—25, and 2 Cor. xii. 7—9. Nothing in the life of Christ could furnish features of an example for our encouragement in cases like these. We need doctrinal statements, such as our Lord has given, of what we should be, and of the means by which we can become such; the example of a perfect model like Jesus, towards which to be conformed; and the example of fallen men in process of restoration by grace to the image of Christ, that through the knowledge of their exercises we may have warning, consolation, and hope. Great encouragement is derived from studying the lives of those who have been among us, and have passed through like difficulties and conflicts to glory. Good biographies are valuable to the saint as an exhibition of the operations of the Holy Spirit, and of God's gracious dealings with those in course of deliverance from the dominion of sin. With these marks so numerous—thus compassed about with so great a cloud of witnesses—we need not wander, as did Joseph, and get bewildered when seeking his brethren with their father's flock in Dothan, Gen. xxxvii. 15; but are enabled to ask for the old paths, where is the good way, and find rest for our souls. Jer. vi. 16.

"And feed thy kids beside the shepherds' tents!" While Jacob was waiting at the well, Rachel came with her father's sheep, for she kept them, Gen. xxix. 9; and the daughters of the priest of Midian came and watered their father's flock. Exod. ii. 16. The direction to the spouse is, In feeding thy kids, keep near to the shepherds' tents, and thou shalt find mo at noon in the midst of my sheep. Jesus said unto Peter, "Feed my lambs," John xxi. 15; and our Lord "shall feed his flock like a shepherd; he shall gather the lambs with his arms, and carry them in his bosom." His ministers are the under-shepherds. Jesus is to be sought by following in the footsteps marked out for his people; and by waiting for him near the shepherds' tents, in the use of the means of a regular ministry, and by "feeding the kids," that is, in the discharge of duties of usefulness to the souls of others, particularly the young. Christ is not to be found in retirement only, "in his chambers:" by following these directions, we may enjoy his presence amid the active duties of life. While religion requires us to be much alone with God, it also requires us to be much with man, especially the brethren and the ministry. They are appointed by Jesus in his stead, and must be esteemed highly for his sake. In the exercise of his sovereignty, God may renew and save souls without the regular means of grace; but this is the exception, not the rule. Grain, fruit, and choice flowers, may be found on remote islands, where no hand has sown or tilled; yet this does not show it is not our duty to labour, if we expect to live. These words include the duty of keeping ourselves under the influence of all the means of the sanctuary, at the head of which stands the ministry of the word. With this, must be joined active usefulness. While bound to offer the sacrifice of praise continually, we must not forget to do good, and to communicate. Heb. xiii. 15. The deepest spirit of love, and of acquaintance with the glory of Jesus, is not found in seclusion, nor in action alone, but in the two combined. Activity, to a certain extent, is the life of our whole being; without this, the body shrivels, the mind withers; nor are we more certainly broken down by over-taxing the powers, than by continuance of sluggish repose. The development of our spiritual life follows the same law. Like the seasons of rest and sleep for the body, times of withdrawal from the world, and of seclusion with our Lord, are essential for recruiting our spiritual energies; but those energies, when thus renewed, will not expand into their full

vigour, unless we use them for running without weariness, and walking without faintness, in the ways and
duties of the Lord. There is something which every
Christian may do, and must do, in feeding the Church
of God, which he hath purchased with his own blood.
"Feeding the kids" requires that we be careful in
training our household in the ways of the Redeemer;
that we do good to those whom we may find, by seeking opportunity, in our daily walk; and that in the
Sabbath-school, we labour according to our situation,
in training the young to follow Jesus. The spirit of
these words has its perfect fulfilment in the faithful
instruction of their children by parents, and in the
unobtrusive but important duties of the teacher in
the Sabbath-school. There, are the young of the
flock gathered under the shadow of the shepherds'
tents, and happy are those servants who are found
thus employed when the good Shepherd appears in
the midst of his fold. "Blessed is that servant whom
his Lord when he cometh shall find so doing." Matt.
xxiv. 46.

VER. 9.—I have compared thee, O my love, to a company of horses in Pharaoh's chariots.

In this encampment, where the bridal company are
now supposed to be, the king would have his most
splendid equipage; the Egyptian horses were celebrated for their beauty, "they were even exported to the
neighbouring countries, and Solomon bought them
at a hundred and fifty shekels of silver, from the
merchants who traded with Egypt by the Syrian

desert."* In modern, as well as in ancient times, the mares are considered in all respects most beautiful, valuable, and desirable. Such a steed in a chariot, like that which Solomon had brought out of Egypt by his agents, for six hundred shekels of silver, was an object of great beauty to the eye, especially when adorned with the costly trappings then usual. The beloved does therefore naturally compare the bride to such a horse in these words, which would be more correctly rendered, "I compare, thee, my love, to my chariot-steed, or mare, from Pharaoh;" or to my Egyptian chariot-steed. Though unusual in the present age, this comparison will appear beautifully appropriate, when we call to mind still further the

---

* Wilkinson's Anc. Egyptians, vol. iii. 35. "It was mid-day before we found a small party that had stopped and were pitching their tents. A young chestnut mare, belonging to the sheik, was one of the most beautiful creatures I ever beheld. As she struggled to free herself from the spear to which she was tied, she showed the lightness and elegance of the gazelle. Her limbs were in perfect symmetry; her ears long, slender, and transparent; her nostrils high, dilated, and deep red; her neck gracefully arched, and her mane and tail of the texture of silk. . . . . Two sheiks rode into the encampment, and hearing that the chief was with us, they fastened their high-bred mares at the door of our tent, and seated themselves on our carpets. . . . . Sofuk was the owner of a mare of match-less beauty, called, as if the property of the tribe, Shammeri-yah. . . . No one can look at the horses of the early Assyrian sculptures without being convinced that they were drawn from the finest models."—*Layard's Nineveh*, vol. i. 91.

The superiority of the mares at the Olympic games is repeatedly referred to in the classic authors.

affectionate adoration and tenderness with which these
animals are regarded by the orientals. Theocritus
has adopted the same illustration:

> As towers the cypress mid the garden's bloom,
> Or in the chariot proud Thessalian steed,
> Thus graceful rose-complexioned Helen moves.*

Having called the spouse "fairest among women,"
in reply to her inquiry after him in ver. 8, the Holy
Spirit proceeds to express the impression had by our
Lord, of the beauty of the saint, by the endearing
words, "my love." This shows the deep, devoted,
pre-eminent, and tender love of Jesus for his people.
Among all his creatures, there can be none for whom
he has a stronger affection than for the redeemed.
Towards these he bears a three-fold love. To the
original affection felt for them as for the holy angels
and all his creatures, is superadded the tenderness
necessarily arising towards those for whom he has
thus suffered, and the love arising from forming them

---

* The words of Horace are well known. Odes, lib. iii. 11.
Thus Sophocles:

> E'en as a high-bred steed, though old, retains
> His mettle still in danger, and his ears
> Pricks upright; so thou us dost onward urge
> And art the first to follow.—*Electra*, 25.

The epithet "magnanimous" is often applied to the horse by
the ancients, as in Virgil, Æn. iii. 704, who speaks of "noble-
spirited horses," produced in the country of the Agrigentines,
who were famous for sending superior horses to the Olympic
games. We need hardly add that the same word is very
commonly applied to heroes.

1

a second time as new creatures. His love for the unfallen inmates of heaven, is the love felt by him as their Creator: his love to the saints has the three-fold strength resulting from creation, redemption, and sanctification.

In Rev. iv. 8, and Ezek. i. 10, the living creatures had faces like different animals, emblematic of various qualities of the mind. The horse is here referred to as the emblem of the saint; and as the best horses came from Egypt, and of these the finest were in the chariot of the king, so whatever excellences this emblem expresses, must exist in the greatest perfection in the believer. Contemplating the saint as following him through the difficulties of pilgrimage in the wilderness, with self-denial, energy, and perseverance, Jesus would intimate by this comparison, that there is in the Christian character something noble, adapted to impress us with respect, and to command our admiration.*   The feeling of unrenewed men towards religion is still the same—"Can any good thing come out of Nazareth?" With them piety is in disrepute, as fitted for base and ignoble minds, as incompatible with true honour. As war was the favourite and most honourable employ-

* These Arabian horses are noble animals, and are no less remarkable for their chivalrous disposition, than for their strength and endurance: gallant, yet docile; fiery, yet gentle; full of mettle, yet patient as a camel. The head is beautiful: the expansive forehead, the brilliant, prominent eye, and the delicately shaped ear, would testify to nobleness in any animal."—*Warburton's Travels.*

ment of the Romans, virtue was in their language synonymous with courage. And the word *honour* will have, among different classes of men, a meaning varying according to the traits of character which, in their view, show the highest excellence. Thus, with some persons, truth is made almost the sole test of honour; and the honourable man, in their judgment, is the man who, whatever other vices he has, will not lie. With others, honour consists in promptitude and severity in avenging an insult.

True honour lies in the possession and practice of the most exalted virtues. Among the irreligious in Christendom, public sentiment has been so affected by religion, that the word *honour* is brought nearer to its true meaning than among even the most refined heathen; yet how glaring and palpable are the vices which the world cherish and associate with what they call honour. That man makes the nearest approach to honour, and has the true claim on our admiration, who has concentrated in his heart, and embodies in his actions, most of the purest moral virtues. He shows something better than the ragged and meretricious excellence in which "gallantry atones for every vice." The trait which has in every age been assumed as the basis of honour, whatever else might be its aspect, is the principle which prompts to exposure of comfort and life to peril for the good of others. This is the principle which stands preeminent in the character of Christ. He exhibits the noblest magnanimity, honour unallied with any imperfection. His

18*

people must be like him in self-denying benevolence,
and expose themselves for the welfare of enemies no
less than friends.

> "Honest courtesy,
> Which oft is sooner found in lowly sheds
> With smoky rafters, than in tap'stry halls
> And courts of princes, where it first was named,
> And yet is most pretended."*

There is nothing on which men of the world pride
themselves, that religion does not give in the full
measure of absolute perfection to the saints. Nobleness of soul, courtesy, excellence of heart, beauty of
appearance, objects of such desire to the fashionable,
are gifts dispensed at the foot of the cross, not to
many rich, not to many wise, not to many noble, but
to the poor of this world, and will be enjoyed at last
in greater perfection by Lazarus than by the proudest
princes. All the excellences that have adorned all
the great and noble of the world, and made their character the admiration of ages, would not form a single
cluster so rich as the many found in the bosom of the

---

* Milton's Comus, 322.—Thus, the following from Æschylus:

Integrity burns a lamp with brilliant beams,
    In smoky cottages,
And crowns with honour purity of life.
But turning with averted eyes away
From gilded prosperity with polluted hands,
    Draws nigh to goodness:
Not honouring wealth stamp'd with a counterfeit impression
    By false applause of men.—*Agamemnon*, 709.

humblest saint.* The world despise religion as over-looking what is honourable, because they judge of piety by what they see in the actions of professing Christians, rather than by the words of Scripture and the example of Christ. And in their judgment of pious men, they overlook their virtues, through eagerness to contemplate their failings. Should the heroes of the world's idolatry be estimated according to the same rule, by neglecting their little excellence and summing up the many vices with which this single good trait is in union, worldly honour would appear a very beggarly and worthless thing. Piety, as seen in God's people here, is at best a conflict of grace with corruption, a yearning and struggling after perfection. Because dishonourable doings are found in those called by Christ's name, it by no means follows these are integral elements of pure religion. Whatever meanness may be seen in God's people, is owing not to their religion, but to their remaining corruptions. If a real Christian exhibit anything of meanness, not-

---

* Sir Walter Scott says: "I have read books enough, and observed and conversed with enough of eminent and splendidly cultivated minds, too, in my time; but I assure you, I have heard higher sentiments from the lips of poor uneducated men and women, when exerting the spirit of severe yet gentle heroism under difficulties and afflictions, or speaking their simple thoughts as to circumstances in the lot of friends and neighbours, than I ever yet met with out of the pages of the Bible. We shall never learn to feel and respect our real calling and destiny, unless we have taught ourselves to consider every thing as moonshine, compared with the education of the heart."—*Lockhart's 'Life of Scott,* vol. ii. 412.

withstanding sanctification is begun, much more of
this would be visible were he entirely without grace.
Charity doth not behave itself unseemly, 1 Cor. xiii.
5; that is, avoids all conduct which may be indecorous,
or, in common estimation, unbecoming a follower of
Christ.

> "The best of men
> That e'er wore earth about him was a sufferer,
> A mild, meek, patient, humble, tranquil spirit,
> The first true gentleman that ever breathed."*

Grace elevates the fallen soul of man; and giving
it a heavenly nobleness, imparts an honour which, like
its courage, is above fear and above reproach. In
their idolatry of heroism the world are willing to
overlook the many defects, even vices, of the hero, in
admiration of his gallant bearing; and to deify one
who has but the single virtue of courage to redeem
a character marked by almost all other imaginable
vices. Let them judge of the nobleness inseparable
from piety, by looking not at the imperfections of the
man, but at his virtues; not at the dark and corrupt
soil, but at the stateliness of the growth and beauty
of the flowers, which the creative energy of the Spirit
is evolving from that mass of corruption.† Homer

---

* Decker.

† "There is not any kind of spirit in the world so noble as
that spirit that is in a Christian, the very Spirit of Jesus Christ,
that great King, the Spirit of glory, as the Apostle calls it,
1 Pet. iv. 14. This is a sure way to ennoble the basest and
poorest among us; this royalty takes away all attainders, and
leaves nothing of all that is past to be laid to our charge, or to
dishonour us."—*Leighton* on 1 Pet. ii. 9.

gives a majestic portrait of his hero on appearing
again to his foes, when Minerva threw over his shoulders her terrific ægis, and crowned his head with a
golden cloud from which burned an all-brilliant flame.
And when God sends forth to the good fight of faith,
to wrestle with wicked spirits in high places, no less
than with flesh and blood, the soul of the believer
weeping for sin; covered with the shield and buckler
of those divine truths more precious and adorned with
richer sculpture than all the gold and silver of all the
shields of the earth; and with that brilliancy of which
the cloud over the mercy-seat was the emblem, burning on his brow; even the hosts of enemies of such
soul, whether evil spirits or evil men, are compelled to
gaze on such a character with reverence, even while
using every exertion to destroy it:

"So spake the Cherub, and his grave rebuke,
Severe in youthful beauty, added grace,
Invincible: abashed the devil stood,
And felt how awful goodness is, and saw
Virtue in her shape how lovely."

A low and sordid disposition is the offspring of man's
corruption, and must vanish as he rises in purity and
fitness for heaven. By the grace which is carrying
our fallen nature back to the perfection of Paradise,
we cannot but be ennobled.

The horse is here mentioned as the emblem of the
energy belonging to piety. Sloth, lack of energy,
indolence, detract from any character. We look for
energy in what we would admire; not the energy of
feverish irregularity, but that which results from the

calm, harmonious movement of well balanced powers. The faculties of the maniac may be vigorous, but are destitute of harmony. There is an energy peculiar to the nature of different beings, and this only can we admire in them. Grace diffuses through the soul the energy which belongs to creatures like ourselves in perfection, but of which we have been despoiled through sin. A healthy mind, of good endowments, is always active, perhaps more or less so, even in hours of sleep. Perfect inactivity is a feature of perfect death; and as the soul sinks down under the influence of spiritual death, the faculties become more enfeebled, and activity becomes a greater effort. Counteracting this tendency, the Holy Spirit opens in the heart a fountain of water springing up into everlasting life; and makes us, while not slothful in business, fervent in spirit; a divine energy rising in the soul, like the waters boiling up in a perennial spring, and flowing with greater fulness as we draw nearer to him with whom is the fountain of life. Indolence is one of the many infirmities from which sanctification sets us free. Industry and perseverance in our calling, whatever that calling may be, prove a duty and a pleasure to the Christian. How are the flagging energies of the soul roused into new life by the presentation of a new motive, like the hope of fame; and the body recruited by the application of a healthful stimulant. The means provided for arresting the decay of the soul and restoring a perfect vigour, are the influences of the Holy Spirit. Compared with these, how weak, how temporary, are all the stimulants which the power of man can bring to bear· on the sinking body or the failing mind. Those who are filled with the Spirit will be active according to their capability; and even when the flesh may be weak, the spirit may be willing. Besides the direct operation of the Holy Ghost feeding the powers with heavenly strength, there are combined in action on the heart the noblest motives from without, heaven, eternal life; and the purest, strongest love within, affection to the dying Redeemer; the greatest of works to be done under the strongest of motives, and with the most encouraging aid. What a calm yet steady energy appears in the example of Christ! From the work-shops of Nazareth, and from the wilderness, from nights spent alone in the mountains in prayer, did he go forth on his ministry, to heal the sick and preach in their cities. How abundant in labours was Paul! in all these the love of Christ constrained him.

The horse may be the symbol of an activity that does not tire. The idea of beauty includes that of an elastic vigour of the frame, light, free from heaviness, and with power of enduring fatigue and exposure.*

---

* "Thus I set my printless feet
    On the cowslip's velvet head,
      That bends not as I tread."—*Comus*, 897.

"E'en the light hare-bell raised its head,
    Elastic from her airy tread."—*Lady of the Lake.*

"Unwearied as in the morning, my gallant mare dashed away over the rocky valley, exulting in her strength and speed. She pressed against the powerful Mameluke bit, as if its curb were but a challenge, and it was only by slackening the rein

These characteristics are imparted in perfection to the body and soul, by grace. So light, elastic, and airy, shall be the tread of the spiritual body, so different from the care-worn footsteps with which we now drag along this body of corruption, that we shall at last be like the angels, not liable to death any more, being the children of the resurrection. Luke xx. 36. While other pursuits bring weariness and satiety, the Christian life grows more interesting and pleasing. Retirement from business, with an independence and full honours, grows burdensome, though desired and laboured for through a long life. After a degree of success, wealth, and reputation, the soldier becomes weary of his triumphs, and longs for repose. But the man who is filled with the Holy Spirit, and cultivates the habits of contemplation and action excited by grace, will find the service of Jesus more and more delightful; every act of duty exhausts not, but renews his strength; and though the infirmity of the flesh, the dullness creeping through the bodily frame, from age, and ardent desire to enjoy the glory of his Lord, may make him anxious to flee away to the rest in heaven, no weariness with the work of holiness and benevolence is felt; he is sensible that as his outward man perishes, his inward man is renewed day by day, he mounts up on wings as eagles', and never is he more willing to remain at the post of

that she could be induced to pause over some precipitous descent, or tangled copse; then, tossing her proud head, she would burst away again like a greyhound from the leash."— *Warburton's Travels.*

duty, never more active in every good work, than when the time of his departure is at hand.

Ver. 10.—Thy cheeks are comely with rows of jewels, thy neck with chains of gold.

The chariot-horses were in ancient times more richly adorned than those used for riding; "the harness and trappings of such were extremely elegant; plumes waved over their heads, or fanciful crests rose gracefully in an arch above the ears, and descended in front to the nostrils; round the neck, immediately at the head, was an embroidered collar, ending in a rich tassel, or bell; the bit, as well as many ornaments of the bridle and trappings, were of gold, and other precious materials."* A drawing given by Layard of the head of an Assyrian horse, thus ornamented, is certainly very beautiful. The mention of the Egyptian steed in ver. 9, naturally suggested the reference here made to the beautiful head-dress of

---

* Layard's Nineveh, vol. ii. 272. "On grand occasions the Egyptian horses were decked with fancy ornaments; a rich striped or checkered housing, trimmed with a broad border, and large pendent tassels, covered the whole body; and two or more feathers inserted in lions' heads, or some other device of gold, formed a crest upon the summit of the head-stall. But this display was confined to the chariots of the monarch, or the military chiefs."—*Wilkinson*, vol. i. 355. Thus when Latinus ordered the ambassadors sent by Æneas to have horses given them on which to return,—in Virgil—

> "At his command
> The steeds caparisoned with purple stand
> With golden trappings glorious to behold;
> And champ betwixt their teeth the foaming gold.

19

the spouse. Olearius tells us, that "all the head-dress that the Persian ladies make use of, are two or three rows of pearls, which are not worn there about the neck, as in other places, but round the head, beginning on the forehead, and descending down the cheeks, and under the chin, so that their faces seem to be set in pearls. This coiffure seems to be very ancient among the Eastern people." Royal brides are represented by oriental authors as dressed after this manner. So, when the Caliph Al Mamon went to receive Touran-Dokht, that prince found her seated on a throne, her head loaded with a thousand pearls, every one of them as big as a pigeon's egg, or a large nut, which rich coiffure the caliph re-solved should be assigned her for her dowry. D'Ar-vieux, who describes the Arab women as wearing pieces of gold coin hanging down by the sides of the face, adds, that they have chains of gold about their necks, which hang down their breasts.*

* Harmer, 206. Females in the East wear an ornament on the forehead, which is made of thin gold, and is studded with precious stones. Tyerman and Bennet say of a bride they saw in China, "Her head-dress sparkled with jewels, and was most elegantly beaded with rows of pearls encircling it like a coronet; from which a brilliant angular ornament hung over her forehead, and between her eyebrows." Curzon, in his "Visits to Monasteries in the Levant," referring to the Jews of Palestine, says, "The women are covered with gold, and dressed in brocades stiff with embroidery. Some of them are beautiful; and a girl of about twelve years old, who was betrothed to the son of a rich old rabbi, was the prettiest little creature I ever saw; her skin was whiter than ivory, and her hair, which

The words of this verse do, therefore, refer to the rows or strings of pearls and jewels ladies were in the habit of wearing as part of the head-dress, and to the rich necklaces with golden chains over the bosom. Speaking to the Jewish church by Ezekiel, chap. xvi. 11, the Holy Spirit says, "I decked thee also with ornaments, and I put bracelets upon thy hands, and a chain on thy neck. And I put a jewel on thy forehead, and ear-rings in thine ears, and a beautiful crown upon thine head. Thus wast thou decked with gold and silver." The comparison of the horse refers to what may be called the vital energy or principle of the Christian life: this verse expresses the virtues which may be superadded by grace. Such allusions are frequent. "They shall be an ornament of grace unto thy head, and chains about thy neck." Prov. i. 9. Wisdom "shall give to thine head an ornament of grace, a crown of glory shall she deliver to thee." Prov. iv. 9. "In like manner, also, that women adorn themselves in modest apparel, with shamefacedness,

---

was black as jet and was plaited with strings of sequins, fell in tresses nearly to the ground." P. 186. The sufa of the modern Egyptian females is a head-dress of beautiful network, hanging down the back, and filled with jewels of various kinds. This ornament is generally made by dividing the hair into a number of tresses, and attaching to each tress three silken threads. These threads have jewels attached to them, and at the end a small gold coin. Mr. Lane remarks, "The sufa appears to me the prettiest, as well as the most singular of the ornaments worn by Egyptian ladies. The glittering of the burck, and their clinking together as the wearer walks, have a peculiarly lively effect."

and sobriety; not with broidered hair, or gold, or pearls, or costly array, but with good works." 1 Tim. ii. 9. " Whose adorning, let it not be that outward adorning of plaiting the hair, and of wearing of gold, or of putting on of apparel; but let it be the hidden man of the heart, in that which is not corruptible, even the ornament of a meek and quiet spirit, which is in the sight of God of great price."

When Pharaoh would honour Joseph, he took off his ring from his hand and put it on Joseph's hand, and arrayed him in vestures of fine linen, and put a gold chain about his neck. Gen. xli. 42. Thus, by the king's command, they put a chain of gold about the neck of Daniel. Dan. v. 29. And when, like Joseph, we are drawn from the horrible pit of our natural condition, and raised by adoption to the second rank in God's glorious kingdom, even to be the sons of God, how pure and rich the robe he throws around us, the same in texture with that worn by Jesus, even his resplendent righteousness; how beautiful those pearls of virtue and chains of heavenly graces, conferred by him, clustered together by the invisible thread of divine influence, while kept steadfast and illumined by the golden clasp of love. These the topaz of Ethiopia shall not equal, neither shall they be valued with pure gold; ornaments so priceless as to be brought down to us by the hands of the Holy Spirit from that world where so excellent are all things, that the very pavement of the streets is pure gold, as it were transparent glass. The Apostle enumerates some of the jewels thus grouped together; "Add to your faith, virtue; and to virtue, knowledge; and to knowledge, temperance; and to temperance, patience; and to patience, godliness; and to godliness, brotherly kindness; and to brotherly kindness, love." 2 Peter i. 5. So beautiful and valuable are these, that a single one of the number is above all price. "If a man would give all the substance of his house for love, it would utterly be contemned." Song viii. 7.

These virtues, the ornament of the saint, are something distinct from his character by nature, and are superadded by grace. There are not in our hearts the germs of graces, lying like seeds in an ungenial soil, awaiting the beams of the summer sun for warming them into life: our sanctification, as well as our regeneration, is not the development of latent goodness of heart, but the creation of those excellences which constitute holiness. No new faculties are added by the work of the Spirit. He does not take of the intellectual powers belonging to a superior order of beings, and ingraft them into our soul. He gives life to the withered hand, strength to the palsied limbs, and sight to the blinded eye of the soul. Like the author of our spiritual being, rising as a branch from the stem or stump of the decayed tree of Jesse, there comes forth, by the energy of grace, from the roots of the fallen trunk of our ruined soul, a shoot that grows by sanctification into a tree of righteousness. By the Holy Ghost, the soul darkened and changed to stone through sin, is inlaid with eyes pure as the seven eyes upon the stone laid before Joshua, Zech. iii. 9; pure

19*

as those seven eyes of the Lamb, Rev. v. 6; and is inlaid with sensibilities alive to the faintest beams of divine goodness; and with ears that gather home to the very core of our being the tones of the melting voice of our God; and with affections which, unfolding more beauteous than Sharon's rose, exhale a perfume grateful even amid the odours of heaven, and gather in their bosom the rays of the Father's love, the drops of the Spirit's dews. What jewels of the spouse, so beautiful as those endowments! What chains of gold, so comely as these clusters of heavenly graces!

VER. 11.—We will make thee borders of gold with studs of silver.

The Hebrew word here rendered "borders," is the same with that rendered "rows," in ver. 10; and would seem to refer here to the same kind of ornaments.* The queen was, however, distinguished by a crown,† Jer. xiii. 18; Ezek. xvi. 12; Esth. ii. 17; and

---

* In the Odyssey, lib. xv., there is much said that refers to the pursuits and skill of the Sidonians, whose intercourse with the Jews in the time of Solomon is well known. Among other things, there is a reference which seems to illustrate this text:

> "A man of theirs, subtle and shrewd, produced
> A splendid collar, gold with amber strung.
> With deep delight, my mother and her maids
> Gazed on it."—*Lib.* xv. 459.

† The Hebrew word rendered "spouse," in Song iv. 8, 9, 10, 11, 12, means a crowned one, derived from a root signifying to make perfect; and then used to express a bride, from the completion put to her attire by the bridal chaplet or crown.

to the crown these words may refer. Struck with her beauty, as adorned with rows of jewels, the king wishes to give the finish to her head-attire, by placing on her a crown of gold, variegated with studs of silver. As in Ps. xxi. 3: "Thou settest a crown of pure gold on his head." There is laid up for every saint a crown of righteousness, which the Lord shall give at that day unto all them that love his appearing. Whatever the exact ornaments here mentioned, the idea is that the beloved would add to the beautiful ornaments already worn by the bride, others of the most precious kind, devised and made by himself. While the graces considered under the foregoing verse, are developing in this life, there are in reserve in the treasury of heaven, crowning glories which shall be received when the chief Shepherd shall appear. "Unto every one that hath shall be given." Those who are faithful to their trust, even though by making their pound gain five pounds, shall be made rulers over cities, kings unto God. Were we presented by some kingly friend with costly jewels, the same in appearance with those worn by himself, he would be little likely to follow those gifts with others equally valuable, did we receive them with eagerness but afterwards appear without them, and allow them to lie neglected, unworn, and bedimmed. Neglect of the ring and gold chain by Joseph, would have certainly drawn on him the displeasure of Pharaoh. By guarding faithfully the treasures committed to our heart by the Holy Spirit, we shall find him constantly adding to them, changing us from glory to glory, till the soul, all glorious within, with clothing of

K.

wrought gold, emerges from its probation on earth
into the unending bridal festivities of heaven, fairer
than the woman clothed with the sun, and the moon
under her feet, and on her head a crown of stars.
Success in amassing wealth depends on keeping and
using properly the amounts acquired from time to
time; no reasonable expectation can be indulged of
its being otherwise in our efforts for gathering the
riches of God's grace.

How much more glorious and desirable must be the
ornaments thus conferred by Jesus, than those which
man elaborates for himself. Desire of personal independence is a besetting sin of our fallen nature.
Among men of the world much is heard about self-
reliance as the spring of success in life: with such
persons the glorification of self is the chief thing;
and they wish the impression made that this fabric of
fortune is the work of their own wisdom and power;
they hate the idea of dependence even on him who
formed the machinery of their intellect, even of their
whole being, and without the stream of whose living
influence that machinery must instantly cease to move.
With the nature of the characters thus formed,
we are familiar. Their portraits are recorded in
colours of selfishness, pride, ambition, and blood.
However ill-disguised by vanity and policy, the smo-
thered sentiments of such hearts, on viewing their
doings, position, and success, are, "Is not this great
Babylon that I have built by the might of my power,
and for the honour of my majesty." Dan. iv. 30.
Reputation, influence, riches, every thing thus rely-

ing on self as its foundation, must be unsubstantial as a fabric resting on the vapour that appeareth for a little time and then vanisheth away. All such hopes and structures of pride are so fragile and unreal, that a breath of air may blast them, and reduce their possessors to a condition as friendless and pitiable as that to which the haughty king of Babylon was brought down by a voice that fell from heaven while yet the word was in his mouth. Like the palace of ice, fairy-like in appearance yet repulsively cold, built on a foundation underneath which was a hidden river ready to swallow it up at the return of spring, all the labours of human pride and self-reliance, for rearing a fabric of happiness and renown, must issue in results equally unsubstantial, and destined to be perfectly lost when the scenes of this wintry world are displaced in heaven by the beauties of an unbounded spring. How much superior the character which is formed by the virtues made for us by God, the Father, the Son, and the Spirit! Casting aside this self-reliance, which is another name for pride, let us substitute therefor reliance on the Holy Ghost; so that to us the words may be addressed, "Ye are his workmanship, created in Christ Jesus unto good works." The results of the artistic skill of this boasted self-reliance are enumerated by one who best knows the heart; which are these—"adultery, fornication, uncleanness, lasciviousness, idolatry, witchcraft, hatred, variance, emulation, wrath, strife, seditions, heresies, envyings, murders, drunkenness, revelings, and such like." Gal. v. 19. The borders of gold, with studs of silver, made for those who depend on the Spirit, include such jewels as, "love, joy, peace, long-suffering, gentleness, goodness, faith, meekness, temperance."

How much honour is conferred on the spouse, and how strong the proof of his love, when the beloved, the king, condescends to make these ornaments himself. He does not say "We will give," but "We will make, &c." There were two reasons for this; none but himself could finish those things in a manner sufficiently royal and splendid; and it is a gratification for him to be thus occupied in labours for the souls he loves. The virtues adorning the redeemed, the beauties of their souls, their spiritual bodies can be the workmanship of none less than Jesus Christ. Growing unto an holy temple in the Lord, we are builded together for an habitation of God through the Spirit; and he by whom we, as living stones, are built up a spiritual house—is one who has been filled to an infinitely greater degree than Bezaleel, the architect of the tabernacle, with the Spirit of God, in wisdom, and in understanding, and in knowledge, and in all manner of workmanship, Exod. xxxi. 3—is Christ the wisdom of God, and Christ the power of God. He cleanses us from sin; he overlays the refined gold of the sanctified heart, with engraving more beautifully than was ever wrought in the gems worn on Aaron's breast; his hands alone set this priceless jewel of a transparent soul in the pellucid shrine of a spiritual body; and deposits it among the peculiar treasure of the King of kings, in the secret of the Most High under the shadow of the Almighty.

And this is to him a labour of love. His affection for us forbids the idea of entrusting this work to other hands, even could any be found equal to the task. The heart of Jesus delights to anticipate our wants, to labour for our good, though in bearing the burden of a cross. He is the artificer of our fortune; he carves out our whole destiny; he makes all that is valuable and beautiful about us; and our only pride is in the consciousness of having nothing which we have not received.

VER. 12.—While the king sitteth at his table, my spikenard sendeth forth the smell thereof.

According to oriental customs the encampment moving from place to place is here supposed to have stopped, and the king to have seated himself for enjoying the society of his friends. Thus Layard says: "When they reached the tents, the chiefs placed themselves on the divan, whilst the others seated themselves in a circle on the green-sward. An abundant repast had been prepared for them. The meaning of the verse is this—My perfume is most fragrant, and while the beloved is enjoying his repast in the circle of his friends, delights him with the richness of its odour.* According to Good, the phrase "gracing

---

* See notes on ver. 3. The spikenard was a very precious and costly unguent, obtained in Judea by foreign commerce from the eastern coast of Africa and from India. The ointment of spikenard used by Mary, John xii. 3, was "very costly;" and Horace, who lived in the same age, promises Virgil a whole cadus, about nine gallons, of wine, for a small onyx-box full of spikenard. "The composition of this unguent is given by Dioscorides, who describes it as being made with nut oil,

the banquet," is in common use among the Persian poets, to delineate an elegant woman. Mary showed her regard for our Lord by bringing very costly spikenard and anointing Jesus while at table, so that the house was filled with the odour of the ointment. John xii. 3. In the same spirit does the spouse here desire to show her affection for the beloved.

After the manifestations of Jesus' love alluded to, in being brought into his chambers, ver. 4, the soul longing for his presence follows hard after him by pilgrimage in the paths of duty, "by the footsteps of the flock." Having found him whom her soul loved, and being brought again into his presence on terms of affectionate friendship by receiving the reviving power of the Holy Spirit under different circumstances from those before noticed, she here expresses, in ver. 12, the effect produced by his presence, in kindling the affections into a lively glow. The presence of Jesus as felt by the divine light beaming in the effulgent cloud of the Spirit's influences continually around him, is unfolded to us at different times, and in various ways. Now, we are revived by entering into that cloud alone in our closet, more retired perhaps, than the three chosen disciples amid the glory

and having as ingredients malabathrum, schœnus, costus, amomum, nardus, myrrha, and balsamum, that is almost all the most valued perfumes of antiquity." Dr. Royle, when in India, near the foot of the Himalaya mountains, found this plant brought down in considerable quantities as an article of commerce; and shows that the Jewish spikenard was most probably derived from these regions.—*Kitto's Cyc. Bib. Lit.*

on Tabor; again, we feel ourselves with him by our hearts burning within us when journeying by the way; and then, we meet with him by grace showered on the soul in the enjoyment of public ordinances, especially the sacrament of the supper. Here, his society is enjoyed not in private communion, his chambers, but in public, at his table, in the circle of his friends.

At this banquet, he presides in person, with kingly majesty. In the Psalms, especially the forty-fifth and seventy-second, to which this Song is allied, the epithet "the king," was held by the Jews to designate, in all cases, except where the context directs otherwise, the Messiah. As here used, this title seems to refer less to what is technically called his kingly office, than to his divine nature. He who receives us into reconciliation and communion, is the King, the most exalted personage in the government of God, is divine, is God. When, after especial blessedness in the private duties of religion, at times when there may be nothing unusual in the Church as a body, we have been cleaving to Christ by patient labours, without any uncommon enjoyment, we find not unfrequently on coming to the sacramental table, the King of saints there refreshing us with the hidden manna for the hungry soul, with the water of life for the thirsting spirit, and with golden censers alive with holy fire and heavenly incense for kindling anew the smouldering affections of the heart. At these seasons of reviving love, we dwell much on the grandeur and divinity of our Lord; and love to feel, "Thou art

20

fairer than the children of men, grace is poured into thy lips."

Sitting together at table was evidence of reconciliation and friendship: "If any man hear my voice, and open the door, I will come in to him, and will sup with him, and he with me." Rev. iii. 20. There is in preparation in heaven a marriage-supper of the Lamb, at which he and those who having been once enemies are reconciled, shall sit down in affectionate fellowship and unbroken peace. Just as, previous to the coming of Christ, the nature of his death was represented by the Jewish sacrifices; so, the nature of that feast of love on high, for which all things in this world are a preparation, is illustrated to us by the services of the Lord's supper. In every sacrifice the part consumed by fire was considered as God's; and the offerer ate a portion to show his restoration to fellowship with his offended king; while the altar was God's table, at which he and the sinner thus met in reconciliation. In the Lord's supper we are partaking, in the only way now possible, of the sacrifice once for all offered on Calvary; and while doing this, show forth the Lord's death, till he come and drink the fruit of the vine anew with us in his Father's kingdom; till the reconciliation through his death, now shadowed dimly through these emblems, shall be perfectly consummated in both body and soul, by sitting with him at table in the New Jerusalem. This feast of love will be enjoyed in perfection in heaven; and all things connected with this sacrament on earth are pledges and foretastes of the fulness enjoyed above. All the sacrificial appointments of the tabernacle were shadows of the blessings we now enjoy; and shadows of them as the beginning of the manifestation of God to his redeemed and their attending joy in heaven. In the camp of Israel, God was in the circle of his friends by the Shechinah; at the supper, he was thus present in the bodily form of Jesus; now at the communion table, in the congregation, and where two or three are gathered in his name, he is there in the influences of the Holy Spirit; and in heaven, he that sitteth on the throne, even the Lamb, shall for ever dwell among them. The covenant made with Israel at the foot of Sinai, was not completed until, after the shedding of blood and its application by sprinkling, the elders, as representatives of the people, went up into the mount, and there seeing the God of Israel, did eat and drink in his presence. In like manner, the new covenant, established on better promises, will not receive its perfect ratification, until all those on whom has been shed the blood of sprinkling, are gathered up into the most holy mount on which rests the purity of the eternal clearness of heaven; and there, led on by a greater than Moses, even by the Lamb slain, drink the new wine at the table where presides the King of kings in the fulness of his glory.

"My spikenard sendeth forth the smell thereof."*

---

* The following, from Chardin's Voyages, illustrates this— mentioned by him for showing how prodigal the oriental females are in the use of perfumes. "I remember that at the solemnization of the nuptials of the three princesses royal of

This was the oil of spikenard, the most costly, precious, and grateful perfume, with which the spouse was anointed according to the practice of using such things profusely at entertainments. In this communion with Christ, our presence is as agreeable to him as the fragrance of spikenard, and his society is delightful to us as a bundle of myrrh or cluster of camphire. With these perfumes of the oil of gladness, the great governor of the feast is anointed without measure; and as the virgins love him because of the savour of his good ointments, so his delight is with none among the sons of men but those who have received an unction from the Holy One. The use of fragrant oils was not a more necessary preparation for the society of friends at a feast, than is the anointing of the Spirit requisite to fit us for seeing God. This unction must come from himself. Hence

Golconda, whom the king, their father, who had no other children, married in one day, in the year 1679, perfumes were lavished on every invited guest as he arrived. They sprinkled them on those who were clad in white; but gave them into the hands of those who wore coloured raiment, because their garments would have been spoiled by throwing it over them, which was done in the following manner. They threw over the body a bottle of rose-water, containing about half a pint, and then a large bottle of water tinted with saffron, in such a manner that the clothes would have been stained with it. After this, they rubbed the arms and the body with a liquid perfume of laudanum and ambergris, and they put round the throat a thick cord of jasmine. I was thus perfumed with saffron in many great houses of this country, and in other places. This attention and honour is a universal custom among the women who have the means of obtaining this luxury."

the Psalmist says, "Thou anointest my head with oil." The graces of the holy heart, so acceptable to God, are the work of the Spirit. He makes us partakers of the excellency of the fulness of Christ, even grace for grace. He brings to us, in this wilderness, from the hills of frankincense on high, those graces of liquid perfume which arise from the alabaster of a heart broken in contrition, in odours of prayers, desires, and affections, most grateful to this kingly friend. Love, holiness, all the desires unfolding purity of heart, are the things well pleasing to our Redeemer. The unction of the Holy Spirit diffuses around us a refreshing perfume, by enlivening and developing our graces. As the Spirit is inseparable from the presence of Jesus, every approach of our Lord brings with it an influence which, by enlivening the affections, draws forth the precious exhalations of the spikenard of the heart. Thus does the sun of spring fill the calm, pure air, with fragrance from the landscape's blooms, the garden's flowers, by pouring around their roots the genial unction of his reviving glow. In the sacrament of the supper we are merely expressing by ceremonies that which it is our privilege and duty continually to enjoy. Not the communion service only, but our whole life, is a continual sacramental feast. As such, this feast may preserve our affections always in a glow, by keeping us near to Christ; and when our fervour may have manifestly declined, we shall find that it is not because Jesus has left the circle of his friends, but because we have gone out from among them, like Judas, led by love or

20*

gain or some kindred desire, when, had we, like the beloved disciple, lingered fondly near our Lord, we might have enjoyed a like fervour of affection.

VER. 13.—A bundle of myrrh is my well-beloved unto me; he shall lie all night betwixt my breasts.

The twelfth verse having expressed the agreeableness of the holy heart to Jesus, the thirteenth and fourteenth verses set forth the pleasantness of the society of Christ to the saint. This passage has been much misrepresented. We would read it, My beloved is unto me as an amulet, (a bag, or delicate vessel,) filled with liquid myrrh, that is borne continually in the bosom.* Myrrh was one of the most costly and

---

* "The eastern women, among other ornaments, used little perfume-boxes, or vessels filled with perfumes, to smell at. These were worn suspended from the neck, and hanging down on the breast. Such smelling-boxes are still in use among the Persian women, to whose necklaces, which fall below the bosom, is fastened a large box of sweets; some of these boxes are as big as one's hand; the common ones are of gold, the others are covered with jewels. They are all bored through, and filled with a black paste, very light, made of musk and amber, but of very strong smell.—*Burder.* Among the Egyptians, "Small boxes, made of wood or ivory, were very numerous, offering, like the vases, a multiplicity of forms; and some, which contained cosmetics of divers kinds, served to deck the dressing-table, or a lady's boudoir. They were carved in various ways, and loaded with ornamental devices in relief; sometimes representing the favourite lotus-flower, with its buds and stalks, a goose, gazelle, fox, or other animal."—*Wilkinson,* vol. ii. 356, where may be found much that is interesting on this subject. He gives also, (vol. iii. 107,) an account and drawings of some curious Chinese bottles, which have been found in various tombs, and were evidently brought to Egypt through India at

fragrant perfumes. The shrub was beautiful, with smooth leaves of a dark green on the upper, and a whitish colour on the under surface, with flowers of a reddish purple, and a remarkable odour in the root, branches, leaf, and bloom; so that a cluster gathered therefrom was beautiful and fragrant; yet the liquid obtained by exudation gave the tree its chief value, and is most probably what is here mentioned. Nothing of the kind could be more delightful to the senses, than myrrh thus worn in the bosom. Rich perfume very appropriately represents the influences of the Holy Spirit; and what can illustrate more beautifully than this, those divine influences distilled as dew from the mountain of myrrh and hill of frankincense, and lying with an embalming power and exhilarating fragrance in the very bosom of the soul, the centre of the spiritual heart. This language is not stronger than those passages of Scripture which speak of Christ dwelling in us by his Spirit—"Christ in you the hope of glory," Col. i. 27; "Filled with all the fulness of God," Eph. iii. 19. Jesus says that his Spirit shall be in us "a well of water springing up into everlasting life," John iv. 14. Here, the illustration is varied for showing still further the loveliness and benefit of his presence, by saying that through his Spirit he is in the pure heart, as distillations of liquid myrrh. Lodged at the bottom of the heart, like a

a very remote period. They are about two inches in height; one side presents a flower, and the other this inscription: "The flower opens, and lo! another year." They must have been filled with some precious ingredient, whose value may be inferred from the size of the vase.

cluster of liquid or pulverized myrrh, the love of Jesus, the truths, thoughts, consolations, and influences of the Holy Spirit, exhale and roll through all the channels of the soul, with a soothing, exhilarating power, and diffuse there as much as is now possible to be enjoyed of heaven.

VER. 14.—My beloved is unto me as a cluster of camphire in the vineyards of Engedi.

The idea of the foregoing verse is presented in another form; My beloved is like a cluster, or bouquet, of camphire blooms from the gardens of Engedi.* By

* "After the ceremony of anointing was over, and in some cases at the time of entering the saloon, a lotus-flower was presented to each guest, who held it in his hand during the entertainment. Servants then brought necklaces of flowers, composed chiefly of the lotus; a garland was put round the head, and a single lotus bud, or a full-blown flower, was so attached as to hang over the forehead. Many of them, made up into wreaths and other devices, were suspended upon stands placed in the room, to be in readiness for immediate use, and servants were constantly employed to bring other fresh flowers from the garden, in order to supply the guests as their bouquets faded; and, to prevent their withering, they were generally put close to jars of water, into which their stalks were probably immersed. The stands that served for holding the flowers and garlands, were similar to those for the vases, and varied in size according to circumstances. The Greeks and Romans had the same custom; and their guests were, in like manner, decked with flowers and garlands. They not only adorned their heads, necks, and breasts, like the Egyptians, but often bestrewed the couches on which they lay, and all parts of the room, with flowers. They also perfumed the apartment with myrrh, frankincense, and other choice odours, which they obtained from Syria."—*Wilkinson*, vol. ii. 215.

the camphire is most probably meant the *hennah*, a plant growing to the height of eight or ten feet, beautiful to the eye and grateful to the smell. "The dark colour of its bark, the light green of its foliage, the softened mixture of white and yellow, with which the flowers, collected into long clusters like the lilac, are coloured; the red tint of the ramifications which support them, form a combination the effect of which is highly agreeable. The flowers whose shades are so delicate, diffuse around the most grateful odours, and embalm with their strong fragrance the gardens in which they grow, and the apartments which they adorn. The women take pleasure in decking their persons and apartments with these delightful blossoms." The best of these flowers grew in Engedi, a part of the fertile plain of Jericho, abounding not only in vineyards, but also in gardens for aromatic shrubs, in the gums and balsams of which the Jews carried on a traffic. In the days of Jerome, this region was remarkable for the balm of Gilead. To persons thus familiar with these beautiful and fragrant clusters, nothing could be more expressive of the loveliness of the presence of another, even of the Lord Jesus Christ. How could we express otherwise, or more intelligibly, than by these emblems, the apprehension had of Jesus as lodged in our hearts by his love, and of that love as hoarded by us, and the source of inexpressible pleasure; as grateful, not merely in public, like the incense burning on the altar, but in private, withdrawn from society. The love of Christ, his consolations and joys, are to us not unstable and evanescent, like fragrance floating on a passing breeze; but are, in the depths of the soul, a perpetual fountain of exhilarating perfumes, refreshing as myrrh, beautiful as the clusters of camphire. And when we are most alone, his presence makes us realize something delightful and delicately beauteous to our spiritual perception, and inseparable from us, as the bundle of myrrh or camphire, which may attend us with an influence pleasant to others, no less than ourselves, in the public assembly, in our closet retirement, or in our private walks.

By our precious Lord there is given to us something better than the golden vial full of odours; the heart of the pure in spirit is a richer vial, and the love of Christ imbedded there in the myrrh of Scripture truth, holy desires, and heavenly anticipations, is a more precious incense. The promises and Scripture truths gathered from time to time, from different parts of the word of God, and borne in our bosom, in clusters, as we need them, are the clusters of camphire, flowering and fragrant with the love of Jesus:

> "A flower which once
> In Paradise, fast by the tree of Life,
> Began to bloom; but soon for man's offence
> To heaven removed, where first it grew, there grows;
> And flowers aloft, shading the fount of life,
> And where the river of bliss through midst of heaven
> Rolls o'er Elysian flowers her amber stream."*

In the fragrance of this divine love thus diffused around us, we are breathing sweeter odours than

---

* Paradise Lost, book iii. 353.

known by Adam in Eden, such as are even now reviving those who are under the shadow of the tree of life in the midst of the Paradise of God. There is in the love of Christ something refined and etherial, to which the most sublimated extracts from the most elegant things of earth cannot approximate; very different from the gross pleasures of sense, better than wine; and as the wind is the best emblem of the Holy Spirit, John iii. 8, so the wind loaded with such fragrance as the myrrh and camphire blooms, is the best illustration of the Holy Spirit in his office of conveying to the soul the exhilarating love of our Lord. In what perfect contrast are the enjoyments of the glutton, and the drunkard, and "all that wallow in the sensual sty," to the pleasures inhaled from a cluster of myrrh or camphire blooms. While the presence of Christ diffuses a pure and elevating influence through the soul, from the influences of the Holy Spirit gathered like liquid myrrh at our heart, it does also gratify the sight by visions more delicately exquisite than the flowers of the camphire. How fragrant does this presence render our retirement, and cause us to linger fondly there while the world are pitying our loneliness. The Scriptures, this precious volume, the visible means of our communion with Christ, with the exquisite net-work of its literary materials and style, filled with words fitly spoken, is more beautiful and valuable than a basket of silver filled with apples of gold; and no golden vase on a centre-table of the purest marble, containing clusters of camphire mingling their fragrance with the odour of distilled myrrh, can diffuse so pleasant an incense as that filling the retired room of the believer, in which the central ornament is this book of life, this golden urn of salvation, filled with the pure water of life, with clusters gathered in the heavenly Paradise, and fragrant with truths in unfading bloom.

VER. 15.—Behold, thou art fair, my love; behold, thou art fair; thou hast doves' eyes.

While thus entertained by Jesus, what is the language addressed by him to the believer? No tenderer epithet could be used, "My love;" or, as the Hebrew word strictly means, a female friend, a companion—the import of the language is, thou art indeed beautiful, my friend, my companion; my love, thou art beautiful. So literally true are the words, "As the bridegroom rejoiceth over the bride, so shall thy God rejoice over thee," Isa. lxii. 5. There are among his creatures none that he loves better than the redeemed. He who is altogether lovely, who is love, shall he not know what is lovely? and shall not his love be of great worth? He that planted the ear, shall he not hear? He that wove the texture of Sharon's rose, shall he not know what is beautiful? Yet, he says to us, "My love, behold thou art fair." Feeling our depravity and knowing our short-comings, we wonder what there can be in us to admire; but he whose all-present eye sees pure gems in the deep caves of ocean, and delicate flowers in secluded retreats of the wilderness, penetrates beyond the outward appearance, and notices what is beautiful in the heart, which may still be too much like the troubled sea when it cannot rest.

An unseemly shoot ingrafted into a tree grows more beautiful by growing into the tree, till at length it bursts into bloom. We are ingrafted into Christ; and as we become more and more one with him, our beauty increases by his beauty becoming ours. The parent looks on the infant as beautiful according to the likeness to himself, though there is much weakness and infirmity in the child, and very much beauty remains to be developed. In his created works, God does not wait until they are perfectly finished, before he can see beauty in them; he traces it in all things, from the first, as there forming; and the unfolding of beauty in the several stages of its progress towards maturity cannot be less interesting to him than the view of its full perfection. There is pleasure in training the tender plant; in watching the bursting bud and fragrant bloom of spring, as well as in enjoying the golden fruits of autumn. As soon as born again, the soul begins an assimilation to Christ, which is scarcely seen in the body, and must be much hidden from those who see the body only, while the lineaments of this loveliness must be apparent to those who can behold the soul. We are made one with Christ by justification; and sanctification then transfers to our soul the excellences existing in Jesus. Beauty is inseparable from holiness, as deformity is inseparable from sin. Jesus is making us what he pleases, with none to interfere; and he certainly cannot wish to make us otherwise than beautiful.

"Thou hast doves' eyes," or literally, Thine eyes are doves. The doves of Syria have eyes remarkably

21

large and beautiful. The eye, as here mentioned, seems to combine the beauty of the brilliant, light-blue eye of Minerva, with that of the tender, melting, languishing eye of Venus, to represent which her statues have the lower eyelid drawn up a little over the eye. All poets dwell on the eye as a most expressive feature. Every one is familiar with the varied epithets on this point in Homer, and the description of a beauty in Anacreon, Ode 28:

> " And paint her eye Minerva's blue,
>   With Venus' melting, languid hue."

The eyes of Agamemnon enraged, "were like blazing fire;" those of Minerva, a mild, sparkling, animated blue; Juno's large, round, and full, "ox-eyed." The countenance has been called "the living telegraph of all that is felt within;"* especially may this be said of the eye. As in Milton's Penseroso,

> "Thy rapt soul sitting in thine eyes."

And an oriental poet, "All his soul sparkled in his eyes." As the soul of the saint is the shrine wherein

---

* The Body and the Mind, by Dr. Moore, p. 85.—" The sagacious traveller, Nicolai, states that he saw the most divinely beautiful female countenances among women who were most devout. The calm contemplation of loveliness where affection blends with adoration, seems to act most powerfully in tranquilizing and exalting the features. Doubtless the apprehension of spiritual truth being absolute, the reflex of the divine mind would possess the mind with a more heavenly idea, and correspondingly transform the whole being." P. 86.

lies the sacred fountain of divine love, the eyes of doves, the emblem of affection, are the best expression to others of this inward emotion. The eyes are transparencies through which the soul may look out on surrounding things; and as through these we do, as it were, come nearer than in any other way, getting glimpes of the soul, the expression of the eye is an index of the passions within, as of anger, envy, guilt, innocence, or love. Hence the language, "An evil eye," Matt. xx. 15; "Eyes full of adultery," 2 Pet. ii. 14; "An high look and a proud heart," Ps. ci. 5. The dove is an emblem of gentleness, innocence, and love; and has been chosen by the Holy Ghost for representing his divine nature and offices towards man. As the Spirit changes us to his own likeness, and makes us harmless, guileless, or pure, as doves, Matt. x. 16, the eyes must acquire an expression like the eyes of doves. Not the haughty air of the devotee of fashion, not the proud bearing of the soldier, not the selfish cast of the miser, not the fierce glare of malice, not the ill-concealed vanity betokening, under the guise of feigned humility, a hungering and thirsting for admiration; but the eye bespeaking gentleness, purity, and love, is the expression of countenance agreeable to our Lord. As the man, who is the head of the woman, 1 Cor. xi. 3, does every thing requiring energy, defence, danger, and resistance, while the woman in her sphere acts, but confides and loves; so we must do all things in love, feeling that the head of every man is Christ; and not avenging ourselves, but committing our cause to him in well doing, and sensible

that with this well doing our business now is, as the
spouse of Christ, to confide and love.

> " They tell of things which no gross ear can hear,
> Till oft converse with heavenly habitants
> Begin to cast a beam on th' outward shape,
> The unpolluted temple of the mind,
> And turns it by degrees to the soul's essence,
> Till all be made immortal."*

Ver. 16, 17.—Behold, thou art fair, my beloved, yea,
pleasant: also our bed is green. The beams of our house
are cedar, and our rafters of fir.

We love him because he first loved us; we presume
to call him our beloved, because he first calls us his
love. It is much for such unworthy creatures to have
the right of saying this; much to have the feelings
and desires which prompt this language. When Jesus
speaks to our heart, as in the 15th verse, there arises
the trepidation of warm affection; and we would gladly
give utterance to the strongest expressions of love;
but we are so overwhelmed with his grandeur, and our
unworthiness, as to hesitate in using words our emotions would justify. Hence the Holy Spirit has in-
dited this language, and assures us we cannot do wrong
in thus speaking of our Lord. Jesus is well pleased to
have us call him our beloved.

"Thou art fair." How fair? Fairer than the sons
of men; adorned with greater beauty than any of
our fallen race; fairer too than the angels. Heb. i.
" Grace is poured into thy lips;" and when, in conse-

* Milton's Comus.

quence of this, we wonder at the gracious words which proceed out of his mouth, we delight to add, "Yea, pleasant." The pleasures of refined society, of society ennobled by intellectual culture and polished manners, in combination with the grace which purifies the heart for seeing God, are the most delightful possible for man The society of Jesus, far from being gloomy and irksome, is captivating and delightful. In him are united all conceivable charms, princely dignity, mind of infinite compass, illimitable influence, beauty, knowledge, and wisdom divine, a nature that is its self love. When in the form of a slave, in the flesh, emptied of his glory, there was a wondrous charm about his person, his presence, his conversation. "Never man spake like this man." What, therefore, must be the charm investing him now in glory. Those who have been admitted to the gatherings in which the hospitality of high rank loved to assemble the courtly, the powerful, the learned, and the influential, delighted in those privileges as their happiest hours, and cherish the remembrance of them fondly in declining age.* Of such privileges the humble saint may be deprived; but he mingles intimately in a more refined, more intellectual, more fascinating society—a gathering wherein he who presides is the king in the circle of his friends. How pleasant is the society of Jesus, when he unfolds to us the way of salvation, opens the promises, encourages in difficulty, comforts in trouble, and speaks of the blessedness of heaven!

* Final Memorials of Charles Lamb, p. 238.

21*

How rich the influence around his presence! In his presence is fulness of joy. When on earth, he must have possessed great attractions, to draw multitudes after him into the wilderness, and retain them there for days without food. The indifference of the believer to the highest society among the irreligious, is the result of a deep and intelligent conviction of the superiority of the society of Christ. Entranced with his pleasantness, enchained with his wisdom, and rapt by the glorious visions of the ideal world unfolded by his promises, we exclaim, "This is my rest for ever; here will I dwell. Whom have I in heaven but thee? and there is none upon earth that I desire beside thee."

"Also our bed is green," or, the green flowery turf is our place of repose. The scene in which these words, and possibly all from verse 12 are used, seems to be laid in the kiosk or summer-house in the royal garden.*   Oriental gardens were without the city,

---

* "The next day we went to visit the gardens, and to spend a day there. The place was about a mile out of town. It afforded us a very pleasant summer-house, having a plentiful stream of water running through it. The garden was thick set with fruit-trees, but without any art or order. Such as this are all the gardens hereabouts: only with this odds, that some of them have their summer-houses more splendid than others, and their waters improved into greater variety of fountains."—*Maundrell*, p. 130. In Kitto's Illustrated Commentary, Deut. iii. 11, is a drawing of what he calls "a garden bedstead," which is in fact a kiosk, and illustrates precisely what is meant in these two verses. "The Egyptians spent much time in the cool and shady retirement of their gardens, where, like the Romans, they entertained their friends during

and from half a mile to a mile distant from the houses of the persons to whom they belonged. "In the gardens around Aleppo, commodious villas are built, for the use of the inhabitants, to which they retire during the oppressive heats of summer. Here, amid the wild and almost impervious thickets of pome-

the summer-season, as we may judge from the size of some of the kiosks which occur in the paintings of the tombs."—*Wilkinson*, vol. ii. 187. Thus the following from Plato: "How beautiful a retreat! For this plane-tree is very wide-spreading and lofty, and the height and shadiness of this agnus castus are very beautiful; and being now in full bloom, it makes the place exceedingly fragrant. Moreover, there flows under this plane-tree a delightful fountain of very cold water, to judge from its effect on the foot. It appears from these images and statues to be sacred to certain nymphs, and to Achelous. Observe again the freshness of the spot, how charming and delightful it is, and how summer-like and shrill it sounds from the choir of grasshoppers. But the most delightful of all is the grass, which, sloping gently, gives an easy support to the head as we recline."—*Phædrus*, 5.

Edw. Atherstone, describing the bower of Achushta, says:
"With fragrant moss the floor
Was planted, to the foot a carpet rich,
Or, for the languid limbs a downy couch
Inviting slumber."

Milton mentions—
"Beds of hyacinth and roses,
Where young Adonis oft reposes."

And Theocritus—
"On soft beds recline,
Of lentisk and young branches of the vine."

"My tent was pitched on a carpet of soft, green sward, under the wide-spread arms of one of the old cedars."—*Warburton's Travels*.

granate, and other fruit-bearing trees, the languid
native and exhausted traveller find a delightful retreat from the scorching beams of the sun. A similar
custom of retiring into the country, and taking shelter
in the gardens, at that season, appears to have been
followed in Palestine, in ages very remote. The
exquisite pleasure which an oriental feels, while he
reclines under the deep shade of the pomegranates,
the apple, and other fruitful trees, in the Syrian gardens, which, uniting their branches over his head,
defend him from the glowing firmament, is well
described by Russel: "Revived by the freshening
breeze, the purling of the brooks, and the verdure of
the groves, his ear will catch the melody of the nightingale, delightful beyond what is heard in England.;
with conscious gratitude to Heaven, he will recline on
the simple mat, and bless the hospitable shelter."
Lady Montague writes, "In the midst of the garden
is the kiosk, that is, a large room, commonly beautified with a fine fountain in the midst of it. It is
raised nine or ten steps, and enclosed with gilded
lattices, round which vines, jessamines, and honey-
suckles, make a sort of green wall. Large trees are
planted round this place, which is the scene of their
greatest pleasures." Speaking of the plain of Sharon,
a traveller remarks, "The fields were decked with
thousands of gay flowers, forming an enamelled carpet, that perfumed the air, and offered a scene re-
plete with every thing that could gratify the eye, or
charm the imagination. In such a place, and on such
a couch, are the beloved and the spouse here repre-

sented as reposing. This picture is common in poetry. Thus Thomson:

> "There on the verdant turf and flowery bed,
> By gelid founts and careless rills to muse."

And Homer—

> "Beneath them earth
> With sudden herbage teem'd at once **upsprang**
> The crocus soft, the lotus bathed in dew,
> And the crisp hyacinth with clustering bells;
> Thick was their growth, and high above the ground
> Upbore them. On that flowery couch they lay,
> Invested with a golden cloud that shed
> Bright dew-drops all around."*

From such scenes does the Holy Spirit draw the means of illustrating the loveliness of the society of Jesus. His presence can make the desert itself delightful. When he brings his beloved into the wilderness for speaking to her heart, Hos. ii. 14, he makes the wilderness and the solitary place glad, and the desert rejoice and blossom as the rose. To the charm of his society is added the beauty of the place in which it is enjoyed. The word *bed* here expresses the place where, in a pastoral scene, the two friends may recline on the verdure, and share the pleasures of each other's company. We would read, Our couch or place of repose is spread with the verdure and flowers of spring; the roof, the ceiling of our summer-house or kiosk, our canopy, is cedar interspersed with fir, richly carved. As if it were said, The place where I rest

* Iliad, book xiv. 347.

and enjoy the society of this beloved friend, is invested with the freshness and richness of vernal beauty, amid green grass and blooming flowers. The same idea is expressed, in different words, in Ps. xxiii. 2, "He maketh me to lie down in green pastures;" and in Isa. xi. 10, "His rest, or place of rest, shall be glorious." And when the same prophet would show that the dwelling-place of God among men shall be adorned with the most attractive beauty, he says, "The glory of Lebanon shall come unto thee, the fir-tree, the pine-tree, and the box together, to beautify the place of my sanctuary; and I will make the place of my feet glorious." Chap. lx. 13. Into the oriental gardens, many of which were very extensive, the owner delighted to go with a few friends, and sitting down in some shady place, most commonly a small open structure or summer-house, elegantly made, there enjoy the cool shade, the refreshing breeze, the foliage of the groves, the fragrance of the flowers, and the golden luxuriousness of the ripening fruits, while the ear was pleased with the murmuring of the rills and the melodies of the nightingale. By such scenes as this, would the Holy Spirit represent that in our communion with Jesus we are surrounded with pleasantness and peace.* There are many barren tracts and wilds in our pilgrimage; but he who comforts Zion, "will make her wilderness like Eden, and her

* Plato says, "Love does not settle on any spot where flowers are not, or where they have fallen off; but wherever is a spot flowery and fragrant, there he settles and fixes his abode."

desert like the garden of the Lord; joy and gladness shall be found therein, thanksgiving and the voice of melody." Isa. li. 3. The curse cannot encroach on the spot where the Lamb slain reposes with his redeemed;* the earth, cursed for the disobedience of the first Adam, receives through the righteousness of the second Adam, a deliverance from the bondage of corruption; the first fruits of which we now feel clustering around us in hours of communion with Jesus. Like the early violets, the harbingers of spring, these incipient joys of holiness bespeak the vernal glories of heaven nigh. Heavenly pleasures can no more be separated from the presence of Jesus, than flowers can be separated from the spring. He is to this blighted world, what spring is to the dreariness of winter, the resurrection and the life. Feeling already the first fruits of that better order of things when

"The storms of wintry time will quickly pass,
And one unbounded spring encircle all;"

we read in these earthly beauties, the patterns of

---

* "When the conscience discovers the favourable sentence of God concerning man, and intimates the same to itself, and at the same time bears testimony of its unfeigned piety towards God, it spreads a surprising serenity and calm over the whole soul. Consequently, the peace of God necessarily brings with it peace of conscience, and much confidence in God. The soul nowhere reposes itself more comfortably, than in that bed of tranquillity, and in the bosom of Jesus, its loving, lovely spouse, singing at that time to its adversaries, 'Know that the Lord hath set apart him that is godly for himself. I will both lay me down in peace and sleep, for thou, Lord, only makest me dwell in safety.' "—*Witsius on Spiritual Peace, Cov.*, book iii. 9. 13.

things in the heavens; and with the eye of faith resting on the blessedness of the second Eden, exclaim
with triumphant exultation,

"Come, gentle spring! ethereal mildness! come;
And from the bosom of yon dropping cloud
Of balm of Paradise and heavenly dews,
While music wakes around, veil'd in a shower
Of shadowing roses, on our plains descend."

From the presence of Jesus, however manifested,
nothing can be separated that is delightful. He
makes all things work together for good. How sweet
is our repose when we sit down with him in the hour
of repentance, in times of refreshing, in seasons of
prayer, amid his gracious providences, in the ordinances of the sanctuary. He makes even the valley
of Baca a well; he sheds down divine blessings, as
the rain that filleth the pools. Around his footsteps,
around the place of his rest, the desert blossoms
abundantly, and rejoices even with joy and singing.
The heavenly host still attend him with more of glory
and of melody than at his appearance on the plains
of Bethlehem; and when we are thus with Jesus,
"the angels with their silver wings, o'ershade the
ground thus sacred by his presence made." They
yet delight to praise God for every display of his
good will to man; their music spreads around us a
sea of harmonious undulations; so that

"The place is full of noises,
Sounds, and sweet airs, that give delight and hurt not;
Sometimes a thousand instruments melodious

Will murmur round our ears; and sometimes voices,
That if we then had waked after long sleep,
Will make us sleep again; and then in dreaming,
The clouds will seem to open and show riches
Ready to drop upon us."*

And though shut out from these airs by "this muddy vesture of decay," there are frequently effects produced on the soul, which force on us the impression that we are in the midst of such a chorus; and that these harmonies are quivering faintly through the flesh, and trilling in upon the heart. No couch of flowers, not even of Sharon's roses, can excite sensations of pleasantness at all equalling those felt by the soul thus reposing in the society of Jesus. All, all is peace, love, harmony; with the surrounding harmonies our disordered soul grows more in unison.

"We lay the head
In golden slumber on a bed
Of heaped Elysian flowers, and hear
Such strains as sweetly win the ear
Of spirits from the flesh set free."†

"The beams of our house are cedar,‡ and our raf-

* Tempest, Act 3, Scene 2.
† Milton's Allegro.
‡ "Hardly any kind of wood unites so many good qualities for building as the cedar: its wood not only pleases the eye by its reddish stripes, and exhales an agreeable smell, but it is hard and without knots, and is never eaten by worms, and lasts so long that some persons consider it imperishable. Hence it was used for rafters and boards, either to cover the houses or floors."—*Burder.*

22

ters of fir."* Our place of repose, while thus beautiful, is not open to the rays of the sun, nor to the
rain, but is protected by a shelter, a roof with rafters
of cedar, and a ceiling of fir or cypress, adorned with
exquisite carved work.† These were materials used

* The Hebrew word here used, seems to be only the Ara-
mæan pronunciation of the word which, in most passages
where it occurs, is translated cypress in the old Greek and
Syriac versions. "The wood of the cypress is hard, fragrant,
and of a remarkably fine, close grain, very durable, and of a
beautiful reddish hue, which Pliny says it never loses. According to this author, 'Th statue of Jupiter in the Capitol,
which was formed of cypress, had existed above six hundred
years, without showing the least symptom of decay; and the
doors of the temple of Diana at Ephesus, which were also of
cypress, and were four hundred years old, had the appearance
of being quite new.' This wood was used for a variety of
purposes, as for wine-presses, rafters, and joists."—*Kitto's
Cyclopedia.*

† "The ceiling was slightly arched, and clustered with stalactites of purple and gold, that appeared to have oozed out
from some rich treasury above. The walls were of panelled
cedar, or some such dark and fragrant wood, exquisitely
carved; and curtains of Damascus silk were gathered into
thick folds between pilasters of cedars, polished, yet rugged
with rich carving."—*Warburton's Travels.* "The ceilings were
divided into square compartments, painted with flowers, or
with the figures of animals. Some were inlaid with ivory,
each compartment being surrounded with elegant borders and
mouldings. The beams, as well as the sides of the chambers,
may have been gilded, or even plated with gold and silver;
and the rarest woods, in which the cedar was conspicuous,
were used for the wood work."—*Layard's Nineveh,* ii. 208.
There are some beautiful "patterns from Egyptian ceilings,"
in Wilkinson, vol. ii. 125.

in the temple; in their nature rich and enduring.
The ceilings of oriental houses, in the present day,
as well as in the time of Solomon, are beautified with
carvings and arabesques, with highly coloured paintings.   According to Josephus, the roof of the temple
was of cedar; and that part of the roof that was
under the beams, was made of the same materials,
and had ornaments proper for roofs; also the royal
palace of Solomon was supported by fluted, quadrangular pillars of cedar, and adorned with sculptures,
whereby were represented trees and all sorts of plants,
with the shades that arose from their branches, and
leaves that hung down from them; the leaves were
wrought so thin and subtile, that you would think
them in motion.   He made the whole building entirely of white stone, and cedar wood, and gold,
and silver: he also adorned the roofs and wall with
stones set in gold.   The idea then seems to be, that
the spouse was enjoying this pleasant society of the
beloved, reclining on a bed of grass and vernal
flowers, over which was spread the protection of a
ceiling of durable materials and exquisite carving,
and open on every side to the pleasing prospects and
balmy airs.   One emblem, or set of emblems, was not
enough; the Holy Spirit, in a kind of anxiety to set
forth our privileges, brings together whatever is most
beautiful in nature and in art—beds of flowers, rural
beauty, the shelter of a palace without the confinement of its walls.   The true conception of happiness,
as connected with our restoration from the curse, is
that of being amid such scenes as those in Eden, and

sheltered from the smiting of the sun by day, and of the moon by night. Ps. cxxi. 6. This protection is set forth as a cloud and smoke by day, and the shining of a flaming fire by night; as a shadow from the heat; as a shade; as a shadow of a great rock; as a covering of us with his wings; here, by the figure of a durable, beauteous, costly ceiling.

That protection is nothing less than the divine nature of Jesus Christ. Nothing can harm us beneath this heavenly shade. Evil, Satan, affliction, death, the chill dews of sin, cannot strike us there. Homer represents the god of the sun coming down gloomy as night, and by his arrows scattering death through the Grecian camp; from which protection was sought in vain: in the cloud lowering with wrath over our guilty world, the angel of death, the minister of divine justice, has his stand; but from his arrows of death, our pardoned spirits are more secure than she, who reposed with the beloved beneath this ceiling, was from the withering rays of the sun. As on the ceiling of ancient temples might sometimes be seen beautiful paintings, and in the roof of this summer-house was curious carving; so, in this overshadowing defence of the divine nature of Jesus, are all the excellences of the Godhead. The arch spread over us at midnight, with its stars, nebulæ, and constellations, does not present to the eye, assisted by the best telescope, any thing comparable with the overshadowing divinity of Christ. While, like the roof, it is our shelter; like the evening sky, it sheds down dews on the thirsting soul, refreshing airs on the fainting heart, guiding

light on the bewildered spirit; and reveals to our enraptured contemplation, transcendent and inexhaustible glories. As God inhabited a pillar of cloud and
of fire, that was the protection of the camp of Israel;
and did at the same time commune with them through
the form of a man supposed to be seen between the
cherubim, so that while the divine nature of Christ is
our glorious covering, he in whom dwells all the fulness of the Godhead bodily, communes with us through
the human nature of Jesus Christ. In the quaint language of Francis Quarles—

> "Hath thy all-glorious Deity no shade,
>   Where I may sit and vengeance never eye me?
> See, here's a shadow found: the human nature
>   Is made th' umbrella to the Deity."

This shelter can never decay: He is the same yes-
terday, to-day, and for ever. We may wander to the
verge of creation, without being beyond the limit of
this defence. The temples and palaces of earth are
crumbling; its fortresses, even the tower of David,
and the stronghold of Zion, are in ruins; the temple
of Solomon, with its marbles, its cedars, and gold, is
in the dust; but this spiritual covert of the soul, reared
for us hard by the tree of life in the paradise of God,
stands, and shall stand, through ages of ages, pure,
fresh, and undecaying: and when the heavens shall
have passed away with a great noise, and the earth,
with all that is in it, be consumed, this refuge, the
place of repose of the Beloved and his redeemed, shall
be seen emerging from the ruins, towering on the

22*

Rock of ages in imposing grandeur, and crowned with that cloud of glory which is the light of the upper world.

———

CHAPTER II.

VER. 1.—I am the rose of Sharon, and the lily of the valleys.*

RECLINING thus on a bed of grass and flowers, and beneath such a shade, with the beauties and odours of an oriental paradise spreading around, the beloved and the bride naturally speak of each other in language drawn from the beautiful objects under their notice. The plain of Sharon was particularly rich in flowers. The orientals have ever been fond of images

---

* Patrick, Henry, and Scott, take this verse as the language of the beloved, and consequently the rose and lily as the emblems of Christ. We interpret these as the words of the spouse, for several reasons. 1. The scope of the passage requires this view; because the evident design is to put the spouse in contrast with the beloved, by comparison of the rose and lily with the majesty of the citron-tree. 2. The lily is in the next verse expressly applied to the spouse; and these two verses are parts of the same continuous sentence; so that it is unreasonable to apply the lily as the emblem of Jesus in the former clause, and then find it restricted to the saint in the latter. 3. The Jewish interpreters in general are of this opinion. 4. With us also agree the best Christian expositors, such as Rosenmüller, Delitzsch, Dopke, Cocceius, Michaelis, Vatablus, Ainsworth, Harmer, Percy, Fry, Good, &c.

The Septuagint and Vulgate render the Hebrew word "rose," by "flower;" and Sharon they translate, not as a proper name,

derived from the rose. The Great Mogul, in a letter to James I. of England, compliments him by comparing him to this flower. A modern eastern poet has the same thought, when speaking of Nischabur, the city in which he resided: he says, "I, like Atthar, that famous poet, came out of the garden of Nischabur; but Atthar was the rose of that garden, and I am only a bramble." Pliny reckons the lily the next plant in excellence to the rose. In the East, as with us, it is the emblem of purity and moral excellence. So the Persian poet Sadi compares an amiable youth to "the white lily in a bed of narcissuses;" because he surpassed all the young shepherds in piety, goodness, and vigilance. The spouse is evidently speaking of herself in a modest, humble manner; and the em-

but "a plain," making the words together mean "a flower of the field." Hence Bishop Percy reads, "I am a mere rose of the field." Kitto, however, truly remarks, "There can be little doubt that the rose is really intended by the Hebrew word. Even if in the general sense it should mean but a flower, we should still infer that when applied in a particular sense, it means a rose; for this would be according to the usage of the East. Thus the Persian word *gul* describes a flower in general, and the rose *par excellence;* and the Arabic term *ward* is employed in the same acceptations." In the East, still more than with us, the rose is the queen of flowers. In May, the hills towards Rama and Joppa, as going from Jerusalem, were found covered with white and pink roses; the gardens of Rama were filled with roses of a powerful fragrance. Mariti states that in the hamlet of St. John, in the desert of that name, "the rose-plants form small forests in the gardens." Burckhardt was struck with the number of rose-trees he found among the ruins of Bozra, beyond the Jordan.

blems of the rose and lily do, therefore, illustrate the
Christian character as possessing a beauty in which
delicacy, lowliness, and purity, are leading characteristics.

Nothing could be more delicate than the texture,
hues, and fragrance of the rose and lily. When even
Sharon's vale was filled with such beauteous flowers,
so soon to fade and wither under the wintry frosts of
the curse, shall the same creative power form with
less delicacy those souls which are to flourish in the
freshness of immortality, as the spiritual roses and
lilies by the river of life, in the heavenly Paradise?
Piety refines our whole nature. It is a cleansing from
the coarseness and defilement of sin. It purifies the
heart, the motives, the views, the aspirations, the
soul; and so completely does it bring the body into
subjection to this spiritual purity, that we are at last
invested with a corporeal frame so pure that its nature can be expressed only by calling it a spiritual
body. This purity sheds through all our powers, and
all our actions, an increasing and delightful delicacy
of sentiment, thought, and feeling. The import of the
word "reverence," in Heb. xii. 28, is the spiritual
modesty, the delicate sensibility, diffused through the
soul by the pervading influence of the Holy Spirit,
which brings spontaneously a blush over the heart,
at the very appearance, or mention, or thought of sin,
without our taking time to think of the consequences
of the act, or its hatefulness in the sight of God.
Coarseness of feeling, as well as of language and of
action, is the offspring of the impurity of sin, and must

disappear under the purifying energy of divine grace. The human eye, which is the bodily organ attempered to the various degrees and shades of light, the most subtile form of matter known to us, is the most delicate of the faculties of sense, and would be unfitted for its office, were it less exquisite in its texture; but the splendour of the stars, the grandeur of the sun, the tints of the rainbow, are merely representations of the excellence of him who points to light as the best emblem of his spiritual purity; and as the pure in heart shall see God, not through the drapery thrown around him when he clothes himself with light as with a garment, but in his unveiled glory; who can tell the delicate sensibility requisite in a soul for beholding such visions; for thus contemplating the beauty of holiness; a sensibility which the Holy Ghost is now diffusing through the whole fabric of our being by sanctification, as the preparation for our dwelling evermore under the shadow of the Almighty, and enjoying the unutterable beauties there unfolding to the view.

Like Jesus, whose yoke we bear, the believer finds rest for his soul in meekness and lowliness of heart.*

* "The soul of a true Christian, as I then wrote my meditations, appeared like such a little white flower as we see in the spring of the year; low and humble on the ground, opening its bosom to receive the pleasant beams of the sun's glory; rejoicing, as it were, in a calm rapture; diffusing around a sweet fragrancy; standing peacefully and lovingly, in the midst of other flowers round about; all in like manner opening their bosoms to drink in the light of the sun."—*Edwards' Works*, vol. i. p. 21.

Love is not more certainly the distinguishing virtue of the pious character, than is humility its vital grace. Love being the fruit which holiness bears in the heart, humility is the root by which it is nourished. When the righteous flourish like the palm-tree and grow like a cedar in Lebanon; when he grows as the lily and casts forth his roots as Lebanon; when his branches spread and his beauty is as the olive-tree; then is humility the root which spreading beneath, as the branches develope above, supplies life and nourishment to all the graces of godliness. Our piety may ever be judged by our humility. When Jesus would cause holiness to grow, he places us in situations where humility may expand. The rose and the lily could hardly be expected to grow with vigour, or, if growing at all, to put forth the fulness of their beauty, in a public thoroughfare, the streets of a city, or the halls of fashionable life: in secluded retreats of the country, in lowly meadows, they find a genial soil. In scenes withdrawn from the world and depressed, unthronged with the crowds who seek and bestow the honours coming from man, scenes kindred in loneliness to those so loved by him who was meek and lowly in heart, does the Lord of the vineyard place those whose holiness he would have to blossom as the rose; whom he would have to spread out their root by the water, and the dew to lie all night on their branch.

> "He sprang from a stock of lowly parentage
> Among the wilds of Scotland, in a tract
> Where many a sheltered and well-tended plant

Bears, on the humblest ground of social life,
Blossoms of piety and innocence."*

Before honour is humility. When God is about to
exalt to honour or usefulness one on whom his love is
placed, he prepares him therefor by humiliation;
and when the blessings of the Holy Spirit are
poured on the soul in an unusual degree, we find the
way was prepared for them by humility, and by
humility are they attended. The richest crowns are
beautified with gems, gathered in untrodden regions;
the freshest chaplets are woven of flowers bathed in
the dews of secluded meadows:

"Like virtue, thriving most where little seen."

So calm is the prospect, so bracing the airs of the
valley of Humiliation, the believer says with Mercy,
"The place, methinks, suits with my spirit. I love
to be in such places, where there is no rattling with
coaches, nor rumbling with wheels: methinks, here
one may, without much molestation, be thinking what
he is, whence he came, what he has done, and to what
the King has called him: here one may think, and
break at heart, and melt in one's spirit, until one's
eyes become as the fish-pools of Heshbon. Behold
how green this valley is; also how beautiful with
lilies."

Like the lily of the valleys, the pious soul is invested with a loveliness combining purity with delicacy
and lowliness.

"Our thoughts
Pleasant as roses in the thickets blown,
And pure as dew bathing their crimson leaves."*

* Wordsworth's Excursion, book ii.

Purity and holiness are inseparable. Perhaps we may say holiness is immaterial purity, the moral spotlessness of spiritual beings. Holiness works purity; sin works corruption. Taking the sinner in the midst of his pollution, with a body tending to corruption, because the dwelling-place of a soul under the dominion of guilt, the Holy Spirit unfolds by degrees that newness of life which swells at last into the perfect holiness and dazzling glory of both body and soul in heaven. A person who might possibly be unacquainted with the growth of plants, would hardly believe that the unsightly root of a lily, or even the stalk in its greenness, could be developed into so rich and fragrant a flower. The same Almighty energy whose Spirit causes the seed or root to grow amid earth and corruption itself, into the flower no less pure and beautiful than the lily or the rose, is even now carrying forward, amid our corruption of soul and body, a growth of holiness which shall ripen into the purity and beauty of heaven. Like the flower of the lily full-blown, perfect sanctification, with a spiritual body, is the consummation of our redemption. The lilies that shall adorn the meadows amid which winds the pure river of water of life, are the souls of an innumerable multitude "without spot or wrinkle, or any such thing," who have washed their robes and made them white in the blood of the Lamb. When the Holy Spirit first dawns on the heart at the new birth, we are surprised at the degree of our impurity. Often will it seem as though our prayers and struggles against the tide of impure thoughts and desires were in vain; yet, "shall we know, if we follow on to know the Lord; his going forth is prepared as the morning." Over the soul thus clouded with darkness and sin, the day shall break and the shadows flee away. By nature, in a state of darkness, like that of the night laden with chilling mists and noxious vapours, the soul receives the influences of the Holy Spirit, at first faint and gradual, as the early dawn: like the morning light which goes on and shines not only to sunrise, but to high noon; (more literally, the fixed part of the day, when the sun seems to stand immovable in the zenith;) and then, every vapour sunk, every cloud vanished away, lights up all the atmosphere with purity, and rains down brilliancy on earth and heaven; the faint streaks of light and holiness shooting over the darkened soul in the new birth, go on increasing to the brightness of mid-day splendour in heaven, where all will be purity and glory, as the Sun of Righteousness from the zenith showers on the heart his soft, enlivening rays.

Ver. 2.—As the lily among thorns, so is my love among the daughters.

While combining these excellences, the disposition of the believer is very different from that of the world. As the lily among thorns, so is the believer, during his probation, "among them that are set on fire, even the sons of men, whose teeth are spears and arrows, and their tongue a sharp sword." Ps. lvii. 4. The wind bloweth where it listeth, and bears on its bosom

23

seeds scattered at random, and springing up unno-
ticed in desolate places; even as the Holy Spirit,
according to his sovereign will, causes the seed of the
word to take root in souls scattered far and wide
among the nations, to grow here, as in their nursery,
until fit for transplanting to heaven.   The saint must
expect to find himself, while in this world, among
uncongenial and hostile spirits.   Holiness, however
perfected, will not alter this state of things.   Spotless
though he may be, as the lily, he is yet the lily among
thorns.   Through his first disciples, the Lord Jesus
said to his servants in all ages, "Behold, I send you
forth as sheep in the midst of wolves." Matt. x. 16.
Still is the carnal mind enmity against God, and
against the sons of God; still the wicked watcheth
the righteous, and seeketh to slay him.   Our position
is surrounded with those whose evil passions, pride,
haughtiness, envy, malice, avarice, sensuality, vindic-
tiveness, bristling from their hearts on every side,
make it difficult for us to move without encountering
something keener than thorns or drawn swords, by
which deep and excruciating wounds are inflicted on
the delicate sensibility of the heavenward spirit.   We
cannot move through the world without feeling more
or less of these lacerations.   Because of the voice of
the enemy, because of the oppression of the wicked,
how often does the bleeding heart feel, "O that I
had wings like a dove, for then would I fly away and
be at rest."   As much care is necessary in dealing
with the wicked, as in handling a thorn bush; yet
will those who use the greatest prudence, frequently

find themselves wounded. With the best wishes, offences cannot be always avoided: "As far as in you lies, live peaceably with all men." Those whose souls are brought by grace nearest to the delicacy of holiness set forth by the lily, and who move with most of steady, undeviating Christian energy through the world, are made to feel most sensibly that the believer is here a lily among thorns. Even in Christian countries, the hearts of the wicked are armed with as fierce passions against piety and the pious, as at any former age; and though they may be kept out of view by the civilities of life, change of circumstances often brings us in contact with them where we had hoped they did not exist. Accordingly, our Lord warns us that in becoming his disciples, we must take up the cross, must prepare for suffering. Ignorant of the true state of things here, we expect too much of the world, and thereby injure our peace. Deceived in men thought worthy of confidence, and finding those who are under the greatest debt of gratitude treating us with persecution the most bitter, we would not think our lot singular and hard, did we feel that ingratitude is an inseparable feature of sin, and that as Jesus was a man of sorrows, the disciple cannot be above his Lord. As we are liable to do even good deeds from improper motives, God has kindly placed us in a world where we are thus repelled in our disinterested acts; and are laid under the necessity of doing good and following after holiness, not from any recompense likely to be got from men, but from principle, from love to God. And the believer who examines carefully his infirmities, and the peculiar discomforts and afflictions meeting him, will most probably find that these ills are just what was necessary for counteracting his besetting sins, for weakening his propensities which are unduly strong, and for strengthening those which are disproportionately weak; so that his life, however checkered and painful, may constitute a course of discipline most wisely adapted for bringing his soul into the perfect balancing of all its powers, which is perfect holiness. Hence, one course of life, one series of sorrows, which may be the best possible for the chastisement and discipline of a heart with one class of infirmities, would not be at all applicable to the spiritual wants of another with failings very different. One man on whom God has set his love, may be of such a disposition that riches would ruin him; and it is necessary for his preparation for heaven that these be denied him, and he be tried with something of a different kind. Another may be so constituted that praise would foster vanity and pride; and he can be kept humble most safely by being depreciated and maligned; while another may pass through the fiery ordeal of worldly applause with less danger of injury. Hence those who are called to greatest holiness are called to greatest mortifications; and the apostle exhorts his son Timothy no less than ten or twelve times in his second Epistle, to bear with evil, to endure hardness. Too often, alas, is this hardness to be borne from brethren from whose hearts the remains of sin have not been removed by grace. Well did Luther say, "If thou art the lily and the rose of Christ, know that thy dwelling-place is among thorns. Only take heed lest by impatience, rash judgments, and pride, thou thyself become a thorn."

VER. 3.—As the apple-tree among the trees of the wood, so is my beloved among the sons. I sat down under his shadow with great delight, and his fruit was sweet to my taste.

Having given in the two foregoing verses the character of the believer as represented by the rose and the lily, the Song sets forth in these words the charms of him, who is the object of the believer's love. These illustrations, the rose, the lily, and the apple-tree, are such as would naturally fall under the view of persons reposing on a bed of flowers in an oriental garden, as seen in chap. i. 16. Comparisons drawn from the tree are not unfrequently applied to Jesus in the Scriptures. Isaiah says, "There shall come forth a shoot from the stem of Jesse, and a branch shall grow out of his roots; and the Spirit of the Lord shall rest upon him." The promised Messiah was called the Branch, foreshowing that like a shoot or twig springing from the stump of a tree, he should spring from the stock of Judah, through the family of Jesse. The two natures of the Lord Jesus are here pointed out—his coming forth as a branch, representing him to be the Son of man, while the Spirit of the Lord resting on him shows him to be the Son of God. He is here represented under the figure of that shoot or branch full grown, of a tree. The citron-tree seems to be the one here in-

23*

tended. The name is derived from the fragrance it
exhales. The foliage is perpetual; there is no time,
not even mid-winter, when there may not be seen on
it a profusion of flowers; there is throughout the
year a continual succession of blossoms, young fruit,
and ripe fruit, at the same time; the fruit was of the
colour of gold, very pleasant to the taste, very fragrant, and reviving to those who were ready to faint;
the leaves are studded with small glands to which the
tree owes its rich fragrance. The shade of this tree
is deep and refreshing.* Maundrell speaks of the

---

* Shade is an article of oriental luxury. "In this fairy-like
garden, there were very few flowers; but shade and greenery
are every thing in this glaring climate; and it was passing
pleasant to stroll along these paths, all shadowy with orange-
trees, whose fruit, 'like lamps in a night of green,' hung
temptingly over our heads. The fragrance of large beds of
roses mingled with that of the orange flower, and seemed to
repose on the quiet airs of the calm evening. In the midst of
the garden we came to a vast pavilion, glittering like porcelain, and supported on light pillars, which formed cloisters
surrounding an immense marble basin, in the centre of which,
sparkling waters gushed from a picturesque fountain. Through
the clear depths of the waters gleamed shoals of gold and silver fish."—*Warburton.* "That variety of fragrant lemon
called the 'citron,' attains its highest perfection in Palestine,
and is very abundant; and by the consent of the Jewish writers themselves, as well as from the probability of the case, we
apprehend that 'citron' is always to be understood by the
word translated 'apple' in the common version. That the citron was well known to the Hebrews, we learn from Josephus,
who mentions that on one occasion, at the feast of tabernacles,
King Alexander Jannæus was pelted in the temple with citrons, which the Jews had in their hands—for which he assigns

very great beauty of the orange garden or citron grove, at Beroot, attached to the emir's palace. The walks were shaded with orange-trees of a large spreading size, and all of so fine a growth that nothing could be imagined more perfect, and "gilded with fruit hanging thick upon them. Around were booths, and summer-houses, and other apartments, very delightful." The difference between citron and orange-trees is hardly discernible except by the fruit, which in both is of the same golden colour. Such a tree, therefore, as the citron, standing among the trees of the forest, must be an object of pre-eminent beauty and strong attraction. Thus is Jesus distinguished "among the sons." Him hath God anointed with the oil of gladness above his fellows, Heb. i. 9; that is, through the Holy Spirit given without measure to Christ, God has conferred on him a nature more excellent than that of his fellows, those associated with him in the work of redemption, whether angels, or prophets, or saints. As the citron-tree stood in an atmosphere of perfume rising in continual freshness from its perennial bloom, the human nature of Jesus dwells in the midst of the spiritual fragrance breathing in his divine nature, and encompassing him for evermore on every

the reason, that the law required that at that feast every one should have bunches of the palm-tree and the citron-tree. The fruit of the citron-tree is much used by the oriental ladies to smell to, for which purpose, they often have it in their hands, or within reach, and, as its fragrance is considered most reviving, it is employed for much the same purpose as a scent-bottle in this country."—*Kitto.*

N

side in the infinity of the fulness of the Godhead. Modern poetry has adopted the spirit of this illustration:

> "The mountain ash
> No eye can yet overlook, when 'mid a grove
> Of yet unfaded trees she lifts her head
> Deck'd with autumnal berries, that outshine
> Spring's richest blossoms; and ye may have marked
> By a brook side or solitary tarn,
> How she her station doth adorn.   The pool
> Glows at her feet, and all the gloomy rocks
> Are brightened round her.   In his native vale,
> Such and so glorious did this youth appear;
> A sight that kindled pleasure in all hearts
> By his ingenuous beauty."*

And the meaning of the passage has been well expressed in the words,

> "From Jesse's root behold a branch arise,
> Whose sacred flower with fragrance fills the skies:
> The ethereal spirit o'er its leaves shall move,
> And on its top descends the mystic Dove."†

While the pious spirit is lowly, though beautiful like the lily, with the beauty and majesty of the citron-tree, Jesus towers above all others, in the infinite grandeur of his divinity, as the Son of God.   The crown of glory and honour resting on him who was made a little lower than the angels, is the glorious crown of his eternal divinity.

He is the shade of his people.   The Lord is thy shade on thy right hand.   A shade does not deprive

---

* Wordsworth's Excursion, book vii.
† Pope's Messiah.

of the light of the sun. It so breaks and tempers
the force of the beams as to keep them from injuring
us; and enables us to enjoy their brilliancy and
warmth. Nothing does this more pleasingly than the
stately, spreading boughs of the citron-tree. What
this shade did for the body, the Lord Jesus does for
the soul. Exposed to the full blaze of the justice of
him who is a consuming fire, we must be blasted and
destroyed, did not Christ spread between us and him
whose jealousy burns like fire, that which Israel's
covering of cloud represented in the desert, his own
divine nature. When the soul feels the agonies of
conviction for sin, how sensible is the change, how
reviving the shelter, as we pass under the shadow of
the cross, and feel around us the refreshing influences
of the righteousness of Christ. Within that sacred
shelter, no evil spirit can enter, no affliction injure,
no fiery dart fall.

The apple-tree yielded a profusion of the richest
fruits in uninterrupted abundance. Its fruit was
highly esteemed as sweet to the taste, of refreshing
fragrance, and of the colour of gold. A word fitly
spoken is compared to apples of gold, or the golden
coloured fruit of the citron, in baskets of silver. Prov.
xxv. 11. With richer fruits than these, does Jesus
satisfy the soul that rests under his shadow. He is a
tree of life to them that lay hold on him. Prov. iii. 18.
He alone can satisfy the cravings of the heart. All
attempts to pacify these restless desires, these surges
of conscience, by any amount of property, or things
of the world, is as unreasonable as to try to quiet the

billows of the tempestuous sea, by pouring into its remorseless caverns treasures and gems. From the presence of him whose power was felt on the sea of Galilee, goes forth the influence which carries to the depths of the soul a great calm. Peace he gives unto us, that he may give unto us to eat of the tree of life, which is in the midst of the Paradise of God. This elder brother, a greater than Joseph, who has gone before us into heaven to preserve life, is a fruitful bough, even a fruitful bough by a well, whose branches run over the wall, separating us from the invisible world; and sweet indeed must be the fruits gathered therefrom, when their native soil is heaven, and they are the same which shall throughout eternity satisfy the redeemed.

The weary pilgrim, on coming to the citron-tree, would be delighted with the majesty of its appearance, the protection of its shade, the richness of its fragrance, and the delightfulness of its fruit.* As we come to Jesus, care-worn with guilt and sorrow, he impresses us with the grandeur of his divinity, the excellence of his protecting righteousness, the blessedness shed around us by his Spirit, and the richness of

---

* "At the foot of each tree is a little circular carpet of verdure."—*Warburton.* "There is something peculiarly delightful in the shade of the fig-tree. It is far superior to the shelter of a tent, and perhaps even to the shadow of a rock; since not only does the mass of heavy foliage completely exclude the rays of the sun, but the traveller finds under it a peculiar coolness, arising from the air gently creeping through the branches."—*Mission of Inquiry,* p. 108.

the fruits of holiness found in the Scriptures, in the earnest of the Spirit in the practice of a heavenly temper, and in the anticipation of future glory in heaven. Here are richer than the golden fruits of the Hesperides; and this Angel of the covenant has destroyed the dragon that guarded them, that old serpent, which is the devil and Satan. In this shadow does the soul delight; here would we sit down in the fulness of joy, with the feeling, "This is my rest for ever, here will I dwell, for I have desired it;" here does God abundantly bless our provision and satisfy the poor with bread; here does he clothe his priests with salvation and his saints shout aloud for joy. Ps. cxxxii. 14.

The cool shadow of this lofty, beautiful, and fragrant tree, offered an asylum into which the spouse might well delight to retreat from the oppressive heat of noon. The exquisite perfume, the cooling shade, the beauty of the flowers, and the richness of the fruit, combined to make it a retreat the most delightful. In Jesus, the tree of life, we find the fragrance of the Holy Spirit, the shade of his divine righteousness, the beauties of his nature budding forth in infinite variety, and the precious fruits of his grace and truth—all uniting to render his shadow desirable and delightful. Hence do we sit down under his shadow with great pleasure: "In this shade I desire to sit down." While the desire of the worldling is towards the enjoyments spread around by riches, or fame, or flattery, or ease, looking unto Jesus, we say, "The desire of our soul is to thy name, and to the remembrance of thee." Isa. xxvi. 8. An intelligent traveller in the East could find no other refuge from the heat of summer than a recess cut into the bank of the river where it rose perpendicularly from the water's edge, and formed into a small room by screening the front with reeds and boughs of trees, and covering the whole with similar materials: such places, though infested with reptiles, were the best retreat that could be found.* In what contrast with this stands the shelter afforded by the citron-tree. More uncomfortable and miserable than the former, is the refuge found by those who have their portion in this world; infinitely more delightful than the latter, is the sanctuary found by those whose resting-place is under the shadow of Christ. Around this place of repose the richest fruits continually fall. As entertainments under trees are common in the East, the soul that abides under the shadow of the Almighty Redeemer, feeds on those pleasant words which are as an honey-comb, sweet to the soul and health to the bones. Prov. xvi. 24. These truths do now excite in the depths of the soul sensations as delightful as those which shall be felt in heaven from eating the fruit of the tree of life.

VER. 4.—He brought me to the banqueting-house, and his banner over me was love.

Finding the spouse under the apple-tree, ch. viii. 5, he leads her to the banqueting-house, the house of wine, a place beautified with every ornament, and stored with every thing refreshing and delightful.

* Layard's Nineveh, vol. i. 116.

Among the apartments of his palace, Solomon built,* according to Josephus, "a most glorious dining-room, for feastings and compotations, and full of gold and such other furniture as so fine a room ought to have for the conveniency of the guests; and where all the vessels were made of gold." To this hall reference seems to be made, rather than to the places where their wine was stored. No pains were spared to make such rooms the most splendid possible, as may be still seen in oriental palaces. In a hall of the Alhambra, "the eye is lost in contemplating the rich assemblage of ornamentals which appear in every part of this noble hall. From the pavement to the beginning of the arches the walls are decorated with elegant mosaic; the panels between the arches are filled with a very delicate ornament, which, at a little distance, has the appearance of a plain mass; and the ceiling is composed of stalactites in stucco, and is finished in a style of equal elegance. The distribution of the various parts of this noble apartment is truly enchanting. The balconies above were occupied by musicians; be-

---

* Speaking of Solomon's palace, Josephus says: "It would be an endless task to give a particular survey of this mighty mass of building; so many courts and other contrivances; such a variety of chambers and offices, great and small; long and large galleries; vast rooms of state, and others for feasting and entertainment, set out as richly as could be with costly furniture and gildings; besides, that all the service for the king's table were of pure gold. In a word, the whole palace was, in a manner, made up, from the base to the coping, of white marble, cedar, gold, and silver, with precious stones here and there intermingled upon the walls and ceilings."—*Antiq.* viii. 5, 2.

low sat the women; while a jet of water in the centre
diffused a refreshing coolness through the hall. The
windows in the back-ground are finished in a similar
manner, and look into a little myrtle garden." Something like this must have been witnessed when the
Queen of Sheba saw all Solomon's wisdom, and the
house that he had built, and the meat of his table, and
the sitting of his servants, and the attendance of his
ministers, and their apparel, and his cup-bearers, and
his ascent by which he went up into the house of the
Lord; and there was no more spirit in her. Far more
glorious is the place into which Jesus brings our souls,
on that mountain where he has made unto all people
a feast of fat things full of marrow, of wines on the
lees well refined. Isa. xxv. 6. Here, our dwelling-
place is amid walls formed of divine goodness, Ps.
xxv. 13; our light is the Shechinah of the Spirit's
presence; our food is the hidden manna; our cup salvation; our drink the new wine of the heavenly kingdom; our anointing the oil of gladness; our ministering attendants angels; and the banner over us is
love.

Nothing can be so excellent as the influences of the
Holy Spirit. How excellent the fragrance of the
citron bloom, the effect of wine! no comparison can
be drawn between these and the ethereal excellence
of the Holy Ghost. When we feed on any thing, it
is so brought into contact with us as to nourish our
life; and when the Spirit's influences are so diffused
through the soul as to sustain its life, we may be said
to feed on his grace. Hence it is written, "Man

shall not live by bread alone, but by every word that proceedeth out of the mouth of God." Matt. iv. 4. There is literally such a thing as feeding on truth; and the place where these spiritual provisions are enjoyed in abundance, may well be called the banqueting house. How superior to every thing else in the world, is the banquet spread for us by Jesus! The truths and doctrines of Scripture, so rich, better than thousands of gold and silver, are the means, sacred vessels brought from heaven, for conveying to us this food of the Spirit. Here we banquet on the riches of redeeming love. The man who feeds on fame, flattery, riches, power, has nothing better than the husks of the dying prodigal; while those who are Christ's, share the luxuries of the marriage-supper of the Lamb.

"His banner over me was love." He brings us to this feast, with the exultation of a conqueror returning in triumph with a loved one wrested from the power of an enemy. Jesus is called the Captain of our salvation, Heb. ii. 10, a name which is applied in the New Testament to none but Christ, and signifies a chief or commander, one who leads a column and directs its movements. When Abraham heard that his brother was taken captive, he armed his trained servants, and pursued the enemy, smote them, and brought back Lot, and his goods, and the people: thus has Jesus come to our rescue, and delivered us from bondage to the powers of darkness. He is still "Captain of the host of the Lord," as when he appeared to Joshua before Jericho; and is leading the

spiritual host, who, from a period earlier than that of
Abraham, have been pressing onward towards the
Canaan on high. The banner of this conqueror and
king of glory has its inscription and symbol. Unlike
the military nations of the world, whose lust has been
for war, and whose emblems have been expressive of
their character, as the eagle on the standards of
Rome, he, as the Prince of peace, has the dove as the
symbol of his kingdom; and has a banner woven of
the precious fabric of love. When combatants raise
a red flag, it is for showing a determination to shed
blood; the black flag is the signal that no quarter
may be expected; a white banner bespeaks the desire
for peace. With what propriety therefore is the banner of Jesus said to be love.

A banner rallies to the defence of the person over
whom it floats, all the resources of the empire to
which it belongs: wherever he wanders, this simple
symbol calls up around him bulwarks invisible, but
mighty with an empire's strength. Thus, under all
circumstances in life, and in death, the love of Christ
enlists all the perfections of the Godhead in behalf of
his saint. As the flag shows to what country we belong, so by love we are shown to be citizens of heaven.
As the banner of his country is an object of honourable pride to the good citizen, thus while the wise man
glories in his wisdom, and the rich man in his riches,
and the brave man in his valour, the saint glories
only in the cross of Christ, and in possessing thereby the divine love. Poetry has delighted to por-
tray the affection of the soldier for the flag of his

country; and true to the feelings of human nature, is the dying patriot said to look upwards to its folds,

"And smile to see its splendours fly,
 In triumph o'er his closing eye."

When he who has fought the good fight, and endured hardness as a good soldier of Jesus Christ, finds the dimness of death on his eye, and its coldness on his heart, how will his spirit revive on seeing over him this banner of love! And as a dying patriot requested that the flag under which he had fought and con-quered might be placed under his head for a pillow, as life was ebbing away; then, with our sinking head pillowed on the divine love, while over us floats the banner of love, as paleness comes over the lips, and dimness over the eye, and coldness over the heart, shall the last beat of the heart send up to heaven the shout—Victory through Jesus Christ.

VER. 5, 6.—Stay me with flagons,* comfort me with apples: for I am sick of love. His left hand is under my head, and his right hand doth embrace me.

In these words the spouse expresses the impression made on her by the display of love in the banqueting

* In Kitto's Cyc. Bib. Lit., art. *Wine*, 10, there is a disser-tation on the Hebrew word here rendered "flagons." From it we extract the following, found in Olearius: "The Persians are permitted to make a sirrup of sweet wine, which they boyl till it be reduced to a sixth part, and be grown as thick as oyl. They call this drug *duschab*, and when they would take of it, they dissolve it with water. Sometimes they boyl the duschab so long that they reduce it into a paste. for the convenience of travellers, who cut it with a knife, and dissolve it in water. At Tabris they make a certain conserve of it, which they call

house—"I am sick of love." From the beginning of the Song, we have had illustrations of the soul as led along from one degree to another of holy love, till reaching here the highest degree of spiritual enjoyment possible in the present world. The Holy Spirit may so fill the heart with his influences as to make us literally "sick of love;" purifying our power of apprehension, and exciting irrepressible desires for seeing more of our Lord. As hope deferred maketh the heart sick, these longing desires run ahead of our enjoyment, and, indeed, of our capability of enjoying Jesus; and these desires, thus unsatisfied, make us sick of love. This state of heart is caused by ardour of affection, and inability to enjoy the society of the object of affection fully as we desire; by longings, sometimes so deep as to be expressed only in groanings that cannot be uttered, to behold Jesus in the fulness of his glory. With Moses, we pray without ceasing, "I beseech thee, show me thy glory." "There be some kind of assurances," says Leighton,* "that are more rare and extraordinary, some immediate glances or coruscations of the love of God upon

helwa, mixing therewith beaten almonds, flour, &c. They put this mixture into a long and narrow bag, and having set it under the press, they make of it a paste, which grows so hard that a man must have a hatchet to cut it." This statement reconciles the version in the text with that which is preferred by those who render the word "cakes—such as were prepared from dried grapes or raisins, pressed or compacted into a certain form."

* Sermon on Rom. viii. 35.

the soul of a believer, a smile of his countenance, and
this doth exceedingly refresh, yea, ravish the soul,
and enables it mightily for duties and sufferings."
This was the experience of Bunyan's Pilgrim, when
towards the end of his course, "by reason of the
natural glory of the city, and the reflection of the
sunbeams upon it, Christian with desire fell sick."
Rutherford's Letters abound in expressions of this
state of heart. In the words of John Howe,* "There
will be a sickness at the heart by the delay of what I
hope for, most of all, when sun of my blessedness is
the thing hoped for, and still deferred. They that
never felt their hearts sick with the desire of heaven,
and the blessedness of that state, cannot conceive of
it a tree of life beforehand, nor ever know what
patience in expecting it signifies in the meantime."
Even yet there are souls thus exercised, that are constrained to pray with an ancient saint,* "Lord, with-

* Sermon on Heb. x. 36. An eminent divine now in glory,
than whom no man understood theology better, either in a
didactic or practical point of view, once remarked to us, in a
conversation on this subject, that there were probably more of
these exercises among scattered members of the Church, than
was generally supposed. There can be no doubt this is the
case. Nor are such instances as that recorded of Dr. Green
confined always to the closing scene. "On the Sabbath but
one before his death, after the family had returned from the
morning service, it was observed on entering his room that his
mind was burdened with meditations to which he wished to
give utterance, and that his emotions were producing a rest-
lessness and agitation that were inexplicable. The reading by
a friend of the first chapter of the Gospel of John, not only
allayed that distressing nervous excitement, but seemed to

draw a little, lest the brittle vial of my heart should burst by the rays of thy favour darting too strongly."

> "Then shall thy ravisht soul inspired bee
> With heavenly thoughts farre above humane skil;
> And thy bright radiant eyes shall planely see
> Th' idee of his pure glorie present still
> Before thy face; that all thy spirits shall fill
> With sweete enragement of celestiall love,
> Kindled through sight of those faire things above."*

In this state the predominating feeling of the soul is deep and melting contrition.† It is with the con-

impart a sort of inspiration, by which his faculties were for the time emancipated: his tongue was loosed, and he burst out into an ecstasy of joy and thanksgiving. His voice was loud, his enunciation clear and distinct as it had been in the best days of his ministry; and this elevated strain of praise and holy exultation was continued until his strength was exhausted, and he sunk into a sweet and refreshing sleep."—*Dr. Jones's Life of Dr. Green*, p. 498.

  * Spenser's Hymn of Heavenly Love.

  † My gloom was very often relieved greatly by the highest exercises of a spiritual kind that I have ever experienced. I was made to feel that I could not command them at my own pleasure, and that Satanic influence could not account for their occurrence, without making Satan hostile to his own interests; for their invariable effect was to humble to the very dust, and to exalt the Redeemer, and to fill my mind with love to God and man, in an eminent degree, and a desire to do all in my power to advance the interests of vital piety."—*Life of Dr. Green*, p. 302.

  "Assurance of the love of God never produces self-complacency or pride; but always humility, self-abasement, wonder, gratitude, and praise. The believer sees that the mysterious fountain of this love is in the divine mind; it is not in himself, who is ungodly and a sinner."—*Hodge on Romans*, v. 8—10.

trite and humble spirit that the high and lofty One
that inhabiteth eternity dwells. The more intimately he dwells with us, the deeper will be our contrition.
Like a blinded eye, the soul is insensible to the
splendour of the divine glory and love shining around
us with such brilliancy, until the touch of him who
healed Bartimeus restores our spiritual sensibility;
then the glory of the love of God is the light; and
the sensations of the heart thus made pure, and acted
on by these heavenly rays, are emotions of contrition
and love. The happiest hours on earth, are those in
which our contrition is deepest and most tender. In
this exercise, there is a commingling in the heart of
the two pellucid streams of humility and love: the
nearer we come to heaven, the deeper, purer, and
more tranquil is their flow. Our luxury is to prostrate ourselves at the mercy-seat, and there weep for
sin; weep, not the tears that find vent when bemoan-
ing some crushing sin, but the tears that well forth
in the soul, dissolving in contrition when the Holy
Spirit is within the heart as a fountain of water
springing up into everlasting life. At such hours, we
wish to do what was once done by a contrite heart,
pour out before the blessed Saviour the precious perfume of the affections from the alabaster of a broken
spirit; and as we lie prostrate before him, weeping,
kiss those feet which have been wounded for us, and
bathe them with our tears. The sense of God's
amazing goodness, of his tenderness to such unworthiness as ours, this it is that overcomes us, and makes
us weep. We are thus sweetly subdued, because we

are able in a clearer manner to "behold what manner of love the Father has bestowed upon us, that we should be called the sons of God." The predominating feeling is, "I am not worthy of the least of all the mercies, and of all the truth, which thou hast showed unto thy servant." We sink down in overpowering humility, because overcome with melting love. No wild or boisterous feeling, no nervous enthusiasm, no burst of passion, then disturbs the soul. All, all is perfect peace. Such were the exercises of Mrs. Graham, when on the borders of heaven, a few hours before her death, bathed in tears, she said: "I have no more doubt of going to my Saviour, than if I were already in his arms; my guilt is all transferred; he has cancelled all I owed. Yet I could weep for sins against so good a God: it seems to me as if there must be weeping even in heaven for sin." At a time of the deepest pious exercises, Edwards says: "There was no part of creature holiness, that I had so great a sense of its loveliness, as humility, brokenness of heart, and poverty of spirit; and there was nothing that I so earnestly longed for. My heart panted after this, to lie low before God, as in the dust; that I might be nothing, and that God might be ALL, that I might become as a little child."

"His left hand is under my head." We then feel sweetly sustained by the Lord Jesus, by his imputed righteousness, and by his inward grace. So far from wishing to rest on any merit of our own, we cast from us our righteousness as filthy rags, as a broken reed, on which if a man lean it will go into his heart and

pierce it, 2 Kings xviii. 21. His righteousness, like
the pillars in the porch of the temple, Jachin and
Boaz, firmness and strength; like the pillars of marble set upon sockets of fine gold, Song v. 15, with his
human nature resting on the fine gold of his divine
nature, is mighty to save even to the uttermost all
who come to him, however great their unworthiness
and guilt. By the grace of the Holy Spirit shed
through the heart, the name of Jesus is as ointment
poured forth, more refreshing than the cluster of camphire in the vineyards of Engedi, than the bundle of
myrrh in the bosom; he is full of grace and truth.
As he comes forth from the ivory palaces of the heavenly glory, his garments smell of myrrh, aloes, and
cassia, the excellency of his divine nature sheds a divine influence around us; we rise gently above the
din, the jar, the perplexities of earth; new vigour is
imparted to our faith, new animation to our desires;
the soul is filled with confidence, with joy, with peace;
duty becomes pleasing, toils borne for Jesus seem delightful, for the love that we bear to him; sorrow
ceases to distress, care no longer perplexes; the angel
of the covenant makes us to ride on the high places
of the earth, and drink of the pure blood of the grape
of Israel's inheritance.

"His right hand doth embrace me." While thus
sustaining us, Jesus draws us very near to himself.
Onward, nearer to Jesus! is the ruling feeling of the
saint. We may at times wish it had been our privilege to see Jesus, as the apostles saw him, with bodily

o

eyes. But there is no evidence that their hearts experienced any more joy than may be now felt by the believer. The manifestations of the glory of his divine nature may be made to our hearts as vivid and as enchanting as they were to patriarchs and apostles. The glories of his glorified human nature we are not so unreasonable as now to expect to behold. The time will come for the body to have its share in ministering to our vision of the glory of God. Our happiness now consists not in seeing visions, and hearing sounds; not in bodily exhilaration and rapturous ecstacies; but in feeling God's love, and in being filled with his Spirit. There is no reason for supposing that the emotions of the multitude under the action of the Spirit on the day of Pentecost, were more delightful than the emotions now felt under the reviving power of the same Spirit. In the most glorious visions had by patriarchs and prophets, there was probably no more delight enjoyed than is now the portion of the contrite spirit. We may not see what they saw; but we may feel what they felt. It is doubtful that Jacob at Bethel, or at Penuel, or that the disciples at the transfiguration, had more real joy of heart than is now often experienced under the ministration of the Spirit. In the words of Witsius: "Hence it is, that while his saints are sometimes ravished on high by his Spirit, he surrounds them with the beams of his super-celestial light, gives them a view of his face, shining with the brightest love, kisses them with the kisses of his mouth, admits them to the most endearing, mutual intercourse of mystical love with himself; and, while he plentifully sheds abroad his love in their hearts, he gives them to drink of rivers of honey and butter; and that often in the greatest drought of the parched soul, when expecting no such thing. There are many more mysteries in this secret intercourse with our heavenly Father, which believers sometimes see, taste, and feel, and which no pen of the learned can represent as they deserve."*

"Stay me with flagons, comfort me with apples:" that is, Give me support and refreshment with cups of wine from the banqueting-house, and with citrons from the tree whose shadow was so delightful. The fruits with which the soul sick of love desires to be refreshed, are the precious doctrines of the cross and the promises of the Scriptures. There is then a wonderful avidity for the word of God; we feel what it is to live not by bread alone, but by every word that proceedeth out of the mouth of God. The simple doctrines of the cross are sweeter than our daily food. Here at this fountain of life, where the doctrine of Jesus drops as the rain, and his speech distils as the dew, does the Holy Spirit give strong drink unto him that is ready to perish, and wine unto those that be of heavy heart —that best wine for the beloved, which goeth down sweetly, causing the lips of those that are asleep to speak; yea, here does the afflicted saint drink, and forget his poverty, and remember his misery no more.

* Witsius on the Covenants, book iii. 11, 34.

VER. 7.—I charge you, O ye daughters of Jerusalem, by the roes and by the hinds of the field, that ye stir not up, nor awake my love, (the object of my affection,) till he please.*

As these animals were proverbially timorous, the greatest care must be taken not to disturb them; and

* Some interpreters, among whom are Dopke, Rosenmüller, and Professor Stowe, in an article on the Song in the Biblical Repository, April, 1847, take these as the words of the beloved, applied to the spouse. The reason for this is, that the Hebrew word rendered "my love," is a feminine noun, and the following verb, "till he please," is also of the feminine form. The conclusion they draw from these facts is unnecessary and incorrect; and the meaning adopted in the English version seems the true one. 1. Because it harmonizes best with the scope of the passage. 3. It seems to be required also by the scope of the context in the other places, ch. iii. 5, viii. 4, where the same language occurs. 2. The beloved is compared to a gazelle, or a young hart, ch. ii. 9, and the immediate connection seems to restrict this verse accordingly to the same, if it can be done without violence to the Hebrew. 4. This can be done. The Hebrew word "my love," means "love," then "an object of affection," whether male or female, precisely as the corresponding word is used in the English language. This noun, with this meaning, being thus feminine, the following verb would naturally take the same gender. In this very book, ch. v. 9, where the spouse is unquestionably addressing her female friends, the verb "if ye find," is the second person masculine instead of feminine. Moreover, the masculine form is used for the feminine, not only in the Future, as in Song viii. 4, Isa. lvii. 8, but also in the Præter, in Ruth i. 8; and in the Imperative, in Micah i. 13, and Isa. xxxii. 11. 5. Besides the English version, our view is that adopted by Delitzsch, Good, Fry, and Bishop Percy.

"Among the orientals, it is considered barbarous in the extreme to awake a person out of his sleep. How often, in going

the believer enjoying the manifestations of heavenly love, will be as cautious in avoiding sin, as in watching the gazelle, which bounds away at the rustling of a leaf. Nothing could express more strongly with what carefulness the contrite heart seeks to retain those influences of the Spirit and the society of Jesus. Never have we such intense anxiety in guarding against sin, as when thus filled with intense love. Then do we watch and pray; then do we groan, being burdened; then do we moan for entire conformity to Jesus, that with Jesus we may for ever rest.

VER. 8, 9.—The voice of my beloved! behold, he cometh leaping upon the mountains, skipping upon the hills. My beloved is like a roe, or a young hart: behold, he standeth behind our wall, he looketh forth at the windows, showing himself through the lattice.

The Christian life is a series of visits and withdrawals of our Lord, of revivals of grace in the heart and exposure to trials. After the overpowering display of love in the foregoing verses, the beloved had left the spouse; these words describe his return. When we have been passing through a season of coldness and decline, how often have we been sweetly surprised by an influence coming over the heart,

to the house of a native, you are saluted with, "He sleeps." Ask them to arouse him: the reply is, "I cannot." Indeed, to request such a thing, shows at once that you are griffin, or new-comer. "Only think of that ignorant Englishman: he went to the house of our chief, and being told that he was asleep, he said he must see him, and actually made such a noise as to awake him; and then laughed at what he had done."—Roberts.

we could hardly tell whence, or how, warming the heart, drawing the attention back to the forgotten Saviour, inclining us to prayer, and giving evidence of the return of Jesus. We are taken by surprise; we look up with wondering love, and exclaim, "The voice of my beloved."

At such times, the Saviour encourages us from a distance by his voice; gives tokens of his approach; makes us feel he is about to repeat his visits; and open to us fresh visions of his love. To the soul dead in sin, the idea of now hearing the voice of Jesus is visionary. But the good Shepherd says, the sheep know his voice. John x. 13. And if the friend of the bridegroom which standeth and heareth him, rejoiceth greatly because of the bridegroom's voice; much more shall the bride rejoice when she heareth him. There is herein no visionary enthusiasm; no wonders ringing in the ear of the body. There is a something speaking to the soul; spirit whispering to spirit; tones from the lips of Jesus, adapted to the hearing ear of the renewed soul. Faith, "the evidence of things not seen," gives us the best kind of evidence, that this is indeed the voice of our Lord. Then, when his speech distils as the dew, as the small rain upon the tender herb, and as the showers upon the grass; the lonely soul feels him to be as the dew unto Israel, and that they that dwell under his shadow, shall return, they shall revive as the corn, and grow as the vine, Hos. xiv. 7; then is he to the reviving heart, like a serene heat after rain, like a cloud of dew in the heat of harvest. Isa. xviii. 4.

He comes over all difficulties to visit and revive us;
on or over the mountains or hills, he comes leaping,
surmounting all obstacles with ease. "Here, near
the sea of Gallilee, we saw the gazelle bounding on
before us, over shrubs and rocks and every obstacle,
and felt the exquisite fulness of meaning in the
church's exclamation, 'Behold, he cometh leaping
upon the mountains, skipping upon the hills. My
beloved is like a roe or young hart.' It is the very
nature of this lively animal to bound over the rough-
est heights with the greatest ease, it seems even to
delight in doing so."* And it is the very nature of
the Lord Jesus to come to the souls of his people,
over all difficulties with perfect ease. Nothing, whether the inward sense of unworthiness and guilt, aggravated by nnmerous backslidings, or outward sorrows rising around us, dark and towering as the crags
of the valley of the shadow of death, nothing can separate us from the love of Christ.

He comes to us speedily, unexpectedly. The
roe was an emblem of swiftness: Asahel was as light
of foot as a wild roe, 2 Sam. ii. 18; and certain of
David's men were as swift as the roes upon the
mountains. 1 Chron. xii. 8. The heart is surprised in an unexpected moment, by the appearance of
the beloved. Though keeping afar off for a time,
he comes speedily; his heart was turned; his repent-
ings were kindled; and ere we were aware, his soul
made him like the chariots Ammi-nadib; he came as

---

* Mission of Inquiry, p. 296.

speedily as the angel came to Peter in prison asleep; as when he came to bless the Psalmist, and he rode on a cherub and did·fly, yea, he did fly upon the wings of the wind; as speedily as on the first visit to the disciples after his ascension, when suddenly there came a sound from heaven, as of a rushing mighty wind, and they were all filled with the Holy Ghost. When churches long thirsting for the revival of his work have well nigh fainted under the thought that their sins and unworthiness were so great as to exclude them, perhaps for ever, from the blessing; he has been found among them, as a dew from the Lord, as the showers upon the grass, that tarrieth not for man, nor waiteth for the sons of men. Micah v. 7.

"Behold he standeth behind our wall." In the present life, we are in the condition of prisoners sentenced to hard labour. This world is our prison. The inmate of a penitentiary is not more completely cut off from the community in the midst of which he is confined, from association with the public, from knowledge of general affairs, from open landscapes and glorious skies, than are we, as offenders against God, cut off from associating with the world of spirits, from knowledge of its mysteries, from views of its grandeurs and glories. After all the labours of science, we have no more acquaintance with the universe at large, than the prisoner is able to get of the world, through the bars of his dungeon. Like the fallen emperor of the French, we have lost our principality; the crown has fallen from our head, and we are confined on this earth, as a solitary, desolate island in the ocean of space; an impassable sea is around us, and we know but little, very little of the worlds and peoples lying beyond. Jesus, who has gone away to receive a kingdom for himself, and after preparing a place for us in that kingdom, to return and receive us to himself, does now kindly visit us in our confinement. But dark walls of our dungeon come between—the walls of our earthly house of this tabernacle, the walls that rise between us and the invisible world. How far is Jesus removed from me? He is standing behind this wall. This it is, and this only, which prevents us from having full view of him, from coming very near to him, from hearing distinctly his voice. When the Lord shall descend from heaven with a shout, with the voice of the archangel and with the trump of God; then shall these walls go down more perfectly than those of Jericho, and our souls, like liberated Rahab, be received into the host of the Lord, and into the presence of the Captain of our salvation.

"He looketh forth at the window, showing himself through the lattice,"* or more strictly, glancing

---

* "I passed into a garden, round three sides of which the apartments ranged. A little lake of crystal water lay enclosed by marble banks, and overshadowed by beautiful weeping-willows; little fountains leaped and sparkled in all directions, 'and shook their loosened silver in the sun.' Arcades of orange, and lemon, and mimosa-trees, afforded a quivering shade to the marble mosaic paths, and the parterres of flowers. At one end of this court, or garden, was a lofty alcove, with a ceiling richly carved in gold and crimson fret-work; the walls are ornamented with arabesques, and a wide divan runs round

through the lattice.   The views now got of Jesus, are like the furtive glances which the spouse was able now and then to catch of the glistening eyes of the loved one through the lattice window.   Vines, jessamines, roses, and honey-suckles, grew in luxuriance against and over the walls of the royal palace or summer-house, with their tendrils and bloom often flowering beautifully through the gilded lattices: to this there may be here an allusion, as though in this way; He who is the true vine, John xv. 1, does unfold to us, through the lattice in the walls separating us from the invisible world, some budding flowers of his glory. The ordinances, the sacraments, the scriptures, constitute the lattice through which we now get glimpses of the Beloved; and are enabled to see beauties unfolding, and breathe exhilarating fragrance, which thrill the soul with assurance of the immeasurable fulness awaiting us amid the splendours of heaven.

Ver. 10.—My beloved spake, and said unto me, Rise up, my love, my fair one, and come away.

To the spouse, confined within doors by the cold and rains of winter, the beloved having thus come from afar, addresses motives for alluring her away from her retreat, and abroad among the beauties of spring.   Thus the Lord Jesus encourages us, by pre-

three sides of the apartment, which opens on the garden and its fountains. Next to this alcove is a beautiful drawing-room, with marble floor and arabesque roof, and carved niches, and softened light falling on delicately painted walls; in the midst is an alabaster basin, into which water falls from four fantastic little fountains."—*Warburton's Travels—The Crescent and the Cross.*

senting to the mind the attractiveness of heaven as a place adorned with more than the beauties of Eden. And after the withdrawal of his presence, how kindly does he encourage the soul by making us feel that he loves us none the less because he withdrew for a time; and how does the heart revive on hearing him still call us, "My love, my fair one!" We had thought that he left us because we had alienated his love by sin, and he was displeased by our many corruptions. His first words are, that he loves us as ever, and rejoices in our society as the bridegroom rejoices in the society of his loved one. Such being his love, he wishes to have us with him where he is, that there may be nothing to break the interchange of affection between him and our souls. Bunyan says, that when the summons came for Mr. Standfast to pass over Jordan, "the contents thereof were, that he must prepare for a change of life, for his master was not willing that he should be so far from him any longer." Much is said of the desire of the saint to depart and be with Jesus. We should think more of the desire of Jesus to have the believer depart and be with him in glory. The saint cannot be so desirous for being in heaven, as Jesus is for having us with him in heaven. "Father, I will that they also whom thou hast given me, be with me where I am, that they may behold my glory." John xvii. 24. He wishes us to be absent from the body and present with the Lord; to go forth from the walls of this prison-cell of the body, and walk with him by the living fountains of waters, in the vernal landscape of the heavenly world. How beautiful and attractive, as they are here shadowed forth, are the motives he addresses to the heart, as he says, "Rise, and come away." Never was there a more lovely description of spring, fit emblem of the time when we shall see

> " The various seasons woven into one,
> And that one season an eternal spring."

VER. 11.—For, lo! the winter is past, the rain is over and gone.

In the broad and open domains of that world which lies beyond the walls of our present condition, separating us from the Beloved, the winter is past: there, the reign of sin, the effect of man's guilt, as seen in the very ground, of which winter is so sad an evidence, is no more seen; in those realms of blessedness, there shall be no more curse. Rev. xxii. 3. St. Paul represents the whole creation as standing in earnest expectation of the time when the curse shall be removed. Rom. viii. 19. In those parts of this world most distinguished for the bodily and mental superiority of man, winter seems the order of nature; the warm genial weather of summer is confined to the smaller portion of the year, no more than sufficient for bringing from the bosom of the earth the productions necessary for the support of man; while cold storms and wintry blasts, chilling nights and gloomy days, fill up the greater part of the seasons, and invade with frequency even the few weeks of summer. In the present condition of the body and soul of man under the curse, this state of things is necessary. In those regions where uninterrupted summer reigns, the en-

ergies of the human mind and body wither, and the
ills of the curse rage with greater power. In that
world to which Jesus is drawing us, all these former
things are passed away. There, the ground is no
longer cursed for the sake of man; nor must he sustain life by the sweat of his brow; there, are no
changing seasons, no days of labour, no tedious chilling nights, no pelting storms, no benumbing winds to
breast even in works of mercy, no lightning and hail,
snow and vapours, stormy blasts fulfilling the word of
an angry God. With imagery of this kind, has unin-
spired poetry, even among pagans, loved to invest the
future abode of the blessed.

> " The blissful plains
> Where heavenly Justice in Elysium reigns;
> Joys ever young, unmixed with pain or fear,
> Fill the wide circle of th' eternal year;
> Spring ever smiles on that auspicious clime,
> The fields are flowery with unfading prime:
> From the bleak pole no winds inclement blow,
> Mould the round hail, or flake the fleecy snow;
> But from the breezy deep the blest inhale
> The fragrant murmurs of the western gale."*

In the same spirit, Pindar speaks of that state as
realms where the virtuous enjoy the light of a sun that
never sets, free from all toil, without sorrow, without
tears; where ocean-breezes refresh the isles of the
blessed; where cluster-flowers of gold, some on the
ground, others on beautiful trees, others bathed by
the waters of pellucid streams; while entwining

---

* Odyssey, iv. 564.

crowns and chaplets of these, the happy one follows a life of purity and justice; meads damasked with purple roses form the suburbs of their heavenly city, around which no evening throws its shades; peaceful plenty everywhere blooms; and over those lovely realms balmy fragrance is shed, as those heavenly meadows are shaded with groves of trees laden with gold and incense.*

The winter has thus passed away from the face of nature in that happy world, because the soul of man, on account of whose sin the curse fell on the ground, has been delivered from all his iniquity; his habitation is all pure and glorious, because his spiritual leprosy has been cleansed. No hurricanes of passion can there burst on the soul; no gusts of sin sweep over the heart; no thunderbolts of guilt shiver our peace; no mildew blight our hopes; no canker prey on the objects of our delight; no frosts chill the budding affections; no withering blasts spread desolation over our prospects, or freeze the currents of joy. Every thing proclaims with a voice of gladness, there shall be no night there; they have no need of the sun, neither of the moon, for the glory of God and the Lamb is the light thereof; there shall be no more curse; "The winter is past."

"The rain is over and gone." About the close of winter in the land of Judea, the latter rains were frequent for many days; and while so necessary for ripening the harvest, and the forerunner of the serene sky

* Pindar, 2d Olymp. Ode.

of that joyous season were always unpleasant and chilly. The eastern winter is past by April; but all the showers were not over till May. The time referred to in these verses seems to be the period directly after the ceasing of these spring-showers, when all nature was beautiful with a new-born freshness yet untouched by the withering drought of summer. Between the wintry rain of the curse over us in this world, and the bursting forth of the vernal beauties of that new earth wherein dwelleth righteousness, the believer must pass through many pelting storms of distress and affliction, which, though for the present not joyous but grievous, are necessary for ripening in our souls the peaceable fruit of righteousness. As the latter rain was the herald of spring and the forerunner of harvest, the divine chastisements are the closing evils connected with sin and the heralds of coming peace in heaven. These must be done away when we reach that world where "God shall wipe away all tears from their eyes, and there shall be no more death, neither sorrow, nor crying;" where the rain is over and gone; where the clouds return not after the rain, Eccl. xii. 2; and as a pledge that sorrow is over and gone never to return, He who set his bow in the cloud, that the waters shall no more become a flood to cover the world, has placed a rainbow round about the throne, in sight like unto an emerald. Rev. iv. 3.

26

VER. 12.—The flowers appear on the earth; the time of the singing of birds is come, and the voice of the turtle is heard in our land.

At this time the fields were covered with beautiful flowers, which delighted the eye and filled the air with fragrance. Before the fall, the earth was robed in these vernal splendours, not merely during the few weeks of spring, and in a few spots scattered over its barren surface, but presented throughout the year a wilderness of sweets rejoicing and blossoming as the rose, of which the glory of Lebanon, the excellency of Carmel and Sharon, is merely a shrivelled remnant. Equally glorious shall be the earth when the curse is done away, and all things are created new. The Paradise awaiting the just in heaven, shall not be less glorious than that Eden,

> "Where from that sapphire fount the crisped brooks,
> Rolling on orient pearl and sands of gold,
> With mazy error under pendent shades
> Ran nectar, visiting each plant, and fed
> Flow'rs worthy of Paradise, which not nice art
> In beds and curious knots, but nature boon
> Poured forth profuse on hill, and dale, and plain,
> Flow'rs of all hue and without thorn the rose."

Spring is the living illustration to fallen man of the truth, that there shall be a like resurrection from the barrenness which the curse has spread over our world. Flowers are the most beauteous form that matter, as now known to us, assumes. And when told that in the future world the flowers appear in the earth as the attendants of an eternal spring, we feel nothing could represent to us more pleasingly that there the curse on the ground is repealed, and the face of nature invested with the attractive beauty of Paradise. There, Jesus as our Shepherd will make us to lie down in green pastures, and lead us beside the still waters; nor will the flowers there appearing in the earth soon wither under summer's heat, and fall under winter's frost; they will bloom unfading, undecaying, throughout a spring which shall fill the whole compass of a cycle boundless as eternal life.

"The time of the singing of birds is come." Thus, the following, translated by Sir W. Jones from a Turkish Ode by Meshi: "Thou hearest the tale of the nightingale, that the vernal season approaches. The spring has spread a bower of joy in every grove where the almond-tree sheds its silver blossoms. The roses and tulips are like the bright cheeks of beautiful maids, in whose ears the pearls hang like drops of dew. The time is passed in which the plants were sick, and the rose-bud hung its thoughtful head upon its bosom." Again, in a Turkish song given by Lady Montague: "The nightingale now wanders in the vines; her passion is to seek roses." Good remarks: "The bulbul, or Persian nightingale, is a far more beautiful bird than the European; and the vernal season here referred to, is always a period of general hilarity among the inhabitants of this happy climate. Hence Hafiz sings—

"The charms of spring once more the fields salute:
Ope to the rose, ye nightingales! your suit:

P

Ye Zephyrs, 'mid the meadow-youths that rove,
Bear to the rose, the basil sweet, our love."

Thus the elegant Jami—

"Though countless shrubs of balmiest breath
    Their fascinating forms disclose,
The constant nightingale till death
    Still covets his beloved rose."

When Thevenot visited Jordan on the sixteenth of April, he found the little woods on the margin of the river filled with nightingales in full chorus; and Lady Montague, at the same time of the year, speaks of turtles as cooing on the cypress-trees of her garden from morning till night.* By reference to such things, would the Holy Spirit illustrate to us that in the world to which Jesus would allure us away, all is vocal with enchanting melody, and even the irrational creation are joining in the chorus.

Next to the pleasures of sight are those of sound; nor do we know that they are inferior. Man is not capable of richer pleasure than is felt in hearing delightful music. It has its foundation in the human soul. Both light and music seem to have the power of exciting the nervous energy of the human system, as though there were a more refined body imbedded in this physical frame. No one enjoys music with such exquisite delight as the sanctified believer. This de-

---

* Warburton says: "The air was the balmiest I ever breathed; myriads of birds were singing enthusiastically in the palm and olive-branches. The nightingales were thrilling the dark groves with their song."

light keeps pace with our growing deliverance from
the bondage of corruption, and our growing fitness for
heaven.

> "Heard melodies are sweet, but those unheard
> Are sweeter."

"And thus the associations of a man familiar with
holy truths, carry him away from the confused warfare of this world; the highest harmony belongs to
another sphere, and in his estimation the best music
of earth serves only to introduce us to that of heaven." Among the joys of heaven the Scriptures give
this a very prominent place. In the Jewish temple,
would their songs have been so sublime, and their
choruses so grand, had they not foreshadowed the
praise and chorus in which the worshippers shall join
in that nobler temple, the heavenly Jerusalem? Well
might the Holy Spirit therefore say, that in the world
to which Jesus would allure us, "the time of singing
is come;" the time of mourning and weeping has been
done away; "violence shall no more be heard in thy
land, wasting nor destruction within thy borders; but
thou shalt call thy walls salvation, and thy gates
praise." The mind can conceive of nothing more magnificent than the worship of the heavenly host as
opened to us in the visions at Patmos. Rev. iv. v. vii.
9, 10; xiv. 3; xv. 3; xix. 1—6. The thoughts of
hearing such deeds celebrated in such worship, of lis-
tening to such words set to appropriate harmonies,
sung by such a chorus, under such circumstances;
nay, of being one of the number who could learn and

sing that song, may well-nigh overpower us; and no more of grandeur and of glory can be conceived, than the idea of being in the midst of that host, and helping to swell that burst of praise which is "as the voice of many waters, and as the voice of mighty thunderings, saying, Alleluia, for the Lord God omnipotent reigneth!" Rev. xix. 6. "Alleluia; salvation, and glory, and honour, and power, unto the Lord our God, and unto the Lamb! And again they said Alleluia." Those who with souls most attuned to the worship of heaven, have heard the "Creation" and the "Messiah," have been made to feel how attractive and full of grandeur is this feature of heaven.

> "Such harmony is in immortal souls;
> But, whilst this muddy vesture of decay
> Doth grossly close it in, we cannot hear it."

With the melodies of the host who have lips and heart touched with the coal of the seraphim, will be mingled the voice of Jesus welcoming us to the service of that temple; some saints seem to have caught swells of those harmonies ere these walls of partition had yet gone entirely down in death; and they were enraptured with the sound. Who can imagine the overpowering feelings of the soul, when, in addition to the glorious visions bursting on the view, as the body is thrown aside, those deep-toned harmonies rise on the ear as the murmur of the tranquil ocean, as the sound of many waters; and as the spirit soars onward in the very midst of that chorus, we hear, as enriching and crowning all, tones from the lips of the glorified body of Jesus.

"The music of birds," as has been well observed, "was the first song of thanksgiving which was offered on earth before man was formed. All their sounds are different, but all harmonious, and all together composed a choir which we cannot imitate." In the words of Isaac Walton, "the nightingale breathes such sweet loud music out of her little instrumental throat, that it might make mankind to think miracles are not ceased. He that at midnight, when the very labourer sleeps securely, should hear, as I have very often, the clear airs, the sweet descants, the natural rising and falling, the doubling and redoubling of her voice, might well be lifted above earth, and say, Lord, what music hast thou provided for the saints in heaven, when thou affordest bad men such music on earth?"

> "Nature's sweet voices, always full of love
> And joyance! 'Tis the merry nightingale
> That crowds, and hurries, and precipitates
> With fast thick warble his delicious notes,
> As he were fearful that an April night
> Would be too short for him to utter forth
> His love-chaunt, and disburden his full soul
> Of all its music."*

"And the voice of the turtle is heard in our land." Even yet, in those regions, the time of the blossoming of the vines and blooming of flowers is the time of the singing of nightingales, of which the country may then

* Coleridge's Nightingale.

be said to be full, and of the cooing of the turtle. The
turtle is migratory. Jer. viii. 7.   Aristotle says: "The
ring-dove and pigeon are always to be seen, but the
turtle in summer only; it does not make its appearance in winter."   "The turtle and the crane and the
swallow observe the time of their coming," which is
about the end of April or beginning of May.   The
dove was the emblem of affection; and its mention
here in preference to any other, is for showing that
the key-note of the harmonies of that better land is
love:

> "No war, or battle's sound
>   Was heard the world around:
>   The idle spear and shield were high up hung,
>   The hooked chariot stood
>   Unstain'd with hostile blood,
>   The trumpet spake not to the armed throng:
>   But peaceful was the night,
>   Wherein the Prince of light
>   His reign of peace upon the earth began."

Much more shall all be peace, the result of universal
love, when the reign then begun shall be consummated
by the establishment of the Church triumphant in heaven.   The dove is here mentioned for the same reason
that the dove was afterwards the symbol, to human
eyes, of the Holy Spirit resting on Jesus by the Jordan.   There, will be heard music, but not military
sounds, making the soul frantic for horrors and blood;
not the swells bursting from the heartless halls of revelry and dancing, but the harmonies rising from an
innumerable multitude, which no man can number, of

hearts perfect in love: "Unto him that loved us, and washed us from our sins in his own blood, and hath made us kings and priests unto God and his Father; to him be glory and dominion for ever and ever. Amen.'

VER. 13.—The fig-tree putteth forth her green figs, and the vines with the tender grape give a good smell. Arise, my love, my fair one, and come away.

The fig-tree was now embalming or spicing its tender fruit, by filling it with aromatic juice. The vines were in bloom, with leaves of about two months growth, consequently very shady; and the buds bursting into full bloom with the tender grape forming in the midst of the flower, yielded a delightful fragrance. This was at the time when the rose-trees were in bloom, and the gardens filled with nightingales.

The kiosk, the same meant by the word "bed," in ch. i. 16, stood in the midst of the garden, surrounded with large shady trees, and enclosed with gilded lattices, round which jessamines, honey-suckles, and vines, make a kind of green wall.* So sweet were the flowers of the vine, that the ancients had a practice of putting them, when dried, into new wine, for giving it a pure and delicious flavour, allowing two pounds of such flowers to every cadus, or jar. As in Eden, "out of the ground made the Lord God to grow every tree that is pleasant to the sight and good for food;" the heavenly paradise is equally delightful, and there too grows the tree of life. All that can feast the eye and regale the senses is there spread forth. The new wine

* See Notes on ch. i. 16, and ch. ii. 3, 8, 9.

which Jesus wills to drink with the saints in his Father's kingdom, is even now awaiting us.

How attractive is heaven as thus represented. There, the curse is done away; no barren land is found in those realms of eternal spring; no clouded skies, no sorrows, no toil; the earth covered with unfading flowers, the air loaded with fragrance and with harmonious melodies the tone of which is love; every thing flourishing that can refresh and delight the powers of both body and soul. Hence, from that world of holiness and joy, does Jesus say to us, "Arise, my love, my fair one, and come away." Come away, from the sorrows, the afflictions, the infirmities, the trials, the bereavements, the toils, the chilling nights, the wintry blasts, of this vale of tears: Come away, to this world of endless spring, to the green pastures and living fountains of waters, to the innumerable company of angels, to the spirits of the just made perfect; come away to the skies, where Jesus, the beloved, awaits thee on the mountain of myrrh and hills of frankincense, over which the day breaks and the shadows flee away.

VER. 14.—O my dove, that art in the clefts of the rock, in the secret places of the stairs, let me see thy countenance, let me hear thy voice; for sweet is thy voice, and thy countenance is comely.

Doves in those countries take up their abodes in the hollow places of rocks and cliffs. Hence the words of the prophet, "O ye that dwell in Moab, leave the cities, and dwell in the rock, and be like the dove that maketh her nest in the sides of the hole's mouth."

Jer. xlviii. 28.* And in Virgil we have a like comparison,

> As the affrighted dove, whose darling young
> And nest are in the covert of some rock.

And in the Iliad,

> She weeping fled,
> As to her cavern in some hollow rock
> The dove, not destined to his talons, flies
> The hawk's pursuit.

Thus, those whom Jesus would allure away to himself, are very frequently found in the rugged scenes of life, in situations of trial, affliction, and desolation, alone, away from the world. "Lo! the people shall dwell alone and shall not be reckoned among the nations." Num. xxiii. 9. And the prophet says, "Feed thy people with thy rod, watch over, as a shepherd with his staff, the flock of thine heritage, which dwells solitarily in the wood, in the midst of Carmel." Mic. vii. 14. As God took fallen man out of the garden of Eden, and placed him, for a check on his depravity, in a world blighted by the curse; so, those whom he would redeem, whose corruptions he would uproot, he cuts off from love of the world, by putting them in the clefts of the rock; he brings us, like Israel, "through the wilderness, through a land of deserts and of pits, through a land of drought and of the shadow of death,"

---

* "At such times of noon-day stillness and heat, the larger animals seek shelter in the recesses of the forest, and the birds hide themselves under the thick foliage of the trees, or in the clefts of the rocks."—*Humboldt's Aspects.*

that we may desire a better country, that is, an heavenly; that we may hearken to the admonition of the
still small voice from the holy oracle, the Spirit's
dwelling-place in the sanctuary of our soul, "Arise
ye, and depart, for this is not your rest." Mic. ii. 10.
Affliction is the promised inheritance of the saints in
this world.   They have been left here an afflicted and
poor people, whose trust is in the name of the Lord.

> "So virtue blooms, brought forth amid the storms
>   Of chill adversity; in some lone walk
>   Of life she rears her head,
>   Obscure and unobserved."

The most remarkable displays of God's glory ever
made to man, were made in scenes of loneliness and
desolation.   When the patriarch dreamed, and beheld
a ladder set upon the earth and the top of it reached
to heaven, the emblem of the heavens opened and the
angels of God ascending and descending upon the Son
of man, he had taken the stones of that place and put
them for his pillows, and thus lain down to sleep: The
vision of the burning-bush was when Moses was a fugi-
tive from his countrymen, and had led the flock to the
back of the desert, to the mountain of God, even to
Horeb, so named from its desolation; and when afterwards God would show this servant his glory, he put
him in a cleft of the rock: On this Horeb, the mount
of desolation, stood Elijah, when, unmoved by the
wind, and the earthquake, and the fire, he wrapped
his face in his mantle, as he heard the still small voice.
The transfiguration was on a high mountain apart;

the appointed place for the meeting of Jesus with his disciples, after the resurrection, and for appearing most probably to a body of above five hundred brethren at once, was a mountain in Galilee; the visions of John were on the rocky isle of Patmos; and when the angel would close those scenes by a view of that great city, the holy Jerusalem, he carried him away in the spirit to a great and high mountain. If now he withdraw us not from the world, he accomplishes the same end in spreading desolation around us, by bereavement, by loss of property, by affliction, by blasted hopes and bitter disappointments. "Of the eight beatitudes, five of them have temporal misery and meanness, or an afflicted condition for their subject. As long as the waters of affliction are upon the earth, so long we dwell in the ark; but when the land is dry the dove itself will be tempted to a wandering course of life, and never to return to the house of her safety."*

The person thus addressed as in the cleft of the rock, was so affected with a sense of unworthiness, as to shrink back and stand in need of the exhortation to come forth to her Lord. To such trembling, timid souls, he says, Cut off though you may be from the riches, the honours, and even the comforts of this world, and feeling yourself most unworthy, there is One on whom you may cast all your care, for he careth for you, who speaks to you in language the most affectionate, My dove, my tender, timid one, the object of

* Jeremy Taylor's Sermons on 1 Pet. iv. 17, 18.

my deepest, most devoted love, "let me see thy countenance," for however the world may disregard and despise that expression of humility, in my eyes the countenance bespeaking contrition is beautiful. To the father of the prodigal, far more pleasing than the gayety of the company thronging his halls, was the careworn countenance of his humbled and repenting son. Let me hear thy voice, for it is sweet. The music and dancing were not so sweet to the father's heart, as the humbled tones of his lost son confessing his sin, acknowledging his transgressions, and giving utterance to his reviving love. No sounds are so delightful to Jesus, as the tones of the contrite spirit confessing sin, mourning the absence of his countenance, calling on him in trouble, and seeking advance in holiness.

VER. 15.—Take us the foxes, the little foxes, that spoil the vines; for our vines have tender grapes.

Foxes, jackals, little foxes, are very common in Palestine, and are particularly fond of grapes. They often burrow in holes in hedges round the gardens; and unless strictly watched, would destroy whole vineyards. Their flesh was sometimes eaten in autumn, when they were grown fat with feeding on grapes. Thus Theocritus says,

> I hate the foxes with their bushy tails,
> Which numerous spoil the grapes of Micon's vines
> When fall the evening shades.

And Aristophanes compares soldiers to foxes, because they consume the grapes of the countries through which they pass. They here represent any thing which injures, by stealth and cunning, the graces of those who are the objects of divine love. Hence, as an enemy of God's people, Herod is called a fox by Jesus. Luke xiii. 32. This verse teaches that those who are favoured richly with grace, and whom our Lord is drawing towards heaven, will be careful to guard against sin, and especially against little sins. Heretofore we had to lament, in the words of ch. i. 6, "Mine own vineyard have I not kept;" now we are anxious to guard the vineyard of the heart against the inroad of any thing, however trifling, that may corrode and destroy our graces. Too often we may have been like a boy represented by Theocritus, as set to watch a vineyard, but becoming so absorbed in weaving a chaplet of flowers as not to notice two foxes, one of which was stealthily plundering his food, while the other was making havoc with the grapes. Never is our carefulness in guarding against sin so great, as when most deeply filled with the love of Jesus; against the slightest sins we wish most carefully to guard. The services of the Jewish tabernacle taught the necessity of holiness, even in trivial things. By these little sins, Satan begins the most deadly temptations; he attacks us in an unexpected quarter, in an unlooked for way; and the time for resisting him, is at the very beginning of his insidious assaults. Indulgence in what may seem trifling departures from watchfulness and duty, blinds the mind to the truth of Scripture, corrodes and enfeebles our graces, and grieves the Holy Ghost. While watching with all diligence, our unceasing prayer will be, "Search me, O God, and know my heart; try me and know my thoughts; and see if there be any wicked way in me, and lead me in the way everlasting." Ps. cxxxix. 23.

VER. 16.—My beloved is mine, and I am his: he feedeth among the lilies.

The lily, on account of its beauty as well as fragrance, has been universally admired in all ages: the Greeks and Romans were no less fond of it than the orientals. The beloved, still compared to a gazelle, is here said to feed beside still waters, in green pastures abounding with lilies. A green meadow, in which the gazelle might be seen feeding and reposing among the lilies, was a scene truly beautiful. Lilies grew wild in abundance in the fields. In early spring the plain of Sharon was seen covered with hyacinths and lilies, and the richest scarlet poppies strewed amid the verdant grass. On this grass the roes loved to pasture. Hence our Saviour says, "Consider the lilies of the field." And a Latin poet says,

> Lo, yonder noble stag, calmly at rest
> Mid the white lilies on the meadow's breast.

As in verses first and second of this chapter, the lilies are emblems of the pure in heart, the virgins surrounding the beloved. Thus Hengstenberg remarks on the title of the forty-fifth psalm: "This psalm employs itself on lilies, beautiful virgins, lovely brides. We take the lilies as a figurative description of the lovely virgins whose marriage with the king the Psalmist celebrates." The words " he feedeth among the lilies," do therefore mean, that as the instinct of the gazelle leads him back to his feeding-ground, and wherever he wanders, there is the place of his strongest desire, in which he loves to linger, loves to rest; so the place of our Lord's strongest desire is in the midst of his saints; and however he may withdraw, thither he will most certainly return. There is no place in which he loves to be, better than among his people.

In view of the assurances of love given in the foregoing verses, the spouse says, "My beloved is mine and I am his." Those who thus watch against sin, and are blessed with communications of heavenly love, enjoy the full assurance of hope, and rejoice to know that Christ is theirs, and they are his. It is not said, I am his and he is mine; but first, he is mine, and then, I am his; inasmuch as Christ's being ours is at the foundation of every blessing. While he is separated from us by the walls between this and the invisible world, unable to show us the fulness of his glory; and in the clefts of the rock, we are cut off from so many of the enjoyments of earth, we are permitted to feel that whatever else is wanting, Christ is ours. The whole of the covenant is simply this: Jesus says to us, give yourself to me, and I will give myself to you. On this principle does he act; and to the degree we surrender ourselves up to him, will we ever find him communicating to us his grace and causing us to receive of his fulness. This assurance is a blessing of unspeakable value. A deed is the legal security that an inheritance is ours and cannot be taken from us by law. This assurance, written in new characters on the white stone of the holy heart, by the finger which wrote on the tables of stone on Sinai, is the pledge that heaven, or what is better still, Christ is ours. This charter of our eternal hopes, this title to heaven, is thus laid up in the inner shrine of the heart, so secure that we cannot be plundered of it even by the spoiler Death. We desire nothing more, as he says, "All mine are thine and thine are mine; and the glory which thou gavest me, I have given them." John xvii. 10. In the words of Quarles,

> "He is my altar; I his holy place;
>   I am his guest; and he my living food;
> I'm his by penitence; he mine by grace;
>   I'm his by purchase; he is mine by blood;
> He's my supporting helm; and I his vine:
> Thus I my best beloved's am; thus he is mine."

"He feedeth among the lilies." There, is the place where he is drawn by the strongest desire. We may calculate unerringly on his returning at intervals, to manifest his presence in his Church; for the roe or young hart may forget his pasture grounds, but He can never forget the calm retreats of this world, where cluster his chosen ones robed in the purity of holiness. Yea, more, the mother may forget her infant child, "yet will I not forget thee." Isa. xlix. 15. Where would he be more likely to wish to dwell than among his redeemed ones? Hence his usual mode of expressing his relation to his people, is that of making his abode with them, John xiv. 23; of dwelling in their hearts by faith, Eph. iii. 17; and in heaven, God himself in his tabernacle shall dwell with them, and be their God. Rev. xxi. 3. In times of darkness and sorrow, let us therefore be comforted by the inward assurance, "My beloved is mine and I am his;" and by feeling that more certainly than the roe to his rich pastures among the lilies, will Jesus return to visit and abide with our longing hearts.

VER. 17.—Until the day break, and the shadows flee away, turn, my beloved, and be thou like a roe, or a young hart, upon the mountains of Bether.

While thus comforted during the withdrawal of our Lord, by the assurance of hope, and by the truth that he may be more certainly expected from time to time among the saints, than the roe may be expected in the pastures where he feeds, the desire of our heart is that Jesus would repeat those visits as often as possible, until the darkness now around us flee away. In those hot countries the dawn of day i, attended with a fine, refreshing breeze, much more grateful and desirable than the light itself, beautifully expressed by the words "the day breathe."* Thus, Milton—

"And temperate vapors bland, which th' only sound
 Of leaves and fuming rills, Aurora's fan,
 Lightly dispersed."

As the Hebrew word *Bether* means a section or division, and as it occurs no where else as a proper

* Van Egmont and Heyman state that " the excessive heat on the coast, and in many places of the Holy Land, is very much lessened by a sea-breeze, which constantly blows every morning, and by its coolness renders the heats of summer very supportable." Dr. Robinson, of Cambridge, mentions that

name, we take "mountains of Bether" here to mean mountains of division—spoken of a region cut up or divided by mountains and valleys, rough, craggy, and difficult to cross. Over these the spouse intreats the beloved to come like a roe or a young hart. See ver. 9. In the spirit of these words, Wordsworth says,

> "When like a roe,
> I bounded o'er the mountains, by the sides
> Of the deep rivers and the lonely streams."

As Jesus sees fit sometimes to withdraw, we pray for the repetition of his visits to the soul as often as possible. These visits are necessary for our advancement in holiness; they are both sunlight and shower. They give the greatest joys we can now have; they are foretastes of heaven. Jesus is the great attrac-

---

"every morning about sunrise, a fresh gale of wind blew from the sea across the land, which from its wholesomeness in clearing the infected air, is always called "*the doctor*."

"At the approach of morning, the stir of life that seemed, like leaven, to ferment the surface of the world round, was very striking; first, the partridge's call joined chorus with the nightingale, and soon after their dusky forms were seen darting through the bushes, and then bird after bird joined the chorus; the lizards began to glance upon the rocks, the insects on the ground and in the air; the jerboa peeping from its burrow, fish glancing in the stream, hares bounding over the dewy grass, and—as more light came—the airy form of the gazelle could be seen on almost every neighbouring hill. Then came sunrise, first flushing the light clouds above, then flashing over the Arabian mountains, and pouring down into the rich valley of the Jordan: the Dead Sea itself seemed to come to life under that blessed spell, and shone like molten gold among its purple hills."—*Warburton—The Crescent and the Cross.*

tion of heaven; and how comforting to know that
although we cannot at present be with him amid the
glories of heaven, he will come frequently, over all
intervening obstacles, and visit us amid the darkness
and ruins of earth, "until the day break and the
shadows flee away."   The ancient philosophers call
this world the dark cavern of the imprisoned soul;
and Plato* says, "Behold men, as if dwelling in a
subterranean cavern."   Our world is now involved in
shadows dark as night; and well does the Apostle
say, the "night is far spent, the day is at hand."
Rom. xiii. 12. The morning star has long since
risen; in the influences of the Holy Spirit, we feel
the breathing of breezes from heaven, harbingers of
an eternal day; in the increasing light of sanctification, we hail the brightening day-break of eternity.
Like a person who might have been born in the
depths of the Mammoth Cave, and wandering for
years therein, without a sight of the glorious world
above and around him—the impenitent are equally
in darkness, living, wandering in caverns more desolate and gloomy to the soul, and with as little knowledge of the splendours of the invisible spiritual
world.   Should the poor offcast born in the cave,
meet with some one from the outer world, penetra-
ting with a torch into those chambers of death, with
what interest would he listen to an account of the
green earth, the morning sun, the starry heavens;
with what feelings must he gaze on the brightening
light, in his approach to the mouth of the cavern.

* Repub., book vii., chap. 1.

How great the transition, when having left those labyrinths of darkness, he stands gazing on the morning star overhanging the brightening dawn of a day in spring, hears the singing of the birds, feels the refreshing breath of the pure breeze, and is exhilarated with the fragrance filling the air from the dewy flowers and trees in bloom. Far, far more delightful are our sensations, when our spiritual perception fixes on Christ the bright morning star, and on the dawning light of heavenly blessedness; and we hear swells of music from that better world, and feel the refreshing breezes of the Holy Spirit, laden with balm from the fields the Lord has blessed.

Then, our view of the boundless universe of God shall be enlarged, as is our view of the landscape under the rising sun; we shall mingle with an innumerable company of angels, with the spirits of just men made perfect; the truths now so precious, will be seen more clearly, and in wider relations; mysteries of Providence will be cleared up; God will be more fully known; Christ will be revealed in all his glory.

———

CHAPTER III.

VER. 1.—By night on my bed I sought him whom my soul loveth: I sought him, but I found him not.

THE portion of this book from chap. ii. 8 to chap. vii. 9, contains three leading motives addressed to the soul by Jesus for alluring us away from the world. Between these there are introduced, chap. iii. 1—5, and chap. v. 2—8, two seasons of spiritual desertion, differing from each other in this respect, that in the latter the beloved is repulsed by the neglect of cold indifference, while in the former, here under consideration, nothing of that kind seems mentioned. This verse is connected with the close of chapter second, and illustrates the earnestness of the soul in seeking Jesus during a time of his absence. God's way of carrying on our sanctification is by repeated visits and withdrawals, at seasons "put in his own power." When thus absent, he returns in different ways. Sometimes, as in chap. ii. 8, he surprises us with his grace, almost before he was expected, Isa. lxv. 1; then, as in this passage, he waits for us to seek him with earnestness. This verse expresses, that in the absence of Jesus, we seek him with desires so strong as to surmount the most necessary cravings of the body, even sleep.

No desire is so intense as the craving of a healthful soul after Christ. This is different from the thirst of the mind for intellectual pleasures. In the state of mind here set forth, there are as the basis of this craving—1. Foregoing manifestations of the love and loveliness of Jesus through the Holy Spirit; 2. A disclosure of the beauty and glory of heaven; 3. The assurance of hope; and, 4. Strong desires for beholding the glory of Christ. What was wanting, was a sense of the presence of Jesus. Now it is possible to have all these without the last. This is exceedingly desirable, and should be sought; but the want of it is no evidence God has cast us off, and is displeased.

Many good people mistake at such time, by despairing and reproaching themselves, instead of seeking him. Through the disposition to walk by sense or sight, rather than by faith, they despond when the manifestations of the presence of Jesus are withheld. But they should feel the absence of these is no proof of want of acceptance; these withdrawals are for a wise end, and are essential in our preparation for heaven.* They test the strength of our faith and steadfastness of our love; they lead to deeper searchings for secret sins; they advance humility by making us feel our weakness and our dependence on God. If this inward spring of divine influence flowed without intermission, in a current always full, we would

---

* "Although it is not possible that any who is admitted into peace and friendship with God should altogether fall from it, yet the sense and relish thereof are often interrupted. For, 1. God doth not always show his pleasant countenance to his friends; sometimes he hides himself, Isa. viii. 17; standeth afar off, Ps. x. 1; admits them not into familiarity with him, nor fills them with the abundance of his consolations; he hears not when they call, Ps. xxii. 2, 3; as if he regarded them not. 2. Nay, he thrusts them from him with a kind of contempt; and 'is angry against their prayer.' Ps. lxxx. 4. 3. He terrifies them with many sorrows; not only by hiding his face, without which there is no joy, but by his fierce anger going over them. 4. He seems to deal with them as an adversary, and holdeth them for his enemies, and writes bitter things against them. 5. Gives them up sometimes to be vexed and buffeted by the devil. Job ii. 6. After that the light of the divine countenance is set, immediately the beasts of the forest come forth against the soul, the young lions roaring after their prey."—*Witsius on Spiritual Peace, Cov.*, book iii. 9, 21.

be in danger of spiritual pride. Says Rutherford,
"As nights and shadows are good for flowers, and
moonlight and dews are better than a continual sun;
so is Christ's absence of special use, and it hath some
nourishing virtue in it, and giveth sap to humility,
and putteth an edge on hunger, and furnisheth a fair
field to faith to put forth itself."

How unreasonable to doubt the love of a friend
when necessarily withdrawn: to love him only when
under our eye betokens infant-like weakness. With
love to Jesus, of a manly, vigorous cast, in seasons of
spiritual desertion, far from despondency, with its
attending inactivity, we will cherish a faithful, devoted
affection, incapable of diversion from its cherished
object by all the seductions of the tempter. How
longs and seeks the soul for Christ, in times of
temptation, of trial, of affliction, of spiritual desertion!
How strong the feelings with which we think, at
night on our bed, of those who are loved, but separated from us by distance or by death! When mourning the absence of him whom our soul loveth, how
often have we made our bed to swim, and watered
our couch with tears. After displays of his love,
Christ gives us up to the power of the devil, within
certain limits. In various ways, Satan will try to
lead us into sin, if not against the moralities of the
world, against the truth and faithfulness of God;
failing in this, he will lead us as near as possible to
sin, if perchance we may in an unguarded moment
fall; repulsed in these attacks, he will then resort to
slander, to worldly perplexity, to bodily affliction.

Thus in his chapter on "the glory of Christ in the
mysterious constitution of his person," Owen quotes
this passage, and adds: "The Lord Christ is pleased
sometimes to withdraw himself from the spiritual
experience of believers, as unto any refreshing sense
of his love, or the fresh communications of consolatory
graces. Those who never had experience of any such
thing, who never had any refreshing communion with
him, cannot be sensible of his absence; they never
were so of his presence. But those whom he hath
visited, to whom he hath given of his loves, with
whom he hath made his abode, whom he hath refreshed, relieved, and comforted, in whom he hath
lived in the power of his grace, they know what it is
to be forsaken by him, though but for a moment.
And their trouble is increased, when they seek him
with diligence in the wonted ways of obtaining his
presence, and cannot find him. Our duty in this case
is, to persevere in our inquiries after him, in prayer,
meditation, mourning, reading, and hearing of the
word, in all ordinances of divine worship, private and
public, in diligent obedience, until we find him, or he
return unto us, as in former days."

VER. 2.—I will rise now, and go about the city in the
streets, and in the broad ways I will seek him whom my
soul loveth: I sought him, but I found him not.

"The broad ways" seem to mean the broad open
places at the gates of oriental cities, where the inhabitants were accustomed to assemble for public business.
Not only in the streets, but in these public places, did
the spouse seek her beloved. All the difficulties of

this passage vanish when the Song is taken as an allegory for illustrating the love of the saint towards Christ.   The heart warmed with thoughts of him, like a spring, boiling or bubbling up with deep emotions, Ps. xlv. 1, impels us to seek him in the way of self-denial.   Time was when Jesus was sacrificed to the pursuit of worldly enjoyments, and pleasures of sense; now every thing else is left, even sleep itself sacrificed, for finding the presence of Jesus.   This verse is another way of setting forth the state of heart expressed in Ps. lxiii. 1, 2, and in Job xxiii. 8—10; more fully in the forty-second Psalm.   This state is different from that noticed in chap. v. 3. The latter is a condition of spiritual sluggishness arising from absence of the Holy Spirit; here the affections are alive, the heart warm by the action of grace; but a sense of the presence of Christ is wanting.   In such times of desertion and trial the soul seeks him with great earnestness; periods of conflict, peril, and sorrow, when we feel our best resolutions are nothing before the power of the devil, when the passions of the soul will struggle as though they would burst the cords of the heart asunder; and the fury with which they roll round through the chambers of the soul, reminds us of Virgil's description of the fury of the winds in the cavern of Æolus:

"Where struggling winds and roaring storms he rules
  With sway imperial; curbs with prison, chains.
 Impetuous rage they round their mountain-cave:
 Did he not check their wrath, forth would they burst;
 Land, sea and heav'n in a wild tempest sweep,
 Uptorn from their foundations, through the air."

Even more terrible than these, were the elements which burst so suddenly on the patriarch Job, and buried him under the ruin of his property, his family, his bodily comfort, his friendships, and his spiritual peace. In his passage onward to heaven, every believer has to pass through the valley of the shadow of death; some find it darker and more terrible than others, and have to encounter at its entrance Satan in fiercer mood. There are times of outward desolation and inward trial, when we say with Jacob, "All these things are against me;" and cry with the Psalmist, "Deep calleth unto deep at the noise of thy water-spouts, all thy waves and thy billows are gone over me." The most painful part of these struggles arises from the fiery darts of the devil. They seem at times to fall almost like hail; and attack is succeeded by attack, as though he was determined to weary us out by the very continuance of his assaults. Ever struggling hard, with desperate determination, we may find ourselves giving ground; like Christian, we may be almost spent, almost pressed to death, so as to despair of life, and notwithstanding all we can do, be wounded in the head, hand, and foot; may get a dreadful fall; yet is his grace made sufficient for us. No battle can be so terrible as that which the believer does thus sustain against the powers of darkness. With thankfulness do we find hour after hour, and day after day, passing by, and our position yet held against this surging host of deadly foes. Now and then will there be a lull in the conflict, and grace will refresh us with cordials from heaven; but the battle will cease only with the setting of the sun, when around us gathers the nightfall of the grave. But though it be a hard fought day, the sun, like that of Waterloo, will go down on victory. Bunyan understood the spiritual conflict, and has in a few words sketched it with marvellous vigour and truth. When the world see the saint thus enduring "a great fight of afflictions;" see him under fire in the heat of the battle; they, and too often nominal Christians with them, are ready to judge hastily; to censure him for his conduct; to impute to his own love of sin wounds he has got in his desperate and uncompromising resistance against sin; and congratulate themselves on being perhaps better than he, because they have escaped wounds incurred by him, when, had they been exposed, in conflicts through which he has passed, their courage might have failed, and their souls perished. Every believer who knows his own heart, will adopt the words of Mr. Great-heart concerning Christian's conflict with Apollyon: "No disparagement to Christian, more than to any others whose hap and lot it was. But we will leave the good man, he is at rest, he also had a brave victory over his enemy: let Him grant that dwelleth above, that we fare not worse, when we come to be tried, than he."

    "Through all stations human life abounds
With mysteries;—for, if Faith were left untried,
How could the might, that lurks within her, then
Be shown? her glorious excellence—that ranks
Among the first of powers and virtues—proved?"

So necessary are conflicts for ripening the excellences of character, and attaining noble rewards and enduring fame, that poetry has made the illustration of this the theme of some of its noblest efforts. Such is the tenor of Spenser's Faery Queen. And in the poem of King Arthur, "The hero thus purified and enlightened by sorrow, is ready to seek the sword, the possession of which confers immortal renown, and could not be won unless by a champion, who, through resistance of strong temptations, had been proved to possess noble moral endowments. The shield is next to be won by heroic valour shown in desperate combat against appalling enemies; not by the valour of the knight, but by the moral greatness of the man; not by warlike deeds, but by resistance to strong temptations, and by clear perception of the relative importance of conflicting duties."* Thus the Scriptures, "Blessed is the man that endureth temptation, for when he is tried he shall receive the crown of life, which the Lord hath promised to them that love him." Jas. i. 12.

VER. 3.—The watchmen that go about the city found me, to whom I said, Saw ye him whom my soul loveth?

The loneliness and gloom of the spouse wandering at night through the streets, deserted by all save the watchmen, sets forth the darkness and desolation of the soul searching for Christ in these times of desertion and trial. The final state of the Church in glory

* King Arthur, by Sir E. Bulwer Lytton. Ed. Rev. No. 181.

is represented by the beauty of a city, as in Heb. xii. 22, and Rev. xxi. Now the Church is the city of the living God, but like Israel in the camp in the wilderness, rather than when established in the palaces on Mount Zion. The watchmen above are angels, Rev. xxi. 12; here they are men. Isa. lxii. 6. This class of men have the important trust of guarding the interests of the Church, warning of danger, instructing and comforting troubled souls. "They watch for souls as they that must give account." Heb. xiii. 17. They are stars in the right hand of Christ. Their aid must we seek in times of darkness and sorrow.* They are expected to know more than others about experimental religion; their duty is to study this as the end of all their investigations. If it was necessary that Jesus should be made in all things like unto his brethren, ministers of the word should be led

---

* "It is most advisable for tempted persons to consult some able, judicious minister, or compassionate and established Christian, whose counsel and prayers may be singularly useful in this case; observing the assistance which Great-heart gave to the Pilgrims, in passing through the valley. Sometimes temptations may be so multiplied and varied, that it may seem impossible to proceed any further; and the mind of the harassed believer is enveloped in confusion and dismay, as if an horrible pit were about to swallow him up, or the prince of darkness to seize upon him. But the counsel of some experienced friend or minister, exciting confidence in the power, mercy, and faithfulness of God, and encouraging him to 'pray without ceasing,' will at length make way for his deliverance." —*Scott's Notes on the Pilgrim's Progress.*

by the Holy Spirit through these exercises of the heart wherein they are to lead and comfort others.

VER. 4.—It was but a little that I passed from them, but I found him whom my soul loveth: I held him, and would not let him go, until I had brought him into my mother's house, and into the chamber of her that conceived me.

Very shortly after leaving them she finds the beloved. Jesus is always to be found near the watchmen, the ministry, the means of grace. How often when we have been seeking Jesus without any comforting sense of his presence, have some bright views of his glory burst upon the soul. Some truth shines forth adapted to our need, some promise precisely suited to our want, some warning that may arouse us from danger. He appears to us as unexpectedly as to the disciples on the way to Emmaus; and like the wise men from the East, on seeing the infant Jesus, we rejoice with exceeding great joy.

"I held him, and would not let him go." With eagerness does the soul then lay hold on our Lord. By night had those holy women been seeking Jesus, at early dawn while it was yet dark on the morning of his resurrection, sorrowful and in tears, when he "met them saying, All hail, and they came and held him by the feet and worshipped him:" this is the manifestation, in a different way, of the feeling now had by us on finding again our Lord. They did in form precisely what we now do by faith. Among the emblematical representations of truth in the Old Testament, this has its illustration in the wrestling of Jacob with the angel. It was night, he was alone, in a lonely place, and about to encounter a dangerous enemy in Esau. Convinced that this being in human form had power to deliver, he laid hold on him and refused to let him go without a blessing. His importunity prevailed, and in that person he found the Lord Jesus.

"I brought him into, &c." Speaking of oriental houses, Dr. Shaw says, "Their chambers are large and spacious, one of them frequently serving a whole family. At one end of each chamber there is a little gallery raised four or five feet, with a balustrade and doubtless a veil to draw in the front of it. Here they place their beds." Hence we have no difficulty in understanding why the bride speaks of her own apartment as connected with her mother's chambers. In this and in the other passage where reference is made to the mother and the mother's apartments, see chap. viii. 2, this is evidently for guarding against the idea of any thing improper in this love. In the house and under the eye of a mother, a virgin must be supposed under the very best safeguard against any thing like impropriety. The love here contemplated is that chaste, ideal affection, not entirely like any thing known on earth, which combines the ardent affection of the marriage relation with the devotion of a brother's and sister's heart, without any unhallowed feeling associated therewith. Hence the expression so frequently used, "my sister-spouse."

Thus finding Jesus, we are anxious to commune with him in secret. In chap. i. 4, he is represented as bringing us into his chambers, drawing us into secret com-

munion with him; here we are set forth as spontaneously drawing him into private communion, seeking
intercourse with him by prayer. Though ever dependent on the Holy Spirit as our strength, and as the
originating spring of every holy emotion and holy
action, there are times when grace seems to visit,
enliven, and draw us again to Christ, and there are
periods when we feel that reviving grace cannot be
expected without offering up supplications with strong
cries and tears. Delightful as are ordinances and
public duties, we wish, after deliverance from spiritual
desertion, to have Jesus much to ourselves in study of
the Scriptures, in meditation, in contrition, and in
secret prayer. Seeking thus to enjoy confidential fellowship with Jesus where there may be no intrusion,
the soul again expresses anxiety to guard against any
thing likely to make him withdraw: "I charge you,
O ye daughters of Jerusalem, &c." ver. 5. See chap.
ii. 7.

VER. 6.—Who is this that cometh out of the wilderness
like pillars of smoke, perfumed with myrrh and frankincense, with all powders of the merchant.

The first grand motive in the series here brought to
bear on the heart, is the desirableness of heaven as a
place. Chap. ii. 10. After a season of heavenly delight,
and glimpses of heavenly glory, we are exposed to
spiritual desertion and assaults of the devil, that the
power of these motives may be put to test. When we
are restored to the joy of his salvation, he allures by
assurance of the security and grandeur of our conveyance thither. Dejected because he left us, as in ver.

1, we are told that however we may seem forsaken, we may be sure our souls are during the darkest hours in a chariot paved with love. As though he says to us, 1. Be not discouraged by these withdrawals of Jesus, for there is a state of glory awaiting you in heaven; 2. Do not despond under the heaviest trials, for you are on your road to glory in a conveyance guarded by angels, encompassed with the intercession of Christ, and made of materials precious as love; 3. Though Jesus may at times hide his face and expose us to trials, he loves us even more strongly than is shown in chap. iv.

The Scriptures speak of God's dwelling in heaven, yet coming down to us on earth; of his being continually around us, yet drawing near to us by his Spirit. Persons may be "absent in body but present in spirit," 1 Cor. v. 3; may be near each other, yet effectually separated by difference of disposition and by enmity. Thus God may be near us in one sense and afar off in another. Hence there is a spiritual coming to Christ, and there is also a bodily coming to him. The former is by exercising the holy affections now wrought by the Spirit; the latter is by our having a spiritual body and going to be with him in glory. Phil. iii. 21; 1 John iii. 2. Redemption extends to both body and soul—first to the soul, then to the body. All the decay of our bodily system began with spiritual death working in the soul. The condition of the body is determined by the foregoing condition of the soul, of which it is the earthly tabernacle. Spiritual death, when not arrested by redemption, has its consumma-

R

tion in the dissolution of the body in the grave. Now
spiritual life follows the same order; first a new life is
imparted to the soul, as in regeneration and sanctification, and then, when the soul has been thus renewed,
God gives us a new body, a body adapted to the nature of the soul thus restored to newness of spiritual
life, and hence characterized as a spiritual body.
These two things are here distinguished: the seeking
of our Lord mentioned in the former part of this
chapter, is the seeking of him with our spirits, but in
the mean time we are in our way to meet him in his
glorified body, when we shall be made like him by
having a spiritual body.

In ver. 6—11 we have, 1. The splendid appearance,
ver. 6.   2. What that cortege consists of, viz: his
palanquin and its guard, ver. 7, 8.   3. A description
of the palanquin, ver. 9, 10.   4. The king awaiting
the arrival of this company, ver. 11.

As the leading of Israel through the wilderness was
a representation of the progress of the saints towards
glory, and as this book sets forth the love of Christ
and his people, the words of ver. 6 may find their
illustration in the camp in the desert.   The object in
bringing Balaam up to the high places, &c., Num. xxii.
41, was to have patriarchism pronounce an excommu-
nication on the Jewish church.   The patriarchal religion had been superseded by this; but it would not
die without an effort, as was afterwards the case with
Judaism in reference to Christianity.   How imposing
was the sight, when from one of the mountain-tops near
Pisgah, he beheld the goodly tents of the host of Jacob

and Israel coming up from the wilderness, Num. xxiv. 5, 6, beautiful as gardens by the river's side, as the trees of lign-aloes which the Lord hath planted, as cedar-trees beside the waters, the pillar of cloud and of fire overshadowing the whole, with the tabernacle in the midst, and with these, combined the idea of a nuptial procession, as in Homer—

> "When from her halls through evening streets they lead
> The bride, with blazing torches, and the scund
> Of hymeneal gladness; rings of youth
> Dance to the melody of flutes and harps;
> And matrons standing in their doors, behold
> The joyous tumult with a wondering smile."*

The region lying between this world and the world where Jesus glorified is awaiting his saints, is as certainly a lonely wilderness as the desert lying between Egypt and Canaan. The angels standing at the gates and on the battlements of the New Jerusalem, see this procession coming up towards the Holy City, and are filled with wonder. As the metropolis of the universe, that city had been heretofore visited by various companies from different quarters of the dominions of the King of kings, but by none presenting an appearance so unusual. Those hitherto have come in a different way; these are drawing near by "a new and living way." Hence the inquiry, "Who is this that cometh out of the wilderness?"

"Like pillars of smoke, &c."† There is not here

---

* Iliad, book xviii.

† "Oily liquids might be burnt as well as powdered gums, in their censers; and it is by no means impossible that the lamps

one pillar, as in the Jewish camp, but pillars, many
rising and towering on every side, and spreading into
a canopy—or, according to the suggestions of the
original word, going up like a palm-tree, straight upward for a distance, and then spreading out like the
branches. Perfumes were used in great profusion
at eastern marriages; the garments were made to
smell richly of myrrh, aloes, and cassia; as they came
forth from the ivory palaces, persons led the procession with silver-gilt pots of perfume, and the air was
rendered fragrant by burning aromatics in the windows of all the houses in the streets through which
the procession was to pass. Here these perfumes were
burnt so freely, that they rose in pillars, and combined
all possible richness capable of being furnished by the

that were carried before her, might be fed with odoriferous oils,
and make an agreeable addition to the other precious smoke.
So D'Herbelot tells us, the Eastern princes are wont to burn
camphor, a precious and odoriferous gum, mingled with wax,
to light their palaces in the night; and giving an account of
the rich booty the Arabs found at Madain, in pillaging the
palace of the Persian monarchs there, he tells us they found
magazines of odoriferous camphor, which was wont to be burnt
there, at once to light and perfume that palace: not to take
notice of the frequent mention of tapers in the Arabian Nights
Entertainments, mixed with aloes and ambergris, which gave
an agreeable scent, as well as delicate light. As for the clause,
"all the chief spices," it is visible that plants, whose flowers or
leaves were fragrant, are meant by the word spices, as we may
learn from the use of that word in the 16th verse; and the
chief spices, therefore, must intend the principal aromatic
plants that were known and esteemed in those days."—*Harmer*, 297.

perfumer with all the variety of his spices. If one
pillar was such a protection against the Egyptians,
and such a glory to Israel in the desert, Exod. xiv. 20,
what must be the grandeur and security of these many
pillars of incense around the individuals of the host
passing onward to glory. Those pillars are the righteousness of Christ, a righteousness glorious to the contemplation, mighty to save. In his righteousness is
included all that he did and suffered for us in obtaining salvation; "his intercession is the continued efficacy of his expiatory merit, and has hence been spoken
of by some as a perpetual oblation." We would understand by these pillars of incense, both what he did
on earth, his righteousness, and what he is now doing
in heaven, his intercession. The saint is passing onward to glory, encompassed and protected by both
these. As the Jewish high-priest went into the most
holy place, amid a cloud of incense from the golden
censer, so did Jesus enter heaven, and thus does he
there remain amid the cloud of glorious incense of his
intercession; and thus must his saints enter there, encompassed with the incense of his prayers in our behalf.
His intercession for us is continual in our progress
through this world towards heaven. Hence we have
always an answer in the heavenly sanctuary to the
calumnies of Satan, and may be assured of acceptance
with God through him whose offering is unto the
Father of a sweet-smelling savour. As the phœnix
was fabled to rise from the midst of the fires and sweet
odours in which the parent bird had died in the temple
of the sun in Egypt, and spread its wings toward hea-

ven, as thus beginning an existence running through centuries, so do our renovated souls rise from amid the richer than aromatic fires and incense in which Jesus perished, and mount upward on wings as eagles, covered with feathers more beautiful than ruby and gold, on the cycle of a life running through ages of ages, carrying with us the memorials of the death of him through whom we live, and bearing them away with us to our eternal repose in the temple of the skies.

VER. 7.—Behold his bed, which is Solomon's, &c.

These words are the answer to the question in the foregoing verse, "Lo, it is the palanquin of Solomon." The word "bed" here means a kind of sedan chair or open vehicle, in which persons in the East are carried on men's shoulders. Such was the means of conveying the bride to the house of the bridegroom. When Jesus was received up into heaven, it was by a cloud; when he appears the second time, "behold, he cometh with clouds;" "he maketh the clouds his chariot," and not to mention other places, the appearance in Ezek. i., was with a conveyance or chariot of glory beyond description. Thus, the saint is here represented as passing onward in a conveyance, chariot, or whatever called, towards heaven. When God would represent the glory of the way in which Elijah was taken up, he made visible a chariot and horses of fire—as light is the best symbol of what is pure and glorious. Every saint has a conveyance as real, though not visible to bodily eyes. As it is a chariot for the soul, this cannot be seen any more than the soul. In the case of Elijah, the conveyance was seen, because God was' taking up body as well as soul. When by withdrawing at death the film of mortality now over them, our eyes are opened like those of the young man of the prophet, 2 Kings vi. 17, we shall find our souls in a bridal chariot, in which, from the moment of regeneration, we have been moving onward to the arms of our beloved Lord. While perfectly free in working out our salvation, on him we are dependent; "in him we live, and move, and have our being;" he gathers us in his arm, and carries us in his bosom; yet all this he does through means, by the chariot of salvation, and through the agency of those who are "ministering spirits." Heb. i. 14.

Hence, around this bed, litter, palanquin of the saint, "are threescore valiant men, of the valiant of Israel. They all hold swords, being expert in war; every man hath his sword on his thigh, because of fear in the night." ver. 8.* On account of the audacity of the Arabs, weddings were often turned into mourning by enemies lying in ambush. See 1 Maccabees ix. 37—41. "They went up and hid themselves under the covert of the mountain; where they lifted up their eyes and looked, and behold there was much ado and great carriage; and the bridegroom came forth and his friends and brethren to meet them, with drums and instruments of music and many

* "With the exception of occasional alarms in the night, caused by thieves attempting to steal our horses, we were not disturbed during our visit."—*Layard*, i. 105.

weapons: Then Jonathan and those that were with
him rose up against them from the place where they
lay in ambush, and made a slaughter of them in such
sort as many fell down dead, and the remnant fled
into the mountains; and they took all their spoils.
Thus was the marriage turned into mourning and
their noise of their melody into lamentation."

> "It was the custom then to bring away
>   The bride from home at blushing shut of day,
>   Veiled, in a chariot, heralded along
>   By strewn flowers, torchès, and a marriage song
>   With other pageants."

Around the saint are enemies lying in ambush amid
the gloom shrouding from us the invisible world, and
anxious to do us every possible injury. The holy
angels are our guard against these. "The angel of
the Lord encampeth round about them that fear
him." They are sent from heaven as a guard, an
escort for us during our passage through this wilderness to heaven.

> "Millions of spiritual beings walk the earth
>   Both when we wake and when we sleep; the soul
>   Made in this wilderness the Spirit's shrine,
>   A thousand liveried angels lacky her,
>   Driving far off each thing of sin and guilt."*

And when at death the believer finds his eye opening
on the mysteries of the unseen world, hitherto around
him, but invisible to flesh, he sees battalions of angels
waiting as a triumphant guard, and they close their

* Milton.

shining ranks around the heir of heaven, and with the proud tread of victory, escort him safe through the regions of the dead; and the prince of darkness from afar looks with dismay on another soul wrested from his grasp; and the exulting band approach the New Jerusalem with strains of triumphal music; and they enter in through the gates into the city. In the text, the number of sixty is mentioned, a definite for an indefinite number, a sufficiency for any possible emergencies; and they are called "the valiant of Israel," not a band of mercenaries who cannot be relied on, but native-born soldiers, faithful to their sovereign and his interests, from patriotic attachment; thus we may feel this angelic guard is sufficient for repelling any foes, and will ever be steadfast to us through their devotion to our king.

VER. 9, 10.—King Solomon made himself a chariot of the wood of Lebanon. He made the pillars thereof of silver, the bottom thereof of gold, the covering of it of purple; the midst thereof being paved with love, for the daughters of Jerusalem.

The word "chariot" here is explanatory of "bed" in ver. 7, and means a sedan, a portable couch, or palanquin. The object of these verses is to set before us the remarkable beauty and excellence of the conveyance provided by Solomon for his bride. Such vehicles are even yet in use in the East, and are of equal magnificence. In the year 1796, the British government presented the Nabob of the Carnatic with a carriage of this kind, thus described at the time: "The beams are solid gold, the inside beauti-

fully decorated with silver lining and fringe throughout: the panels are painted in the highest style of
finishing, and represent various groups and heads of
animals, after the manner of Asia, beaded with gold
richly raised above the surface, and engraved. The
stays and different other ornaments are of embossed
silver." Such litters were in use among the Egyptians. Wilkinson gives a copy of a representation of
a person of distinction carried in an open palanquin
by four bearers, followed by an attendant with a sort
of parasol. Those yet in use in the East are couches
with a canopy supported by pillars at the four cor-
ners, and hung round with curtains, to protect the
person within from the sun, and carried on men's
shoulders, or in their hands, by means of poles by
which they are supported. They are long enough
for the rider to lie down at length, and about three
feet broad, though varying in size and richness
according to the wealth of the owner.* In this of
Solomon, "the pillars" were silver; "the bottom" as
in our version, or more correctly, "the railing"
around it, was gold; the seat—English version, "cov-

* Robert Fitch, in his voyage to the kingdom of Pegu, in
1591, speaking of its sovereign, says, "The king keepeth
great state. When he rideth abroad, he rideth with a great
guard, and many noblemen; oftentimes upon an elephant
with a fine castle upon him, very fairly gilded with gold; and
sometimes upon a great frame like a horse-litter, which hath a
little house upon it, covered overhead, but open on the sides,
which is all gilded with gold, and set with many rubies and
sapphires, whereof he hath infinite store in his country, and is
carried upon sixteen or eighteen men's shoulders."

ering"—was purple; the midst thereof being checkered or tesselated with love, "for the daughters of
Jerusalem." Among the different interpretations of
these words, this seems the best, and in accordance
with the Hebrew; this chariot was made thus rich
and beautiful for their benefit; the last clause being
thus understood as referring not merely to the midst
paved with love, but to the whole structure of the
vehicle.

It seems no part of the mind of the Spirit that we
should take this description to pieces, and try to
allegorize the several parts. The intention is to represent to us the fact that the believer is carried
onward to heaven in a conveyance as costly and
glorious as that here described; that the materials
are of the richest, choicest, most durable character;
that the midst is paved or tesselated with love. The
provision made, the means provided for bringing us
to glory, are of a rare and splendid nature. After
exhausting the things most valuable among men,
making the pillars silver, the railing gold, the seat
or couch purple, he adopts a feature in the description entirely new, and says the midst is curiously
wrought with something more precious than silver or
gold, even with love itself—showing that the saint,
while thus passing through the wilderness between
this world and heaven, between our state of guilt and
our state of glory, is in a palanquin of the most costly
make, borne up in the hands of angels, surrounded
by an armed angelic guard, and reclining on a soft

couch beautiful as purple, the most costly colour, with the midst of the litter formed of love—the many acts of divine love from Father, Son, and Holy Spirit, there combining underneath us like the different pieces in a beautiful mosaic, tesselated pavement. In the spirit of this passage, those who wait on the Lord are said to renew their strength; and he will give his angels charge concerning such, to bear them up in their hands, lest at any time they dash their foot against a stone. Isa. xl. 31, Ps. xci. 12. With the author of our faith finishing his temptation in the wilderness, it may be said of every saint passed away to glory:

> "A fiery globe
> Of angels on full sail of wing flew nigh,
> Who on their plumy vans received him soft
> From his uneasy station, and upbore
> As on a floating couch through the blithe air;
> Then in a flowery valley set him down
> On a green bank, and set before him spread
> A table of celestial food, divine
> Ambrosial fruits, fetch'd from the tree of life,
> And from the fount of life ambrosial drink."*

The redeemed soul is a "peculiar treasure," Ps. cxxxv. 4; this litter is the casket, the conveyance, in which it is carried towards heaven by the hands of angels, sent by Jesus, our elder brother, gone away to prepare a place for us in a better land than Egypt, and more fitted to cheer our fainting spirits than the wagons sent by Joseph, which so revived the heart of

* Paradise Regained, book iv. 581.

Jacob.* To human appearance, we are in the condition of the prophet who ran by the side, while Ahab was within the chariot; yet as the hand of the Lord was on Elijah for enabling him to glide along before the swift-rolling vehicle of the king; and to angels' eyes he was in a chariot far more glorious, unseen by flesh, of a spiritual fabric; thus are we in reality moving towards heaven, while around us, amid the darkness of our present state, angels and the spirits of just men made perfect see "the shining of a flaming

* With this representation we may compare the following from Pindar, where in the ninth Pythian Ode, he is speaking of Cyrene: "Whom the long-haired son of Latona snatched away from the recesses of Pelion echoing with the wind, and in his golden chariot brought the virgin huntress, where he constituted her sovereign of the realms teeming with flocks and transcendently fertile. And the silver-footed Venus, gently touching with her hand, received the Delian stranger, as he alighted from his heaven-built car."

Thus, in the Iliad, Dolon says of the chariot of Rhesus,

"With gold and silver all his chariot burns."

And the same poet thus describes the chariot of Juno:

> "Hebe to the chariot roll'd
> The brazen wheels, and joined them to the smooth
> Steel axle; twice four spokes divided each,
> Shot from the centre to the verge. The verge
> Was gold, by fellies of eternal brass
> Guarded, a dazzling show! The shining naves
> Were silver; silver cords, and cords of gold,
> The seat upbore; two crescents blazed in front.
> The pole was argent all, to which she bound
> The golden yoke with its appendant charge
> Inserted braces, straps and bands of gold."—*Iliad*, v. 719.

fire," Isa. iv. 6, even the splendour of the righteousness of Jesus. The angel of the covenant who appeared to Manoah, when the flame of the sacrifice
offered on the rock went up toward heaven, ascended
in the flame of the altar, "as in a chariot," ὥσπερ
ὀχήματος· says Josephus; and like him, the souls of
the redeemed pass up towards glory in this precious
chariot of salvation, pillowed on love, surrounded by
an escort of angels, amid pillars of incense of the
intercession of our divine Redeemer, and wrapped in
the splendour of the righteousness of the sacrifice
offered for us on the altar of the divine nature of
Christ, even "the Rock of ages."

VER. 11.—Go forth, O ye daughters of Zion, and behold
king Solomon with the crown wherewith his mother crowned him in the day of his espousals, and in the day of the
gladness of his heart.

These words show the reception awaiting us on our
arrival in heaven. While the magnificent cortege
just noticed are coming up through the wilderness,
that greater than Solomon, the Prince of Peace, is
standing ready to receive us with all the gladness of
a marriage festivity. The daughters of Zion, a general expression for the inmates of heaven, while gazing
on this sight, are called on to behold the splendour of
the appearance of Jesus and of his retinue as awaiting
his redeemed in glory. The Jews knew nothing
richer than the attire of a bridegroom; hence even of
the sun, "He cometh forth as a bridegroom out of his
chamber." It was here sufficient to mention merely
the nuptial crown. The use of nuptial crowns was

very ancient and very general.* Selden has gathered the information on this subject in his Uxor Heb. lib. 2. Among the Greeks and Romans, these crowns were usually chaplets of flowers. The Talmud states that the crown of the bridegroom was of gold or silver, or else a wreath of roses, olives, or myrtle; that the bride's crown was of gold or silver, in the shape of a tower, like those represented on the head of the heathen goddess Cybele. Jesus is crowned with many crowns. Rev. xix. 12. There was no crown given by the ancients for distinguished conduct, which is not merited by our Lord. But on the reception of his ransomed ones, here referred to, there is peculiar propriety in mentioning only the nuptial crown.

* "It was usual with many nations to put crowns or garlands on the heads of new-married persons. The Mishna informs us that this custom prevailed among the Jews; and it should seem from the passage before us, that the ceremony of putting it on was performed by one of the parents. Among the Greeks the bride was crowned by her mother, as appears from the instance of Iphigenia in Euripides, v. 903. Bochart supposes this the nuptial crown and other ornaments of a bride, alluded to in Ezekiel xvi. 8—12. Georgr. Sacr. p. 2, c. 25. The nuptial crowns used among the Greeks and Romans were only chaplets of leaves or flowers. Among the Hebrews they were not only of these, but also occasionally of richer materials, as gold or silver, according to the rank or wealth of the parties. The original word used in the text is the same used to express a kingly crown in 2 Sam. xii. 30; 1 Chron. xxii. 2; and is often described to be of gold, Esth. viii. 15; Ps. xxi. 4; but appears to have been worn by those who were no kings, Job xix. 9, and was probably often composed of less valuable materials; as of enamelled work, also of roses, myrtle, and olive-leaves."—*Bishop Percy.*

30

We naturally inquire, How will Jesus receive me on my approach to heaven? The answer is here. He is awaiting us, not as he appeared when discoursing on the mount, when sitting at Jacob's well, when weeping over Jerusalem, when ascending from Olivet, or even as when appearing to John at Patmos; but invested with all the glory of heaven, and with the affection of the bridegroom receiving the bride. For "as the bridegroom rejoiceth over the bride, so shall thy God rejoice over thee." Isa. lxii. 5. That time will be a day not of trouble and war, but of marriage festivity; the conflict over; his soul not exceeding sorrowful unto death, as in Gethsemane, but exulting in having finished the work of redemption by the destruction of even the last enemy death, and in having nothing henceforth, but the uninterrupted enjoyment of the society of the bride, the wife of the Lamb. To this period had he reference continually in his humiliation. "For the joy that was set before him, he endured the cross, despising the shame, and is set down at the right hand of the throne of God." Heb. xii. 2. "The Lord shall rejoice in his works," Ps. civ. 31; especially shall he rejoice in the completion of redemption, and in the finishing stroke of the bringing of many sons unto glory. Amid the discouragements, the conflicts, the gloom of earth, with our souls passing onward to heaven in a chariot paved with love, borne in the hands of angels, and with Jesus crowned with glory and honour, crowned with a nuptial crown, awaiting us, well may we rejoice even in tribulation, and sing, "I will greatly rejoice

in the Lord, my soul shall be joyful in my God; for
he hath clothed me with the garments of salvation,
he hath covered me with the robe of righteousness, as
a bridegroom decketh himself with ornaments, and
as a bride adorneth herself with her jewels." Isa.
lxi. 10.

CHAPTER IV.

THE soul, thus conveyed to the bosom of Jesus, is
oppressed with a deepening sense of unworthiness,
and finds difficulty in believing there can be so glorious a destiny awaiting us; conscious of our corruptions and short comings, we cannot understand
how the pure eyes of Jesus can see anything in us
attractive. Hence, he takes special pains to enlarge
on this point, and assure us how greatly he delights
in beholding our ripening graces. This is the portion of the Scriptures which sets forth what is thought
by Christ, the King of glory, concerning those who
are despised and offcast by the world.

When Zeuxis would paint Helen the most beautiful
of women, he copied the beauties from several different persons, and by concentrating these in an individual, represented a beau ideal of feminine grace.*

* These principles have been laid down by Cicero for eluci-
dating another subject. "We can conceive of something more
beautiful than even the statues of Phidias and the pictures I
have mentioned, than which we can think of nothing more
perfect in their kind. Yet that artist when about to make the
statue of Jupiter and of Minerva, did not draw his representa-

S

In these following descriptions of both the bride and
the beloved, the same course is pursued by the Holy
Spirit, save that the beauties are here embodied in
words instead of colours, and are represented by comparisons drawn from the beauties of nature. Yet it
is entirely according to the rules of poetry and the
laws of nature, that the beauty of a person be illustrated by the beauty of natural objects. Lord Jeffrey
says, " Our sense of beauty depends entirely on our
previous experience of simpler pleasures or emotions,
and consists in the suggestion of agreeable or interesting sensations with which we had formerly been
made familiar by the direct and intelligible agency of
our common sensibilities; and that vast variety of
objects to which we give the common name of beautiful,
become entitled to that appellation, merely because
they all possess the power of recalling or reflecting
those sensations of which they have been the accom-
paniments, or with which they have been associated
in our imagination by any other more casual bond of
connection." The same, or very similar effects, may
be produced on the mind from different sources and
by different causes. A picture may make impressions of beauty very like those raised by a landscape
of which it is the copy; music may be so composed
as to start feelings of the same kind; a relic, a
memento may be the occasion of reviving a whole

tion from any visible thing, but there was abiding in his mind
an imaginary form of beauty, and studying this attentively, he
fashioned his representations after this image."—*Cicero, Ora-
tor. 2.*

cloud of remembrances; things very unlike in point
of fact may awaken the same sensations in the breast,
by suggesting analogies: as when Ossian says, "The
music of Carryl was like the memory of joys that are
past, pleasant and mournful to the soul." "The
grounds or causes of beauty, while the result or in-
ternal emotion is always identical in its nature, are
multiplied and various. In other words, beauty in
the mind is one, while outward beauty, or rather the
causes of beauty in outward objects, is many."

Now, in these descriptions, Jesus wishes to give us
an idea of the impressions of beauty and pleasure he
has in contemplating the souls of the saints. Hence,
he must use resemblances, and those of things we can
see and enjoy. He might have used comparisons
drawn from the angelic host and superior beings; but
such illustrations could not have done us any good, for
they could not convey to us any idea. Nor would it
answer to use references to others of the human race;
for there is no perfection on earth, and the Scriptures
are for the benefit of mankind at large in all ages; so
that the reference should be to things which may be
essentially lasting. Here we find an unbounded field
opened in the beauties of nature. The resemblance
in these comparisons consists not in any outward
likeness, but lies in the views and effects produced in
the views and sensations of the soul, in the pleasure
had in contemplating these natural objects. Here is
light combining seven different colours; how would
the philosopher represent what he sees in it, to an
ignorant man? He would say, One of these is like

30*

the violet, another blue like the sky, a third like the verdure, another like the rose. In these comparisons, the only resemblance is in the effect produced on the mind by the colours. These natural objects and the rainbow, so unlike in other respects, agree in this—in making certain impressions on us which are expressed by our words for those colours. Now the pure in heart are growing like God, who is light; and Jesus, in pointing out what hidden beauty he sees in the soul, says, those graces of the Christian life produce on him impressions more pleasing than those made on us by the lovely objects there specified in nature. And the mode of some interpreters in explaining these, is as unreasonable as it would be to run the parallel farther than the mere colour, out into the most minute particulars; between the tints of the rainbow and the objects by which they might be illustrated.

This is exactly what might be expected in cases like the present. Christ is a spiritual being; and though invested with a body, that is a spiritual body. There can therefore be no outward resemblance between him and these material objects; nor between these and the renewed soul as it appears in his eyes. That likeness must therefore exist in the emotions and impressions made on the soul.

VER. 1.—Behold, thou art fair, my love; behold, thou art fair; thou hast doves' eyes within thy locks.

See notes on chap. i. 15.* The large beautiful eye

* "It was pleasant, now and then, to look up from one's book, as the window was darkened by a slight turban from

of the Syrian dove appears even more beautiful when
seen amid its native groves of noble trees and rich
foliage; and hence the eyes of the saint are spoken
of as embowered within her locks.* The point of the
words does therefore seem to be this, that Jesus contemplates the expression of love beaming from the
soul of the pure in heart, with a pleasure greater than
what is felt by us in gazing on the large, sparkling,
melting eyes of the Syrian dove, amid the wild beauty
of its native groves.

which rich tresses hung over the shoulder, and dark but gentle
eyes shone beneath it. The bosom was generally open, or but
partially enclosed by the crape garment within; a light turban,
or a handkerchief of Damascus silk, covered the head, from
which the rich hair flowed free, or was plaited into two long
braids. Suddenly the door opened, the tapestry that hung
over it was moved aside by a beautifully rounded arm, on
which jewels gleamed, and there stepped forth a female form
which fascinated my attention as if it had been a vision. She
had a light gauzy turban, with a glittering fringe falling gracefully over the shoulder; masses of black and shining hair,
that made the forehead and delicately browned cheek look as
fair as a Circassian's; if a thought of luxury hovered upon the
richly rosy mouth, it was awed into admiration by the large
dark eyes, so fearless, yet so modest, glancing round as if they
read a meaning in every thing, and everywhere, yet calm and
self-possessed in their consciousness of power."—*Warburton's
Crescent and Cross*, ii. 132.

* We retain the rendering "within thy locks," rather than
"within thy veil." 1. The same Hebrew word is translated
"locks," in Isa. xlvii. 2. 2. The Arabic root, as given in
Gesenius and Winer, favours this. 3. The connection requires
this meaning. 4. Locks adds to the consistency of the portrait;
and the Jewish females carefully cultivated a luxuriant growth
of hair.

Thy hair is as a flock of goats that appear from mount Gilead.

The Hebrew here reads, "Thy hair is as a flock of goats that lie down from mount Gilead;" that is, like a flock of goats lying along the sides of mount Gilead from the top towards the bottom, so that they seem to hang from it. The hair of the oriental goat has the fineness of silk, and is expressly observed by an ancient naturalist to bear a great resemblance to the fine ringlets of a woman's hair. The Angora species of goat is probably meant here. The country of Gilead was most beautiful and fertile, and abounding in rich pastures and aromatic growths, among which was the celebrated balsam. The whole region is covered with groups of limestone mountains, intersected by fertile valleys, and includes the territory east of Jordan, as far south as the Jabbok. Hills rising behind hills in pleasing elevations, clothed with luxuriant verdure; the finest trees and noblest oaks; lovely slopes opening in the forest, and affording the best pastures and most lovely flowers; valleys murmuring with limpid rills; and the romantic wildness softened by lovely park-like scenes; all combined to form a landscape so delightful that the beholder could hardly persuade himself it was real. Such mountain scenes were more beautiful when on their slopes might have been seen a flock of these beautiful goats lying down. The comparison of a fine head of hair to the long, silk-like fleece of such goats in such a scene, was natural. Few things could be more beautiful than the sight of such a flock reclining on the verdant, balmy slopes of Gilead, on a clear, calm day. Now in conveying to us an idea of the satisfaction Jesus has in dwelling on his saints, he here gives an additional particular, and says, that in contemplating us, another group of delightful impressions is gathered into his heart, like that felt in gazing on a flock of those goats, with long, silky hair, amid the richness, beauty, and grandeur of Gilead.

VER. 2.—Thy teeth are like a flock of sheep that are even shorn,* which came up from the washing; whereof every one bear twins, and none is barren among them.

Rather, "thy teeth are like a flock of sheep all of the same size." The word rendered "bear twins" is in Exod. xxvi. 24, "coupled together," speaking of the boards of the tabernacle, and may refer to the flocks standing close together; as "none is barren" expresses the perfection of the flock. Coming up from

* The word "even shorn," means of an equal size. 1. This is not the common word for shorn in the Hebrew. 2. The word, in other places, has a meaning in accordance with what we here give. 1 Kings vi. 25, "were of one size;" also, 1 Kings vii. 37, "one size." "This expression," says Rosenmüller, "embodies the idea, that two or more things, whether of wood or stone, had been so wrought that the same relative proportion was preserved among them. By a metaphor thence derived, this Hebrew word is applied to sheep, for showing that throughout the flock they were as much alike as if they had been fashioned from wood or metal, after the same pattern." 3. The design of the comparison requires it, as applying to the teeth, to mean they were of equal size. 4. The idea of perfection is intended; this is not associated with sheep shorn; their being of equal size, and coming up from the washing-pool immediately before shearing, represents them as in all respects perfect.

the place of washing, they had fleeces in perfection of
growth as well as whiteness. The beauty of the
teeth is spoken of by Lucian: "When laughing, she
showed her teeth; in what way shall I express how
white they are, how symmetrical, how perfectly fitted
together? They are like a very beautiful necklace of
pearls glistening and of the same size, thus ranged in
regular order. They received additional beauty from
the redness of the lips; for they appeared between
them, like the cut ivory in Homer, not some broader,
some larger than others, or separated, as is very frequently the case, but with a perfect uniformity of all
in colour, size, and arrangement."* This is but
another mode of illustrating the same idea, which, to
a pastoral people like the Jews, was more beautifully
represented in the comparison in the text. The illustration of this verse pours into the mind a flood of
delightful ideas, and this goes a step farther in showing the aggregate of pleasing feelings had by Jesus in
contemplating the saint.

VER. 3.—Thy lips are like a thread of scarlet, and thy
speech is comely.

The colour here meant seems to be a deep red,
bright rich crimson: this was the meaning of the word
"scarlet," in the time of James I. The colour now
known as such, was then unknown. According to
Wilkinson, the colour was imparted to the thread
before woven into the cloth. The force of the comparison here lies in the colour; the lips were delicately

* Lucian, Imagines, ver. vi. p. 11.

free from undue thickness, and of the most beautiful
deep red. The Jews knew no more beautiful red than
the bright rich crimson here noticed as appearing in
a skein of thread carefully dyed.

"Thy speech," or, as we should read, by a common
figure of rhetoric, thy 'mouth is beautiful.'* While the
colour of the lips is thus beautiful, the whole mouth is
equally perfect.

Thy temples are like a piece of a pomegranate within thy
locks.

This simile is still common in the East. Thus, in
an anonymous Persian ode, cited by Sir William
Jones, "The pomegranate brings to my mind the
blushes of my beloved, when her cheeks are coloured
with a modest resentment." The word *temples* is
used for the upper part of the cheeks near them, and
the design of this passage is to express the peculiar
freshness, beauty, and ruddy colour of the cheeks.
Some would make allusion here to the flower of the
"pomegranate, rich with its bright green leaves, and
its blossoms of that beautiful and vivid red which
is excelled by few even of the most brilliant flowers
of the East." We suppose the reference is however
to a piece of the pomegranate, which is about the size
of an orange, and contains within its hard, brown
rind, a number of cells divided by membraneous par-

* "Both ancient and modern writers of the East agree in
describing the mouth with simplicity, 'Her mouth small and
vermilion,' says the writer of the Arabian Nights Entertainments. 'Her lips are like a thread of scarlet,' says the Jewish
Poet."—*Harmer*, 289.

titions, in which lie in rows the seeds or grains, pellucid, tinged with red, and shining like crystal. When cut up, or bursting and displaying its seeds, this fruit was of the richest vermilion. Hence the Portuguese poet, as quoted by Good,

> " The pomegranate of orange hue,
> Whose open heart a brighter red displays
> Than that which sparkles in the ruby's blaze."

Among the ladies of Persia the hair is still suffered to fall loosely over the forehead and cheeks, and is generally perfumed with the most exquisite essences. An oriental poet, quoted by Good, says, " O thou, whose lips, which outshine the grains of the pomegranate, are embellished, when thou speakest, by the brightness of thy teeth!" And in the spirit of the foregoing illustrations, is the following: " Thy lips, O thou most beautiful among women! are a bandhujiva flower; the lustre of the madhuca beams on thy cheek; thine eye outshines the blue lotos; thy nose is a bud of the tila; the cunda-blossom yields to thy teeth."

VER. 4.—Thy neck is like the tower of David, builded for an armoury, whereon there hang a thousand bucklers, all shields of mighty men.

This tower of David was probably the noblest of the towers built by him, of white marble, on a summit of Zion. Sandys says, " Aloft on the uttermost angle of mount Zion, stood the tower of David, whose ruins are yet extant, of a wonderful strength and admirable beauty, adorned with shields and the arms of the

mighty." Speaking of Tyre, the prophet says,
"They hang their shields upon thy walls round about;
they have made thy beauty perfect." Ezek. xxvii. 11.
Thus Pausanias, concerning the temple of Jupiter at
Olympia: "On each corner of the roof is placed a
gilded vase, and on the top of the pediment a statue
of Victory, gilded likewise, under which is hung up a
golden shield, with a figure of the gorgon Medusa
carved upon it. The inscription on the shield imports
it to have been a gift of the Tanagreans for a victory
gained over the Argives and Athenians. On the
cornice, which runs round the temple on the outside
over the columns, are hung one and twenty gilt shields,
a present from Mummius, the Roman general, who
took and destroyed Corinth." According to Layard,
"The castles of the maritime people, whose conquest
is recorded by the Kouyunjik bas-reliefs, are distinguished by the shields hung round the walls. Around
the sides of the vessels were also suspended the shields
of the warriors."* The ancients bestowed great care
on their shields, adorning them with precious metals
and elaborate engraving, as may be seen from the description of the shield of Achilles in the Iliad. "King
Solomon made two hundred targets of beaten gold.
And he made three hundred shields of beaten gold;
three pounds of gold went to one shield; and the king
put them in the house of the forest of Lebanon."
1 Kings x. 16. When the text says, "all shields of
mighty men," it means simply all were shields the
most costly and beautiful. As the Jews built their

* Layard's Nineveh, vol. ii. 296.

31

nobler edifices of white marble, a tower of this kind rising on the summit of mount Zion, hung around with shields of gold like those of Solomon, would furnish an exquisite simile for illustrating the beauty of the graceful neck of the bride, adorned with the rich ornaments and necklace of those bygone ages. We can conceive of nothing more appropriate and beautiful. The shields of the warriors associate with the beauty of the tower the recollection of the noble deeds and triumphs in which those shields had been borne; as the pleasure had by Jesus in contemplating his saints is increased by the remembrance of his sufferings and victories in working out their salvation.

VER. 5.—Thy two breasts are like two young roes that are twins, which feed among the lilies.

All the monuments and pictures of ancient Egypt, show us that the ancient oriental ladies dressed so as to leave the busts fully open to view, and of course there could then be no impropriety in alluding to, or describing that part of the person. It may be added, that this is the custom of modern oriental,* as well as of ancient oriental dress. Lilies abounded in

* "The virgins wore their hair floating in exuberant curls over their shoulders: their dress is indescribable by male lips; all I·can say of it is, that it is very graceful and pretty, and lavishly open at the bosom."—*Warburton.*

Theocritus puts the following into the mouth of Grecian virgins, on a nuptial occasion:

"While we, descending to the city gate,
  Arrayed in decent robes that sweep the ground,
  With naked bosoms, and with hair unbound."

Idyl. **xv.** 134.

their pasture-grounds; and the young twin roes, with eyes uncommonly black and large, creatures so exquisitely beautiful, that their name, as here used, signifies loveliness in general, would present a scene of the greatest pastoral beauty, while feeding in meadows overspread with those delightful flowers. In Proverbs there is a like allusion, "Rejoice with the wife of thy youth. Let her be as the loving hind and pleasant roe; let her breasts satisfy thee at all times, and be thou ravished always with her love." Chap. v. 19.

Now, in the comparisons of the foregoing verses, the thing to be illustrated is the general beauty of the pious soul in the eyes of Jesus. The point around which they are all clustered is stated in ver. 1, "Thou art fair:" this is repeated in ver. 7, "Thou art all fair." This is the golden thread which runs through this part of the allegory, and unites these poetical allusions in one string of unearthly pearls. Losing sight of this, most commentators have marred the passage by separating these emblems from one another, and appropriating them to other uses than the one intended by the Holy Spirit. What would be thought of a person who, under the plea of heightening the effect of a beautiful picture by a great artist, could cut out the several figures, the trees, the waters, the tinted clouds, and exhibit them apart in every imaginable variety of light and position? This would show something more than want of judgment. No argument would be necessary for making us feel such was never the mind of the artist. The common method of expounding this and the other kindred passages in the Song, seems no less unreasonable. The Apollo Belvidere can be appreciated, not by breaking off and examining severally an arm, a leg, or any other part detached, but by studying the whole, uninjured and untouched. These exquisite portraitures by the Holy Spirit must be viewed in the same way, as they are set constituting a group, a whole; and the various ideas of beauty radiating from them, must be gathered into a focus on the mind. How beautiful the scenes, how rich the pleasure, in contemplating the flock of silken-haired goats on beautiful, verdant Gilead; the even-sized, purely white, in all points perfect, flock of sheep coming up amid the beauties of early spring, from groves beside the pure waters; the deep, rich crimson of the scarlet thread; the vermilion blush of the slice of pomegranate; the tower of David, of white marble, hung round with costly shields, the mementos of noble achievements, rising in delicate majesty on mount Zion; the twin gazelles feeding among the fresh-blown lilies;—what a strong impression of beauty is made on the mind by viewing any one of those scenes at a time; how overpowering the sense of the beautiful, could the heart receive at the same time all the delightful impressions from these different sources, combined in one luxurious, glorious flood. Yet even that, however overwhelming and perhaps impossible for us, could give but a faint representation of the beauty seen by Jesus in the humblest of his saints, and the pleasure had by him in dwelling on their beauties of holiness. We are justified in saying, that the perfection of the nature of the redeemed will be the crowning beauty of all the works of God, the full-blown flower of which universal creation may be called the trunk and stem. Surely the glorified humanity of the Son of God, the nature which is taken into union with the Godhead, must surpass every other manifestation of creative power. That nature, when fully glorified, will differ infinitely more from the same nature seen in its germ in the babe of Bethlehem, than the beauteous flower differs from the humble seed. It is reasonable, it is right, that Jesus should thus honour the nature taken into oneness with his divinity, by making it the highest possible development of created beauty, splendour, and glory. But to this glorified nature of the man Christ Jesus, the nature of his redeemed people shall be made like. "Who shall change our vile body that it may be fashioned like unto his glorious body," Phil. iii. 21; "When he shall appear, we shall be like him," 1 John iii. 2. And with him there is no succession, all is present, so that he now sees in his saints all the glory which shall ever invest them, and which we may be years or ages in beholding; and thus contemplating it, he would give us an idea of his pleasure therein by such language as in the text, by referring us to our delight in gazing on whatever is most beautiful in the present world. The rich, the great, the noble of earth, look on the humble believer, only as Dives looked on Lazarus, to pity or despise; as the Jews looked on him who was in their eyes as a root out of a dry ground, with no form, nor comeliness, nor beauty, Isa. liii. 2; yet as certainly as the human nature of Jesus has been glorified and exalted far above all principality, and power, and might, and dominion, and every name that is named, not only in this world, but also in that which is to come, Eph. i. 21, so certainly shall these despised ones of Jesus be glorified with him, and be with him where he is, that they may behold his glory. John xvii. 24. Why should we heed the censure or praise of the world, when we are thus esteemed by the King of kings?

VER. 6.—Until the day break, and the shadows flee away, I will get me to the mountain of myrrh, and to the hill of frankincense.

While in this world preparing for the day of our espousals, we are not cut off from communication with Jesus. He who views us with the delight set forth in the foregoing verses, has appointed a place where he may always be found by us at present. That place is designated in this verse. For an explanation of the first clause, see chap. ii. 17. When passing over Lebanon and by Damascus, Pompey the Great is said to have passed through sweet smelling groves and woods of frankincense and balsam. "The approach to Lebanon is adorned with olive-plantations, vineyards, and luxuriant fields; and its lower regions, besides the olive and the vine, are beautified with the myrtle, the styrax, and other odoriferous shrubs; and the perfume which exhales from these plants is increased by the fragrance of the cedars which crown its summits, or garnish its declivities. The great rupture which runs a long way up into the mountain, and is on both sides exceedingly steep and high, is clothed from the top to the bottom with fragrant evergreens, and everywhere refreshed with streams, descending from the rocks in beautiful cascades. The cedar-apples growing on the famous cedars must be classed with the scented fruits of the oriental regions; and have perhaps contributed greatly to the fragrance for which the sacred writers so frequently celebrate the mountains of Lebanon."*

The mountain of frankincense is the place where Jesus has established the mercy-seat. Zion, where our Lord dwelt amid the Shechinah, was a mountain of incense gushing from the censer and the golden altar; but the place where Jesus now dwells by his Spirit and meets with his saints, he would represent as fragrant with richer dews, so rich that here the odours come not from one altar or censer, but from groves crowded with trees of incense, every one of which is an altar, and with flowers every one of which is a censer, pouring upon the dewy air unearthly fragrance. Here, too, the point of the comparison is in the pleasing effect produced on the soul: the person who might go up into a hill of myrrh and frankincense at dewy eve, could not have emotions so pleasant as those arising in the heart drawing near unto the presence of Jesus and the sacred atmosphere spread by the Holy Spirit around the throne of grace. Fragrant odours are a favourite emblem in the Scriptures for expressing the gracious influences of the Spirit.

How delightful are the spiritual odours diffused

* Paxton's Illustrations.

T

around the heart at the mercy-seat, called a mountain, because apart from the busy scenes of the world; because the appointed place of God's meeting with his ancient people was on mount Moriah; and because, when Jesus wished to pray, he went apart into a mountain, Matt. xiv. 23; Luke ix. 2. As we come to the mercy-seat with our spiritual apprehensions enlivened by grace, we feel ourselves entering an atmosphere different from that of the world, and breathing an air so pure, so rich, so calm, that it must be a foretaste of heaven. At times of special manifestations of the Holy Spirit, the believer may sometimes feel as though in an atmosphere of calmness, purity, peace, and softened delight, around the soul, different from any thing of this world—something which is to the heart what the air of heaven must be to the spiritual body, than which the air of the Holy City could hardly be more pure, refreshing and pleasant. This is the Holy Spirit diffusing around us more and more of the atmosphere which the soul will breathe in heaven; and at the same time making us feel how appropriately the place where such blessedness is enjoyed, is called the mountain of myrrh and hill of frankincense.

"In the centre of a world whose soil
Is rank with all unkindness, compassed round
With such memorials, I have sometimes felt
It was no momentary happiness
To have *one* Enclosure where the voice that speaks
In envy or detraction is not heard;
Which malice may not enter; where the traces
Of evil inclinations are unknown;

Where love and pity tenderly unite
With resignation; and no jarring tone
Intrudes, the peaceful concert to disturb
Of amity and gratitude."

To this place will Jesus get till the day break and the shadows flee away; till we pass into the final state of glory where all these former things are done away, and there shall be no night there. The mercy-seat is the appointed place of meeting with him till that time. Not only will he come to that place occasionally in answer to prayer, as in chap. ii. 17; he may always be found there. Whenever we wish to meet with Jesus, we have only to betake ourselves to the place of prayer. After the day breaks, he will be found by us in the heavenly Jerusalem, where we shall no longer enjoy his society dimly, as in a grove of frankincense, amid the shadows of night, but clearly, perfectly, knowing even as we are known. 1 Cor. xiii. 10.

VER. 7.—Thou art all fair, my love; there is no spot in thee.

This verse is the first of eight reasons he gives for encouraging us to meet him on the hill of frankincense, at the throne of grace. See chap. i. 15, 16. There, he speaks of the saint as being fair in his eyes; here, as being all fair, "without spot, or wrinkle, or any such thing." Eph. v. 27. How fair were Moses and Elijah when on the mount they appeared with Jesus in glory, being made like him; and his face did shine as the sun, and his raiment was white as the light. Luke ix. 29. Now, with Jesus there is no such thing as time; he inhabiteth eternity; with him there

is no succession, all is present; and we are in his eyes
attired with his glorious righteousness and luminous
with the splendours of his Spirit; we are viewed by
him precisely as we are when our sanctification is
finished.

How kind, therefore, are these words, and how fitted
for encouraging us to frequent the throne of grace.
They express what is precisely the first encouragement
necessary for us in coming to him in prayer. The
more fervent our love, and the stronger our apprehension of his glory, the deeper is the sense of our vileness, unworthiness, and guilt, often so strong as to
make us hesitate, under the impression that he cannot
receive such sinners as ourselves. But he cheers us
to come, assuring us that he has blotted out all our
iniquities; that his blood cleanseth from all sin; that
he will purge us with hyssop, and we shall be clean;
he will wash us and make us whiter than snow. Ps.
li. 7.

VER. 8.—Come with me from Lebanon, my spouse, with
me from Lebanon: look from the top of Amana, from the
top of Shenir and Hermon, from the lions' dens, from the
mountains of the leopards.

Lebanon is well known as the noble range on the
north of the land of promise, "that goodly mountain"
which Moses so desired to visit. Amana was probably the southern part of Anti-Libanus, and was so
named, perhaps, from the river which had its sources
at its foot, called in 2 Kings v. 12, Abana, but in the
margin, Amana. Shenir and Hermon were names for
the same mountain; Hermon perhaps the name for

the whole mountain; and Sirion the name for the part of it belonging to the Sidonians; Shenir for that belonging to the Amorites. All these lay in the same region in the northern borders of Palestine, and while abounding in the grandest and most attractive mountain scenery, were infested with leopards and lions, no less than with robbers, so that they might truly be called "the mountains of prey." Ps. lxxvi. 4. The view from these summits was extensive and unsurpassed.*

Now these mountains, thus beautiful but dangerous, are put in contrast with the mountain of myrrh and hill of frankincense. The beloved would have his spouse leave the former, and seek his society in the retreats of the latter. The verse does then give a second reason for dwelling with Jesus at the mercy-seat. Those mountains are like the world, with its high places and pleasures, attractive but dangerous,

* "The lofty summits of Lebanon were the chosen haunts of various beasts of prey, the print of whose feet Maundrell and his party observed in the snow. But they are not confined to these situations; a recent traveller continued descending several hours, through varied scenery, presenting at every turn some new feature, distinguished either by its picturesque beauty or awful sublimity. On arriving at one of the lower swells, which form the base of the mountain, he and his party broke rather abruptly into a deep and thick forest. As they traversed the bocage, the howlings of wild animals were distinctly heard from the recesses."—*Paxton.*

"We lodged this night on the very top of Libanus. We saw in the snow, prints of the feet of several wild beasts, which are the sole proprietors of these parts of the mountains."—*Maundrell*, 140.

beautiful to the eye, but filled with lurking places of the most stealthy and deadly foes. "The mountain of the Lord's house," Isa. ii. 2, Moriah, was more glorious and excellent, or, as it may better be read, brighter, more glorious, than the mountains of prey, Lebanon, Amana, Hermon, and Shenir; because, however rich the natural scenery of these latter, they were infested with beasts of prey, while the former was the place where Jehovah had in Salem his tabernacle, and his dwelling-place in Zion; where was the word of life, the emblems of heaven, the divine oracle, the cloud of glory overshadowing the mercy-seat.

The world is attractive and beautiful, but dangerous and deadly. Amid its specious scenes are lurking enemies, like the lion, powerful, 1 Pet. v. 8, and like the leopard, stealthy, Eph. vi. 11. In circumstances of the greatest prosperity, our adversary, the devil, with his agents, wicked men, "lieth in wait, secretly, as a lion in his den, that they may privily shoot at the upright in heart." From all these dangers and snares, the throne of grace is a refuge. This is established, not among the mountains of prey, but on the hill of frankincense, on Zion, where is Jehovah's dwelling-place amid the innumerable company of angels: "No lion shall be there, nor any ravenous beast shall go up thereon; it shall not be found there; but the redeemed shall walk there." Isa. xxxv. 9. There, we do indeed dwell in the secret place of the Most High, and abide under the shadow of the Almighty. There is no place of safety on earth, save in that sacred refuge, under that heavenly shade. And while those who are enjoying the world are continually in greater danger than those wandering among dens of ravenous beasts; they who are in the company of Jesus have not only a perfect security against every possible evil, but are breathing an air richer than frankincense, and enjoying confidential friendship with the King of kings. Well may we, therefore, say with the Psalmist, "Because the Lord hath chosen Zion, because he hath desired it for his habitation; this is my rest for ever, here will I dwell, for I have desired it." Ps. cxxxii. 13.

VER. 9.—Thou hast ravished my heart, my sister, my spouse; thou hast ravished my heart with one of thine eyes, with one chain of thy neck.

After all the attempts to alter the shade of meaning by another translation and emendation of the text, the common version seems the best. The idea is, that even a partial glimpse of the beauties and ornaments of the bride, had so filled the heart of the beloved with intense affection, as to unheart, unman him; and the ardour of love thus felt, he gives as another reason for her coming away to meet him at the appointed place, on the mountain of myrrh. He calls her "my sister, my spouse," or, as it might be, "my sister-spouse." The word sister is applied to the wife in Tobit vii. 4, 16. Yet, keeping in mind this book is an allegory, as stated in the Introduction, p. 16, we imagine the appellation of "sister" is here used for expressing more perfectly than "spouse" alone would do, the relation of Jesus and his people. Language can at best give us only a very imperfect expression of spirit-

32

ual and heavenly things. Hence the necessity for mul-
tiplying types, illustrations, and epithets, in the Scriptures. So, while the relation between Jesus and the
redeemed soul may in many respects be represented by
that existing between husband and bride, it is in some
essential points different; and that difference may be
marked by the relation of brother and sister, for separating therefrom all unhallowed and carnal ideas. The
union between Christ and his people is one combining
the purest and noblest characteristics of both the
unions just mentioned, separated from every thing
earthly and sensual, having the ardour of affection and
the oneness of the marriage relation, with the purity
and sacredness of a brother's and sister's love. This
is a distinction of very great importance for understanding rightly the Song. Hence the Holy Spirit is
so careful to repeat the appellation "my sister," as
well as spouse. See chaps. iv. 12; v. 1, 2. This repetition has not been made without design by that
pen of inspiration which never uses a superfluous
word; and the many pitiable interpretations put by
excellent men on some passages, show the necessity
there was for closing the door against those unfor-
tunate misapprehensions which this single word "sister" thus introduced and thus repeated was intended
to prevent. The delicacy and emphasis with which
this is here done by the Holy Spirit, is worthy of all
admiration.

Like the queen of Sheba, of whom it is recorded
that on seeing the glory of Solomon "there was no
more spirit in her," 1 Kings x. 5, the beloved says

his heart was carried away with one of her eyes, with one chain of her neck—a most delicate and forcible way of expressing the very great intensity of his affection. It is not intimated that he was not acquainted with the full effect of all her charms; he seems to use this language as the best mode of setting forth the delight had in her beauty. The heart was ravished by merely a partial view of her loveliness; what shall then be said of the effect produced by the full disclosure of her beauty! Oriental poets often use the same language: "I meditate on the ravishing glances darted from her eye." And again, "Bring speedily to my presence her who has stolen the heart of Mejnún with a glance."* Theocritus speaks of "A most bitter wound inflicted on the breast by the dart of powerful Venus." And speaking of a beauty, Horace mentions the graceful turn of her neck. Wilkinson says of the Egyptians, "Handsome and richly ornamented necklaces were a principal part of the dress both of men and women. They consisted of gold, or of beads of various qualities and shapes, disposed according to fancy, generally with a large drop or figure in the centre. Some wore simple gold chains, in imitation of string, to which a stone scarabæus, set in the same precious metal, was appended. A set of small cups, or covered saucers, of bronze gilt, hanging from a chain of the same materials, were sometimes worn by women; a necklace of which has been found belonging to a Theban lady,

* A Persian poem quoted by Sir William Jones.

offering a striking contrast in their simplicity to the
gold leaves inlaid with lapis lazuli, red and green
stones, of another she wore; which served, with many
more in her possession, to excite the admiration of
her friends."* Withdrawing from the spouse for the
mountain of myrrh, the beloved has a glimpse of
her beautiful necklace and melting eye, as bidding
him adieu; and then in this verse assures her she
would not fail to meet him on the hill of frankincense,
did she know the ardour and intensity of his love.
After the farewell spoken, while casting a longing,
lingering look behind, he found a single glance of her
eye and view of the golden chain of her neck causing
his affection to burst forth afresh, in a vehement
flame; from this she might judge with what delight
he would receive her in the balmy retreats of their
appointed place of meeting.

And from this we may understand with what a
heart-warm welcome Jesus will gather us to his
bosom, when we withdraw to meet him at the throne
of grace. In coming to the mercy-seat we are apt to
draw near rather with a feeling that our Lord permits
it, than with the impression he is deeply anxious to
receive us, and meets us with delight. Through
lingering unbelief, the sense of unworthiness makes
us think he can hardly rejoice to meet us. But,

---

* Ancient Egyptians, vol. ii. p. 375. In the Hecuba of
Euripides, the chorus speak of the daughter of Priam, slain at
the tomb of Achilles, dyed in blood gushing in a dark stream
from her neck adorned with gold. And Homer mentions
Amphimachus coming, like a girl, to the war, arrayed in gold.

"Thou meetest him that rejoiceth and worketh righteousness, those that remember thee in thy ways."
Isa. lxiv. 5. Our besetting sin, the desire for merit,
makes us hesitate. Jesus will love us no better in
heaven than he loves us now. Merit in us, personal
excellence, has nothing to do with his love. This
will be no stronger towards us when invested with the
spiritual body in glory, than it is at present, amid
our infirmities and imperfect sanctification. The
spring and strength of his affection is entirely apart
from us, and independent of any thing like goodness
in ourselves. His love cannot know increase nor
diminution. He cannot welcome us with any stronger
affection to heaven, than that with which he now
welcomes us to the throne of grace. The words of
this verse are but another mode of expressing the
greatness of the love of Christ, and his readiness to
receive us, as a motive for our coming with "boldness
to the throne of grace, that we may obtain mercy
and find grace to help in time of need." Heb. iv. 16.
That love is represented as passing knowledge. Eph.
iii. 19. If it passeth knowledge, it must pass expression; and therefore such language as this must be
viewed as an effort for conveying, though yet in a
very dim way, all that can now be known of this glorious and incomprehensible truth. The person whose
heart has been completely carried away with the
loveliness of a loved one, cannot be so delighted to
welcome her, as Jesus is to welcome us to his bosom
in prayer. He would therefore have us to leave the
attractions of this dangerous and ensnaring world,

for enjoying his society at the mercy-seat; and to come not with the hesitancy of Esther, but with the feeling that he loves us thus intensely.

Ver. 10.—How fair is thy love, my sister, my spouse! how much better is thy love than wine! and the smell of thine ointments than all spices!

The words give a fourth reason for encouraging us to come to Jesus in prayer—the beauty and delightfulness to him of the graces of piety in the believer's heart. Among these excellences, the first mentioned is love. The reason of this may be readily understood from 1 Cor. xiii. Moral beauty is more glorious and admirable than material beauty. The former is the life, the perfection of the latter. Of moral excellence, love is the crown. Love is the glory of the character of God, the sum of his perfections. Love in the believing soul is the image of the love of God, new-forming there by the Holy Spirit. Well might Jesus therefore say, that to him this love is beautiful. This is the beauty of all other beauties, the reflection of his own divine image. The gem is none the less beautiful, none the less valuable, though not set, though in the mine; and this love may be still in its incipient state in the heart, imbedded amid the corruption of our many infirmities, not yet set in the spiritual body, and nevertheless be beautiful in the eyes of Jesus. This love will not be more beautiful hereafter, even in heaven, than it is now. It may there shine with greater brilliancy, not with greater attractiveness. Overwhelmed with the sense of unworthiness, we feel that in us, that is, in our flesh, dwelleth no good thing, Rom. vii. 18; and can only say that amid these corruptions, we see nothing of a redeeming character but love to Christ, while even this is frail and inconstant, borne down too often by predominating infirmities. "Lord, thou knowest all things: thou knowest that I love thee." But on this love, even thus in its incipient state, Jesus looks with delight. This makes our society pleasant to him. Even where persons have no bodily beauty, loveliness of heart and manners will make us forget even their ugliness, and cause us to take more pleasure in their company, than we could do, if they had beauty without loveliness. Looking not on the outward appearance, but on the heart, our Lord welcomes to his presence and companionship all who possess this love. He says, "How much better is this love than wine?" that is, 'None can tell how much more delightful to me than the most exquisite enjoyments of sense, is this love shed abroad in thy heart by the Holy Spirit.' See chap i. 2. Not only is our love thus agreeable to him; equally so are all those graces which are the fruit of the Spirit. Gal. v. 22; Eph. v. 9. How much better "the smell of thine ointments than all spices!" See chap. i. 3. It is indeed hard for us, oppressed as the pious heart ever is with the sense of deep, deep unworthiness, to realize that Jesus will receive us with open arms in prayer. But how can we hesitate when he encourages us by such representations as that contained in this verse? The impression produced on him by these graces of holiness, is more grateful than to us is the combined fragrance of all spices.

VER. 11.—Thy lips, O my spouse, drop as the honey-comb: honey and milk are under thy tongue.

Here he would encourage us in communion with him by assuring us how pleasant to his heart is our language of prayer and praise. This comparison of agreeable speech to honey is very common in ancient profane authors, as well as in the Scriptures. "Pleasant words are as an honey-comb, sweet to the soul and health to the bones." Prov. xvi. 24; v. 3. "How sweet are thy words unto my taste! yea, sweeter than honey to my mouth." Ps. cxix. 103. "More to be desired are they than gold, yea, than much fine gold: sweeter also than honey and the honey-comb." Ps. xix. 10. Hence Xenophon was called the Attic bee; and in consequence of the beauty of the writings of Plato, a swarm of bees was fabled to have settled on his lips when an infant. Speaking of his ode, Pindar says, towards its conclusion,

> "Amid the Æolian blasts of flutes,
> This honey mixed with milk I send."

Thus Homer says of Nestor,

> "Words sweeter from his tongue than honey flowed."

An oriental poet mentions,

> "Those ruby lips whence honied sweets distil."

And again, "O grant me a draught of honey from the lotos of thy mouth."

Thus Milton's description of Belial:

> His tongue
> "Dropped manna, and could make the worse appear
> The better reason."

While the poison of asps is under the lips of the ungodly, Rom. iii. 13, honey and milk are under the tongue of the spouse. So Theocritus,

> "More sweet her lips than milk in luscious rills,
> Lips, whence pure honey, as she speaks, distils."

Nothing could express to the ancients more strongly than such comparisons, the idea of speech, sweet, pleasant, and captivating. The Holy Spirit would therefore assure us by this verse, that to Jesus no language, not even the highest praise of unfallen angels, is more delightful than the words of repentance, faith, prayer, and praise, offered at the mercy-seat by the contrite heart. Our Lord himself is included when it is said, "Joy shall be in heaven over one sinner that repenteth, more than over ninety and nine just persons, which need no repentance." Luke xv. 7. See Song ii. 14. He sees a fountain of this excellent discourse under the tongue. Out of the abundance of the heart the mouth speaketh; and this language of holiness from the lips of the redeemed can never fail, when the Holy Spirit is in the heart a well of water springing up into everlasting life. No music is richer, none more melodious, none more pleasing, than a chorus of infant voices in Jesus' praise; and we can readily see with what pleasure the hosts of heaven, and chief among them, our Lord, must hearken to the pious utterances of those who are now in this world, in the infancy of their spiritual being and eternal life.

And the smell of thy garments is like the smell of Lebanon.

That is, 'Come without hesitation to meet me in prayer, because thou mayest be assured, that nothing, not even the fragrance of Lebanon, can be more grateful to the human senses than is thy presence to me.' See ver. 6. Musæus speaks of "the heights of odorous Lebanon." Lebanon abounded in odoriferous trees of various kinds, from which fragrant gums were extracted, especially frankincense. Maundrell says, "It is clothed in fragrant greens from top to bottom." Its wine had a peculiar fragrance: "The scent thereof shall be as the wine of Lebanon." Hos. xiv. 7. On account of its fragrance, the wood of the cedars of Lebanon was used for making precious pieces of furniture, especially chests for keeping rich garments. Odoriferous garments are thus mentioned in the Odyssey, lib. xxi. 52; and Calypso gave such to Ulysses, lib. v. 264. Speaking of an individual, Moschus says,

> "Whose heavenly fragrance e'en afar exceeds
> The odours breathing from the flowery meads."

Hence the Psalmist, "All thy garments smell of myrrh, aloes, and cassia, out of the ivory palaces." And the patriarch "smelled the smell of his raiment, and blessed him, and said, See, the smell of my son is as the smell of a field which the Lord hath

blessed."* As in chap. i. 3, the perfume expressed
the loveliness of Jesus and the pleasantness of his

* The orientals endeavour to perfume their clothes in various ways. They sprinkle them with sweet scented oils,
extracted from spices, they fumigate them with the most
valuable incense or scented wood, and also sew the wood of
the aloe in their clothes. They are universally fond of having
their garments strongly perfumed; so much so, that Europeans
can scarcely bear the smell. The persons of the Assyrian
ladies are elegantly clothed, and scented with the richest oils
and perfumes; and the Jewish females did not yield to them
in the elegance of their dress, the beauty of their ornament,
and the fragrance of their essences. Such is Virgil's account
of Venus:

"Thus, as she turned away, with roseate hue
Her neck shone beauteous; and her locks bedewed
With perfume of ambrosia, richly breathed
Odours divine; graceful her flowing robe;
And in her gait the goddess true appeared."
—*Æneid*, i. 403.

With this portraiture of the bride in the Song, we may compare Homer's description of Juno:

"Self-closed, behind her shut the doors of gold.
Here first she bathes; and round her body pours
Soft oils of fragrance, and ambrosial showers:
The winds perfumed, the balmy gale convey
Thro' heaven, thro' earth, and all the aerial way:
Thus, while she breathed of heaven, with decent pride
Her artful hands the radiant tresses tied:
Part on her head in shining ringlets roll'd,
Part o'er her shoulders waved like melted gold.
Around her, next, a heavenly mantle flow'd,
That rich with Pallas' labour'd colours glow'd:
Large clasps of gold the foldings gather'd round,
A golden zone her swelling bosom bound.
Far-beaming pendants tremble in her ear,

society to us; in this verse the fragrance of Lebanon, than which they knew nothing of the kind having greater richness, freshness, and excellence, sets forth the very great agreeableness of the humble-hearted saint to our blessed Lord. How can we hesitate in prayer, when Jesus takes as much delight in our society as ever Jew could take in the dewy fragrance of Lebanon!

How animating are the motives thus set forth for encouraging us to dwell at the throne of grace and to persevere in prayer! They are touching and tender in the extreme. Urging us to arise and come away from earth, by the greatness of his affection, as illustrated in chap. iv. 1—5, he instructs us that in the meanwhile, before the dawning of glory, we may find him by prayer on the hill of frankincense, and encourages us to meet him there as often as possible; because, though unworthy in our own eyes, he sees in us, as attired in his righteousness, no spot, nothing but beauty; because this is the only place of safety amid the dangers and enemies of the world; because his heart is enraptured with affection for us; because our love, with its attending graces, is more beautiful to his contemplation than we can now conceive; be-

> Each gem illumined with a triple star.
> Then o'er her head she casts a veil more white
> Than new fall'n snow, and dazzling as the light.
> Last, her fair feet celestial sandals grace.
> Thus issuing radiant, with majestic pace,
> Forth from the dome th' imperial goddess moves."
> —*Iliad*, xiv. 168.

cause our language, in contrition, prayer, and praise, is his greatest delight; because our presence altogether is more agreeable to him, than to our senses such fragrance as was wafted from Lebanon. O what a welcome does then ever await us at the mercy-seat!

VER. 12.—A garden inclosed is my sister, my spouse; a spring shut up, a fountain sealed.

As a seventh reason for encouraging us to meet him at the throne of grace, he states that his delights in the soul of the believer is as great as what is felt by us in enjoying the most beautiful garden. Ver. 12—15. See notes, chap. viii. 13. Thus Isaiah says, "Ye shall be as a garden that hath no water," Isa. i. 30; and again, "Thou shalt be like a watered garden; and like a spring of water, whose waters fail not." Isa. lviii. 11. So Jeremiah—"Their soul shall be as a watered garden." Jer. xxxi. 12.* In Keats' Ode to Psyche, the spirit of the same illustration is adopted:

"Yes, I will be thy priest, and build a fane
    In some untrodden region of my mind,
Where branched thoughts, new-grown with pleasant pain,
    Instead of pines shall murmur in the wind:
Far, far around shall those dark-cluster'd trees
    Fledge the wild-ridged mountains steep by steep;

* "When a man dwells in love, the eyes of his wife are as fair as the light of heaven, she is a fountain sealed, and he can quench his thirst, and ease his cares, and lay his sorrow down upon her lap, and can retire home as to his sanctuary and refectory, and his gardens of sweetness and chaste refreshments."—*Jeremy Taylor's Sermons on Eph. v. 32, 33.*

And there by zephyrs, streams, and birds, and bees,
  The moss-lain Dryads shall be lull'd to sleep;
And in the midst of this wide quietness
A rosy sanctuary will I dress
With the wreathed trellis of a working brain,
  With buds, and bells, and stars without a name,
With all the gardener Fancy e'er could feign,
  Who breeding flowers, will never breed the same:
And there shall be for thee all soft delight
  That shadowy thought can win,
A bright torch, and a casement ope at night
  To let the true love in."

President Edwards says, "Holiness, as I then wrote down some of my contemplations on it, appeared to me to be of a sweet, pleasant, charming, serene, calm nature; which brought an inexpressible purity, brightness, peacefulness, and ravishment to the soul. In other words, that it made the soul like a field or garden of God, with all manner of pleasant flowers; all pleasant, delightful and undisturbed, enjoying a sweet calm, and the gentle, vivifying beams of the sun." Speaking of the church as a vine, the Psalmist says, "Why hast thou broken down her hedges, so that all they which pass by the way do pluck her?" In this passage, chaps. iv. 12—v. 1, there are four points brought out to view. 1. The holiness of the pious heart as set apart for God, ver. 12. 2. The heart thus hedged around by grace is occupied with the precious, odoriferous virtues of holiness, ver. 13—14, and by the Holy Spirit, who is within the soul as a fountain of water, John iv. 14—vii. 38, and whose influences are the very life and nourishment of these pious graces. Ver. 15. 3. The desire of the believer that his soul may be in readiness for the coming into our hearts of the beloved, by the Holy Spirit breathing on our graces and bringing out their fragrance. Ver. 16. 4. The consequence of this prayer—Jesus comes to dwell with us. Chap. v. 1. When keeping the soul thus guarded from the world, and against every one but Jesus, we enjoy the presence of the Spirit, and desire his operations in greater fulness—how great is our encouragement to prayer, in the assurance that even while we are yet asking, our Lord will come down into our souls, and take as much delight in our enlivened graces, as the beloved took in gathering the spices of the garden, and eating its precious fruits.

The Jewish gardens were generally hedged or walled, as indeed Josephus expressly states respecting the gardens near Jerusalem.* The idea set forth in these words, is the same with that in Ps. iv. 3—"Know that the Lord hath set apart him that is godly for himself." Hence the acknowledgment made by Satan concerning Job: "Hast thou not made an hedge about him, and about his house, and about all that he hath on every side." The seclusion of the soul

---

* Speaking of a garden represented in the tombs of Thebes and other parts of Egypt, Wilkinson says, "The one here introduced is shown to have been surrounded by an embattled wall, with a canal of water passing in front of it, connected with the river. The small kiosks, or summer-houses, shaded with trees, stood near the water, and overlooked beds of flowers."—Vol. ii. 144.

from the intrusion of the evil passions and evil spirits overrunning it in a state of nature, and the hedging of it around with the habits formed by Christian discipline, so that the virtues of piety may be undisturbed in their growth, is what the Scriptures really mean by sanctification. To sanctify, is to set apart from a common to a sacred use. In the East, wives are secluded with the greatest care from public gaze, for the company of their lords; and so far from looking on this restraint with disfavour, they seem to estimate the degree of their husband's affection by the watchfulness with which they are guarded. The most flattering epithet that can be applied to an eastern lady, is that of "the concealed treasure," "the guarded jewel," "the well-watched angel." The words, "a spring shut up, a fountain sealed," are a repetition of the idea in the foregoing part of the verse, expressing the sentiments of holy seclusion for Jesus, even more beautifully than does the garden enclosed. Sir John Chardin says, he has known springs locked up in divers parts of Asia on account of the scarcity of water. Among the Persians were fountains of which only the king and his eldest son might drink. Thus, says the Apostle, "Ye are Christ's." 1 Cor. iii. 23. No one has a right to our affections but Jesus. How entirely is the life of the Christian a hidden life; "hid with Christ in God;" hid from the world, as a spring shut up, so that they can neither see fully its excellence, nor reach it in such a way as to disturb or break it up at its source. The holy soul is a fountain of pious affections, shut up from the world, for the delight of him who has redeemed us with his blood, and sealed us with his Holy Spirit. The Spirit is the seal of the King of kings, set upon those spiritual fountains, holy hearts, in this wilderness, which are thereby shown to belong, not to the world, but to himself. The idea of holiness, as separation from earth and all things sinful, and as consecration to God, cannot be more neatly expressed, than by a garden hedged, a spring enclosed and sealed. Jesus will take delight in our society and welcome us to the throne of grace, according to the care with which our soul excludes all other affections, for the enjoyment of his love. This verse shows what the true saint is, or should be; and in its connection teaches that if we would enjoy the presence of Jesus in the heart, we must watch against the intrusion of sin. "Blessed are the pure in heart, for they shall see God." "If I regard iniquity in my heart, the Lord will not hear me." "Keep thy heart with all diligence, for out of it are the issues of life." Jesus takes delight in dwelling only in the soul that is a garden barred or hedged, a spring bolted, a fountain sealed. The same truth is expressed with even more strictness in the words, "Know ye not that ye are the temple of God, and that the Spirit of God dwelleth in you?" 1 Cor. iii. 16. Holiness requires that the soul be as exclusively devoted to God as the enclosed garden, or bolted spring, to its lord; or the temple, to him who dwelt between the cherubim. Over the door of the heart bolted against every one but Jesus, is written,

33*

"Holiness to the Lord." The dream of the heathen that each fountain had its divinity residing in it, is here realized. The Holy Spirit dwells in this fountain of the pious soul, and he is its guardian divinity.

VER. 13, 14.—Thy plants are an orchard of pomegranates, with pleasant fruits; camphire, with spikenard; spikenard and saffron; calamus and cinnamon, with all trees of frankincense; myrrh and aloes, with all the chief spices.

The three following verses give that with which this garden is occupied. The word rendered "thy plants" means not merely shoots and flowers, but any thing issuing, or springing, or sent out from another; and therefore includes every thing which is a product of the garden, or belonging thereto—the well of living waters with its streams, no less than the spikenard and all the chief spices. We understand the word "plants" to include all the things that follow to the end of ver. 15. The word "orchard" corresponds exactly to our word "paradise," and is of oriental origin, signifying the pleasure-gardens and parks, some with, others without, wild animals, around the residence of the Persian monarchs, planted with stately forest-trees and fruit-trees of every kind, well watered, and surrounded with a wall.* As mentioned

* "Behind these were the royal gardens, laid out in the most exquisite taste, and decorated with all that could gratify the eye, regale the ear, or satiate the most luxurious palate; the loveliest shade, the deepest verdure, grottoes of the most refreshing coolness, fruits of the most delicious flavour; cascades that never ceased to murmur, and music that never failed to delight."—*Maurice's Indian Antiquities*, i. 209.

by Xenophon, there was one of these belonging to
Cyrus the younger, at Celænæ in Phrygia, through
the middle of which ran the river Mæander. This in
the text is mentioned as such a park or pleasure-
ground, without the wild animals; and filled with
trees and shrubbery, with the most beautiful flowers, the most delightful fruits, and the richest fragrance.

The pomegranate, still common in Syria and Persia, is considered delicious by travellers, and is highly
prized. The bright and dark-green foliage of the
pomegranate, and its flowers of a crimson colour,
made it an object of desire in these gardens; while
its large reddish-coloured fruit, filled with numerous
seeds, each surrounded with juicy, pleasant-tasted
pulp, would make it valuable as a fruit, in warm
countries. See chap. iv. 3. With the pomegranate, thus mentioned for its beauty and sweetness, this
garden has the most precious fruits in general. Besides, there are all the choice aromatic trees and
shrubs—camphire and spikenard, spikenard and saffron; calamus and cinnamon, with trees of frankincense; myrrh and aloes, with all the chief spices.
See chap. i. 12, 14. Earth can show nothing to
man, more beautiful to the eye, no fruits more precious, no fragrance more delightful, than those combined in this paradise—a fitting representation of the
graces of holiness centring in the believing heart, and
making it a retreat where Jesus our Saviour loves to
make his abode.

VER. 15.—A fountain of gardens, a well of living waters, and streams from Lebanon.

In ver. 12 the "spring shut up" seems mentioned, like the "garden enclosed," for illustrating the idea of the holiness of the believer, or his separation and consecration to God; and to be entirely independent of the idea intended in this verse. Here is mentioned the source whence is derived the life and fragrance of the fruits and shrubbery of this garden. A fountain of gardens means a very copious fountain, sufficient for watering many gardens. This fountain was the best possible. Instead of a reservoir filled with rain water, as was often used, this pleasure-ground was enriched with a well or spring of running water, combining therewith streams, cool, refreshing, and fertilizing, as those coming from Lebanon. These make the gardens of Damascus so enchanting. Their refreshing coolness is mentioned by the prophet: "Will a man leave the snow of Lebanon, which cometh from the rock of the field?" Jer. xviii. 14. Maundrell says, "There is a very deep rupture in the side of Libanus, running at least seven hours' travel directly up into the mountain. It is on both sides exceedingly steep and high, clothed with fragrant greens from top to bottom, and everywhere refreshed with fountains falling down from the rocks in pleasant cascades. The streams all uniting at the bottom, make a full and rapid torrent, whose agreeable murmur is heard over the place, and adds no small pleasure to it." Says another traveller, "We came into pleasant groves, by delightful rivulets that arose from springs, that made so sweet a noise as to be admired by king Solomon." We cannot see that any light is thrown on the real significance of this passage by a detailed description of "The pools of Solomon," about six miles from Jerusalem, on the rout to Hebron.* This valley containing these pools,

* The following is from Maundrell: "This morning we went to see some remarkable places in the neighbourhood of Bethlehem. The first place that we directed our course to, was those famous fountains, pools, and gardens, about an hour and a quarter distant from Bethlehem, southward, said to have been the contrivance and delight of king Solomon. To these works and places of pleasure, that great prince is supposed to allude, Eccl. ii. 5, 6, where, among the other instances of his magnificence, he reckons up his gardens, and vineyards, and pools. As for the pools, they are three in number, lying in a row above each other, being so disposed that the waters of the uppermost may descend into the second, and those of the second into the third. Their figure is quadrangular; the breadth is the same in all, amounting to about ninety paces; in their length there is some difference between them, the first being about one hundred and sixty paces long, the second two hundred, the third two hundred and twenty. They are all lined with wall, and plastered, and contain a great depth of water. Close by the pools is a pleasant castle of modern structure; and at about the distance of one hundred and forty paces from them them is a fountain, from which, principally, they derive their waters. This the friars will have to be that sealed fountain, to which the holy spouse is compared, Cant. iv. 12, and, in confirmation of this opinion, they pretend a tradition, that king Solomon shut up these springs, and kept the door of them sealed with his signet, to the end that he might preserve the waters for his own drinking, in their natu ral freshness and purity. Nor was it difficult thus to secure them, they rising under ground, and having no avenue to

supposed the one referred to by Josephus, and mentioned by Maundrell, Hasselquist, and others, may be the site of the grounds described in the text, and has indeed got from Latin travellers the name of *Hortus Conclusus.* A modern, speaking of a monastery in the Levant, says, "There below my feet lay the convent garden, in all the fresh luxuriance of tropical vegetation. Tufts upon tufts of waving palms over-

them but by a little hole, like to the mouth of a narrow well. Through this hole you descend directly down, but not without some difficulty, for about four yards, and then arrive in a vaulted room, fifteen paces long, and eight broad. Joining to this is another room, of the same fashion, but somewhat less. Both these rooms are covered with handsome stone arches, very ancient, and perhaps the work of Solomon himself. Below the pool here runs down a narrow rocky valley, enclosed on both sides with high mountains. This the friars will have to be the enclosed garden alluded to in the same place of the Canticles before cited. What truth there may be in this conjecture, I cannot absolutely pronounce. As to the pools, it is probable enough that they may be the same with Solomon's; there not being the like store of excellent spring-water to be met with anywhere else throughout all Palestine."

Hasselquist thinks this might possibly be the garden noticed in the text. Mariti says, "Nature has still preserved its original fertility in this valley. Although but little cultivated, the soil still produces a tolerable supply of cotton and various kinds of grain; there are also fine plantations of fruit trees, affording the most juicy fruits in the country. Various flowers, and many fragrant plants, grow there naturally at all seasons, among which are thyme, rosemary, marjoram, salvius, persil, rue, ranunculuses, and anemones." Here may be found various rare plants not to be found elsewhere in Palestine, and which, as an old traveller suggests, may have been propagated from exotic plants which Solomon introduced into his gardens.

shadowed the immense succulent leaves of the banana, which in their turn rose out of thickets of the pomegranate, with its bright green leaves and its blossoms of that beautiful and vivid red which is excelled by few even of the most brilliant flowers of the East. These were contrasted with the deep green of the caroub or locust-tree; and the yellow apples of the lotus vied with the clusters of green limes with their sweet white flowers. Fair branches and flowers, exhaling rich perfume and bearing freshness in their very aspect, become more beautiful from their contrast to the dreary plains outside the convent walls; and this great difference was owing solely to there being a well of water in this spot, from which were constantly drawn the fertilizing streams which nourished the teeming vegetation of this garden."

More beautiful was this spring than that classic fountain whose green, wild margin, with dew-sprinkled mosses, grows undisturbed:

"Nor must the delicate waters sleep
  Prison'd in marble, bubbling from the base
  Of the cleft statue, with a gentle leap
The rill runs o'er, and round fern, flowers, and ivy creep
  Fantastically tangled: the green hills
  Are clothed with early blossoms, through the grass
  The silvery zephyr rustles, and the bills
Of summer birds sing welcome as ye pass;
  Flow'rs fresh in hue, and many in their class,
Implore the pausing step, and with their dyes
  Dance in the soft breeze in a fairy mass;
The sweetness of the violets' deep blue eyes
Kiss'd by the breath of heaven, seems colour'd by its skies."*

* Childe Harold, iv. 116.

This comparison is applied to the soul by Jesus himself: "The water that I shall give him, shall be in him a well of water springing up into everlasting life." John iv. 14. "This spake he of the Spirit, which they that believe on him should receive." John vii. 39. The fountain was the life of the garden; without this there could be no verdure, no growth, no flowers, no fragrance, no fruits, no refreshing shade. Trees not planted by these streams of water, had their leaf to wither, and brought forth no fruit. Ps. i. 3. Nothing could atone for the want of such a stream. Even so it is with the heart. The Holy Spirit is everything to our desolate and sinful souls. He is "as rivers of water in a dry place." Without his influences there can be no spiritual life, no fragrance of piety, no fruits of holiness. When his influences overflow from this hallowed fountain in the heart, every pious virtue thrives, this wilderness and solitary place is glad, and rejoices, and blossoms as the rose; and each grace of holiness becomes "as a tree planted by the waters, and spreadeth out her roots by the rivulet, and shall not see when heat cometh; but her leaf shall be green, and shall not be careful in the year of drought, neither shall cease from yielding fruit." Jer. xvii. 8. The Holy Spirit being thus the hidden spring of the life of holiness, Christian activity is as necessary for developing this life as exercise is for the growth of a child. Life and activity are inseparable. He who has enjoyed the Spirit, welling as a crystal fountain in his heart—

"His life hath flowed
From its mysterious urn a sacred stream,
In whose calm depth the beautiful and pure
Alone are mirror'd; which, though shapes of ill
May hover round its surface, glides in light,
And takes no shadow from them."*

These influences of the Holy Spirit are copious and overflowing; a fountain sufficient for many gardens; more healing to our blinded souls than the streams of Jordan to the leprous Naaman; giving that understanding which is a well-spring of wisdom to him that hath it; making the words of a man's mouth as deep waters, and the well-spring of wisdom as a flowing brook. Prov. xviii. 4. When a heathen could sing,

"Go to the silvery eddies
Of pure Castalia's spring,
And bathed in its pellucid waves
Thy temple offering bring;"†

we feel that much more shall we be fitted for the services of the heavenly sanctuary, by having our souls continually steeped in purer than Castalian dews by this perennial fountain of the Spirit, gushing forth in the heart, and bathing in its silvery streams the roots of all our virtues of holiness. And as Arethusa was fabled to have passed under the sea, and broken forth afresh in a distant island—so this fountain of the soul, passing unseen the sea of death, shall burst forth afresh beyond those gloomy waves, to flow with.

* Talfourd's Ion, act i., sc. 1.
† Euripides, Ion, 95.

34

perennial and pellucid streams in the heavenly paradise.

VER. 16.—Awake, O north wind; and come, thou south; blow upon my garden, that the spices thereof may flow out.

These words give another feature of the heart which may meet Jesus with confidence at the throne of grace. Such soul has been just represented as a garden, lovely in his eyes, filled with the precious plants of the graces of holiness, and watered with the perennial and refreshing streams of the Holy Spirit; here the heart is set forth as having the desire, and using the corresponding means, for being in a state as agreeable and acceptable as possible to the beloved. All those precious plants are not sufficient to picture the loveliness of this garden; fountains and rills must crown the whole. Now, also, cooling winds are introduced for making the abode in this pleasure-garden delightful, and scattering the balmy fragrance through its delightful retreats. The east wind is in Palestine generally withering and tempestuous; the west wind brings from the sea clouds of rain, or dark, damp air; the north wind is cooling and refreshing, its power being broken by the mountain-chain of Lebanon; the south wind, though hot, has its heat mitigated in the upland regions, and is never stormy. The north wind is called on to "arise," because it is more powerful and strong; the south wind to "come," as though it were the soft breathing zephyr. The north wind brought clear weather. "The north wind driveth away rain." Prov. xxv. 23. "Fair weather cometh out of the north." Job xxxvii. 22. Pliny says, that though cold and nipping, the north wind is the most wholesome wind that blows. The south wind was warm and moist. "Dost thou know, how thy garments are warm when he quieteth the earth by the south wind?" Job xxxvii. 17. And the oriental poet, "O gale, scented with sandal, who breathest love from the regions of the south, be propitious."* The bride here calls for the north wind, that thereby all clouds may be swept away, and the sky cleared; and for the south wind, that its genial influence might ripen the fruits of the garden, and draw forth the fragrance of the flowers. Thus Hafiz, as quoted by Dopke, "Send me with zephyrs, roses from thy cheek, that I may breathe the luscious fragrance of thy garden bloom."

The wind is on many accounts the best emblem of the Holy Spirit. Hence our Saviour says, "The wind bloweth where it listeth, and thou hearest the sound: so is every one that is born of the Spirit." John iii. 8. The identity of the Hebrew, Greek, and Latin words for wind, breath, and spirit, shows that the air has the nearest resemblance, of all created things, to the influence of the Holy Spirit, and is therefore a most appropriate illustration. The words of this verse are, then, a prayer that the heart may be prepared for the coming of Jesus, by the action of the Holy Spirit, like the north wind, sweeping away all gloom, error, unbelief, and mists of sin; and like the south wind, warming into vigorous life all the graces of holiness.

* Songs of Jayadeva.

W

To do this, is the prerogative of this sacred agent alone. Gloom overspreads the garden, and the flow of its spices is checked, not because the heavens above are changed, or the sun has ceased to shine, for these are as pure, and glorious, and life-giving as ever; but because clouds have arisen heavily, and intercept the genial influence from on high. Thus from the depths of that heart which in its natural state is like the troubled sea when it cannot rest, arise clouds that separate between us and our God; these influences the Holy Spirit removes by his power; and then, shines into our heart the light of the knowledge of the glory of God in the person of Jesus Christ;—then flows forth the fragrance of our holy virtues. After times of desertion, darkness, and decay, when the Spirit does thus clear the soul, and breathe thereon with more than the reviving power of the south wind, how delightfully is the holiness of the heart felt by all around, "as the smell of a field the Lord has blessed."

Let my beloved come into his garden, and eat his pleasant fruits.*

Having thus sought the preparation of the heart,

---

* With this may be compared the following from Theocritus:

"And now in due return, O heavenly born!
Whose honour'd name a thousand fanes adorn,
Arsinoe gladly pays the rites divine,
Rival of Helen, at Adonis' shrine;
All fruits she offers that ripe autumn yields,
The produce of the gardens, and the fields;
All herbs and plants which silver baskets hold;
And Syrian unguents flow from shells of gold,

the believer now prays that Jesus may enter there
and enjoy the fruits of holiness. Thus, in the Gitagovinda, the lovely Kadha is in like manner invited
to enter the garden or the embraces of her beloved:
"Enter, sweet Kadha, the bower graced with a bed
of asoca-leaves, the bower illumined with gay blossoms, the bower made cool and fragrant by gales from
the woods of Malaya." "Pleasant fruits," or fruits
of pleasantness, as in ver. 13, means all that are most
delicious of fruits. The fruits of the garden are the
products of the garden; and the fruits enjoyed by
Jesus in the believing soul are those virtues which are
there developed by the Holy Spirit; and the text
means that our Lord should enjoy them as really as
we enjoy the most delicious fruits by eating. Well
would it be for us, could we feel that the garden-spot
of Jesus in the whole universe, is the heart of the
saint; and the graces of the soul are to him a source
of more exquisite pleasure than to us are the most

With finest meal sweet paste the women make,
Oil, flowers, and honey mingling in the cake:
Earth and the air afford a large supply
Of animals that creep, and birds that fly.
Green bow'rs are built with dill sweet-smelling crown'd,
And little Cupids hover all around;
And as young nightingales their wings essay,
Skip here and there, and hop from spray to spray,
What heaps of golden vessels glittering bright!
What stores of ebon black, and ivory white!
In ivory carved large eagles seem to move,
And through the clouds bear Ganymede to Jove."
—*Idyl* xv. 109.

precious fruits of the choicest garden. How valuable would we then feel those graces to be, and with what care would we cherish and cultivate them for this blessed friend, not for self-gratulation or self-interest, not for the applause of the world, but for the approbation and love of our Lord.

CHAPTER V.

VER. 1.—I am come into my garden, my sister, my spouse: I have gathered my myrrh with my spice; I have eaten my honey-comb with my honey; I have drunk my wine with my milk: eat, O friends; drink, yea, drink abundantly, O beloved.

THIS verse shows how promptly the prayer in the foregoing verse was answered. It is the eighth reason for meeting Jesus in prayer with preparation of the heart; because he will then come into the soul by his Holy Spirit, and bring around us a host of angels rejoicing to be our guard. When the heart is thus prepared, and anxiously desires the presence of Christ, "It shall come to pass, that before they call I will answer; and while they are yet speaking I will hear." Isa. lxv. 24. The fact of the existence of such desires for him, is evidence of his being with us; as in this passage, in immediate connection with the request, he adds, "I have already come, &c." He was present in the heart, though his presence was not felt; as "when Jacob awaked out of his sleep, and said, Surely the Lord is in this place, and I knew it not;" and when

Jesus was present in the garden with Mary, and she knew it not. John xx. 14.

In the East, banquets are sometimes held in gardens; as Egmont and Heyman, when at the convent of Sinai, dined under the trees of the garden, with a number of the inmates, on one of their festival days. The ancients were in the habit of wearing chaplets of flowers on their heads at feasts. Thus in the book of Wisdom: "Let us fill ourselves with costly wine and ointments; and let no flower of the spring pass by us. Let us crown ourselves with rose-buds before they be withered." Chap. ii. 7. And in the Arabian Nights, a person is represented at Bagdad as buying myrtles, lilies, jessamine, and other fragrant flowers and plants, along with meat, wine, and fruit, as preparations for a repast. Milk and honey still form a luscious and common banquet among many Asiatic nations. Milk is mingled with wine for cooling the latter. Jael gave Sisera, when thirsty, milk to drink instead of water, as preferable; and Clemens Alexandrinus says, wine and milk is a very healthful and profitable mixture. Tibullus mentions "bowls of snow-white milk, mixed with wine." The words "my honey-comb with my honey," are possibly intended to express both the wild honey that was found dropping from trees, and that which was eaten in the comb and was consequently the most delicious. Gen. xliii. 11. In India, says Mr. Roberts, "the forests literally flow with honey; large combs may be seen hanging on the trees, as you pass along, full of honey." The same seems to have been the case formerly in Palestine. Here the beloved found the best honey in perfection, and both kinds, liquid and in the comb.*

The meaning of this verse, therefore, is, that the Lord Jesus comes into the heart prepared for him and desiring him, and draws from the enjoyment of the virtues blooming there, a pleasure that can be best illustrated to man by saying, it is like, in richness and exquisiteness, to the delight had in dwelling amid the fragrance, and feasting on the delicious fruits, of an oriental garden. The willingness of Jesus to answer prayer is set forth in many places of the Scriptures, but nowhere in language more encouraging than this. The idea is the same, and in expressions equally figurative, though not so much amplified as here, in John xiv. 23, "We will come unto him, and make our abode with him;" and in Rev. iii. 20, "I will come in to him, and will sup with him, and he with me." Unbelief, blunting the spiritual apprehension of the soul, keeps us from feeling the power of these passages, and gathering from them due consolation. And in the same tone are the words, "Thus saith the high and lofty One that inhabiteth eternity, whose name is Holy, I dwell in the high and holy place, with him also that is of a contrite and humble spirit." Isa. lvii. 15. God is indeed everywhere present, but he is said to dwell in the places where his presence is

---

* "Honey was of far more importance formerly than it is now. There was no sugar, and honey had to supply its place, besides being eaten in its primary state. Vast quantities of it must, therefore, have been consumed; and the importance assigned to it in Scripture becomes intelligible."—*Kitto.*

manifested in brighter displays of his glory. Size of place, greatness of extent or space, is not requisite for a habitation for him. In comparison with him the grandest world and the most obscure retreat, the most widely extended garden and the contracted limits of the human soul, are equally mere spots; in his sight, the dimensions of the temple on mount Moriah, and of the heart which is a temple for the habitation of God through the Spirit, are marked by no difference worthy of notice. Of all other places, the redeemed soul was especially created for a shrine in which may shine forth the divine glory; and hence, when that glory is thus manifested in the heart, there God is said to dwell. The idea of a banquet and of feasting on the most delicious fruits, as in this verse, is added for illustrating to our comprehension the exceedingly great delight Jesus has in dwelling in such soul and enjoying its graces of holiness, thankfulness, and praise: as we say of the society of a cherished friend, his company was a feast, so the same mode of expression is used here. Even this delight does he take in answering the prayer of his people and manifesting his presence in their soul, when they have sought the preparation of the heart, and are awaiting him in humble faith. And when by his Holy Spirit thus bringing us into union with him by pervading and enlivening our affections, we feel his presence, how truly may he be said to be feeding on the fruits of this spiritual garden; and how deep our tranquil, heavenly enjoyment.

"Eat, O friends; drink, yea, drink abundantly, O

beloved." These words, spoken by the bridegroom to his attendants, express the wish indulged by Jesus to have his own pleasure shared by others, here called "beloved ones." The angels and the heavenly host take a deep interest in redemption; there is joy in heaven among the angels of God over one sinner that repenteth; into these things the angels desire to look. They sang together and shouted for joy when the corner-stone of the earth was laid; they announced his coming at Bethlehem; they attended him at his resurrection and at his ascension; and when the Son of man shall come in his glory, all the holy angels shall be with him. Through all our pilgrimage, these are ministering spirits sent forth to minister for them who shall be heirs of salvation; and at death the soul is carried by the angels to Abraham's bosom. Such being the case, it is not strange that they should be represented as attending Jesus in his visits to the believing soul, and as being allowed to share with him the delight had in hovering around, contemplating and blessing those whose hearts are a sacred spot, a garden enclosed of the King of kings, filled with the fruits of those holy virtues which are the choicest plants in the universe of God. The fellows or associates in the work of redemption, above whom Jesus is anointed with the oil of gladness, include the angels of heaven. The words "drink, yea, drink abundantly," are precisely the same in the Hebrew, with those rendered "they drank and were merry with him," in Gen. xliii. 34. The latter means, to drink to the full, to hilarity. This kind of expression is common in the East—as in the following passage, quoted by Sir W. Jones: "They who walk in the true path are drowned in the sea of mysterious adoration, they are inebriated with the melody of amorous complaints." They simply mean that these holy angels have the privilege of sharing with him his delight in the sanctified soul. They attend on the saints and derive exquisite pleasure from hovering around us by the permission and command of our Lord. By meeting Jesus in prayer, among other motives here mentioned for encouraging us so to do, we have this as the crowning blessing, that there, on the mountain of myrrh and hill of frankincense, we have coming down into our heart the heavenly Shechinah, Jesus, through his Holy Spirit, encompassed with a crown-like host of angels. How great a glory and protection! Well may prayer be said to secure for us a wall of fire round about us, and a glory in our midst. "The angelic host of the Lord encampeth round about them that fear him, and delivereth them." The case of Elisha was but what is enjoyed by the humblest believer now, when, in the midst of perils, "behold the mountain was full of horses and chariots of fire round about Elisha." 2 Kings vi. 17. Thus, for his encouragement, Jacob was permitted to have a view of the angelic bands which, though unseen, had been around him when "the angels of God met him; and when Jacob saw them he said, This is God's host." Gen. xxxii. 1. It was while Daniel was praying, that Gabriel, being caused to fly swiftly, came to him with a gracious promise, and the assurance that he was

greatly beloved. Dan. ix. 20. The bereaved disciples
were all with one accord in prayer, when the Holy
Spirit came with a sound from heaven as of a rushing
mighty wind. While prayer was made without ceasing of the church unto God for Peter, the angel of
the Lord appeared to him, and brought him forth
from prison. And " when Solomon had made an end
of praying, the fire came down from heaven, and consumed the burnt-offering and the sacrifices; and the
glory of the Lord filled the house." 2 Chron. vii. 1.
And it was, when Jesus our forerunner had gone up
into a mountain to pray, and as he prayed, that he
was transfigured, and his face did shine as the sun,
and his raiment was white as the light; and a bright
cloud, the same that had dwelt between the cherubim,
overshadowed them; and behold, the voice of God
out of the cloud. Matt. xvii. 1; Luke ix. 28.

How glorious was the sight in Eden, when amid the
luxuriance of Paradise, man, just created, was overshadowed by the Shechinah, the dwelling-place of
God; and around was gathered the innumerable company of angels—the Lord and all his attendants
rejoicing in the work of his hands. The same Sovereign and his divine attendants take no less interest
now in man formed anew by redemption; and hover
over him with equal glory. The idea here may be
best got by contemplating a beautiful, well-watered
garden, Num. xxiv. 5, 6, as described in chap. iv.
12—15; or even like Eden, with the cloud that
rested over the mercy-seat, dwelling in it as its light
and glory; while an innumerable company of angels

are gathered around in admiration and praise. And when, after seasons of withdrawal, in prayer, Jesus comes again into the garden of our hearts, it is as the coming down of the cloud of glory into the midst of Paradise to overshadow and enlighten it, surrounded by the host of his holy angels.

How encouraging are the motives here brought together for inclining us to prayer! How delightfully are they developed one after another, till ending in a blaze of glory, in the assurance that by faithful prayer we receive Jesus to dwell in our hearts by the Shechinah of his Spirit, and are encompassed by a guardian host of angels!

VER. 2.—I sleep, but my heart waketh.

This passage, to the end of ver. 8, illustrates the exercises of the soul in a time of spiritual sloth and decay. After thus unfolding to us his love, he lets us, as in this passage, see our depravity and indifference. Our religious life consists of a series of revivals and of withdrawals by Jesus, for calling into exercise and putting to the test our graces. When under the influence of first love, we determine never to forget the Saviour, and think the thing almost impossible. After some experience of the deceitfulness of the heart, when at some subsequent period we have had our souls restored and made to lie down in green pastures, beside the still waters, we resolve again to be faithful in close adherence to our Lord, under the impression, that with our present knowledge of the

workings of sin, and the glorious displays made to us
of the loveliness of Christ, and of his love towards us
personally, we shall now at length persevere; but we
soon find to our sorrow, that, left to ourselves, we are
as unsteady and unfaithful as ever. It is surprising
how quickly coldness will succeed great religious
fervour. To the experienced believer it will not appear strange, that this divine allegory should bring
this representation of indifference to the beloved into
such immediate connection with the remarkable expressions of Jesus' love contained in the foregoing
chapter. Where is the Christian who has not found
the truth of this in his own experience? The three
chosen disciples were overcome with lethargy even on
the mount of transfiguration; and immediately after
the first affecting sacrament, they not only fell asleep
in Gethsemane, but all forsook Jesus and fled; while
Peter added thereto a denial of his Lord, with profane swearing. While the bridegroom tarried, even
the wise virgins with oil in their lamps, slumbered
and slept. After endearing manifestations of Jesus'
love, how soon do we find ourselves falling into spiritual slumber—often, like the disciples on the mount,
under the full light of the presence of the Holy Spirit.
And after periods of revival, in the same way will
churches speedily show signs of sinking down into
former coldness.

A Persian poet has almost exactly the same image:
"Last night, my eyes being closed in sleep, but my
good genius awake, the whole night, the live-long
night, the image of my beloved was the companion of

my soul."* We see no necessity for supposing, with some, that Anacreon must have got from the Song the hint of his ode, in which Love is represented as standing at his door at midnight, and begging for admittance, lost in the dark, chilled, and drenched with the dews. Cicero speaks of persons "semisomni," half asleep, beholding the trite farces; and Seneca reflects on some who lay half asleep until mid-day. This phrase is sometimes used to express a sluggish, slothful man, also by Plautus. Here it implies that while the body was overcome with drowsiness, and thus insensible to surrounding things, the heart was unaffected, and still vigorous in its affections, though borne down and controlled by the action of the body. The medium of activity for the mind is through the body; hence, when the body is asleep, though the heart be awake, the individual is in a state of inactivity which cannot be broken till the body is

* Mr. Lane gives the following from odes of the Moslems, sung at their religious festivals. Its likeness to this part of the Song is obvious:

"O gazelle, from among the gazelles of El-Yemen!
I am thy slave without cost;
The phantom of thy form visited me in my slumber:
I said, 'O phantom of slumber, who sent thee?'
He said, 'He sent me whom thou knowest;
He whom love occupies thee.'
The beloved of my heart visited me in the darkness of the night:
I stood to show him honour until he sat down.
I said, 'O thou, my petition and all my desire!
Hast thou come at midnight and not feared the watchman?'
He said to me, 'I feared; but, however, love
Had taken from me my soul and my breath.'"

aroused. The spiritual import of these words is therefore well expressed by John Owen: "Woful sloth
and negligence are apt to prevail in us, in our meditations on heavenly things. 'Though our hearts wake'
in a valuation of Christ, his love, and his grace, yet
we sleep as unto the due exercise of faith and love
towards him. Let them take heed of their aptness to
forget endearing manifestations of special love. When
God at any time draws nigh unto a soul by his Spirit
in his word, with gracious words of peace and love,
giving a sense of his kindness upon the heart by the
Holy Ghost, so that it is filled with joy unspeakable
and glorious thereon; for this soul, upon a temptation,
a diversion, or by mere carelessness and neglect,
which oftentimes falls out, to suffer this sense of love
to be, as it were, obliterated, and so to lose that
influencing efficacy unto obedience which it is accom-
panied withal; this also is full of unkindness. An
account hereof we have in Cant. v. 1—6."*

---

* Madame Guyon speaks of the early part of her residence
at Gex as being characterized by sweet and happy peace of
mind, and the most intimate communion with God. She
mentions, that a number of times she awoke at midnight, with
such a presence and possession of God in her soul that she
could no longer sleep, but arose and spent hours in prayer and
praise, and divine communion. "I felt, even in my sleep, a
singular possession of God. He loved me so much that he
seemed to pervade my being, at a time when I could be only
imperfectly conscious of his presence. My sleep is sometimes
broken—a sort of half sleep—but my soul seems to be awake
enough to know God, when it is hardly capable of knowing
any thing else."—*Life by Upham*, vol. i. 261.

It is the voice of my beloved that knocketh, saying, Open to me, my sister, my love, my dove, my undefiled: for my head is filled with dew, and my locks with the drops of the night.

Our view of the nature of the Song makes it unnecessary for us to say anything in reply to those who view this whole passage as a narrative of what happened in a dream. These incidents, like the supposable incidents of allegories in general, are grouped together for the mere purpose of illustrating certain points of religious experience. This is done with remarkable beauty and delicacy, by this picture showing how a female treated a friend standing in the relation to her of a husband and a brother, as noted, chap. iv. 9, when he sued for admittance at night after a temporary absence. The connection seems to be, When I was sleeping, but my heart waking and intent on my friend, behold the voice of my beloved was heard knocking at the door, and saying, "Open to me, &c." The former clause expressed the condition of the soul sunk down in spiritual drowsiness, sloth, and inaction. This sets forth the tenderness of Jesus in trying to rouse us from our slumbers, and have us to enjoy his society. How multiplied and tender are his terms of endearment—My sister, my beloved female friend, my dove, my perfect one. Chap. iv. 7. The word "perfect one," says Dopke, "does not mean physical beauty, as Klenker thinks, but what we express by, my angel, a pure innocent virgin." A glance will show that while these epithets are of unsurpassed tenderness, they

35*

are used as though with scrupulous care for guarding against the indelicate ideas some have tried to force from this passage. It might be thought that such affecting appeals would have moved in an instant the bride to welcome him with open arms. But to these he adds the fact of his being damp and chilly from the dew, which was very copious, especially in the latter part of the spring and the beginning of autumn. Maundrell says, "We were instructed by experience what the Psalmist means by the dew of Hermon, our tents being as wet with it as if it had rained all night." "My head is filled with dew, and my locks with the drops of the night." Could it be thought possible that such an appeal would be unsuccessful? There is a twofold reference—to his tender love for her, and to his condition as houseless, chilled, wet, and without a place of rest for the night.

Thus tenderly does Jesus appeal to us, for rousing us from our spiritual apathy and slumbers. He is all tenderness. Concerning all his dealings, we must say, "Thy gentleness hath made me great." Ps. xviii. 35. It is a sad evidence of the strength of our corruptions, that after such displays of his love, we should ever sink down into indifference. Even with grace in the soul, with the heart awake, we find ourselves falling asleep, borne down by the business of life, the charms of the world, or the infirmities of the flesh. This condition is one of outward comfort; every thing around us is pleasant, as when reposing at night on our bed; and we are feeling the dangers incurred by the Christian through prosperity. Had the spouse been at this time suffering from pain or fear, so as to be incapable of sleep, and to feel the need of the presence and protection of the beloved, he would have found her watching for his return, and would not have been obliged thus to sue for admission. At such times, in our heartless indifference, how tenderly does he try to regain and rouse our love. What tenderness was there in the look he turned on backsliding Peter; and also in the words, "Simon, son of Jonas, lovest thou me." It might be supposed that the simple words, "Behold, I stand at the door and knock," would be enough to make us leap from our spiritual slumbers, without such subduing language as is here used.

VER. 3.—I have put off my coat; how shall I put it on? I have washed my feet; how shall I defile them?"

These words mean, that as the bride had retired to rest, she could not put herself to the trouble of arising, even to let in the beloved. The bath is mentioned in the Odyssey, in connection with retiring:

> "Give him the bath, arrange his couch with rugs
> Of warmth and costliness, and linen soft,
> There to await the golden-throned morn."

As Lady Montague assures us, the houses of the great ladies are kept clean with as much nicety as those of Holland, this pretence must appear still more frivolous. Taken as an illustration of the nature of the excuses formed by the soul for neglecting to receive Jesus at times of spiritual lethargy, these words are true and instructive. To us, it would

x

seem impossible that the spouse could indulge or give such a reason. Yet the thing signified hereby has happened, how often, in our own experience. When, in our indifference to him, Jesus has stood near and allured by the tenderest influences, how often have we allowed personal ease, worldly pleasure, business, and indeed sheer indolence, to make us indifferent to his tenderness, and cause us to allow him to remain suing for admission to our hearts. The most trivial thing is enough to keep us from running to meet him in the duty of secret prayer, of the social meeting, of scripture-study and self-examination, of attending in the sanctuary, of giving to the cause of benevolence, of co-operating in Christian activity, of ministering to the necessity of saints. The same truth is illustrated in the conduct of those bidden to the supper, when "they all with one consent began to make excuse." Luke xiv. 18.

VER. 4.—My beloved put in his hand by the hole of the door, and my bowels were moved for him.

On the whole, the best explanation of the first clause of this verse, seems to us that which may be got from a statement of Wilkinson, taken with one in the "Mission of Inquiry to the Jews." "The folding doors had bolts in the centre; a bar was placed across from one wall to the other; and in many instances wooden locks secured them by passing over the centre, at the junction of the two folds. These locks were probably on the principle of those now used in Egypt, which are of wood, and are opened by a key furnished

with several fixed pins, answering to a similar number, that fall down into the hollow moveable tongue,
into which the key is introduced when they fasten or
open the lock." "He showed us the key of his cot-
tage, commonly used for the door, which is nothing
more than a piece of wood with pegs fastened in it,
corresponding to small holes in a wooden bolt within.
It is put through a hole in the door, and draws the
bolt in a very simple manner. The large opening
through which the key is introduced, illustrates these
words in the Song." The words, "put in his hand
by the hole of the door," we prefer reading, "withdrew his hand from the hole of the door." This,
perhaps, is more strictly the meaning of the Hebrew,
and gives a sufficient reason for her rising at that
particular moment for opening the door to him. He
might have removed the bolt and entered without her
assistance; but after having put his hand through the
aperture and made a movement towards opening, finding her still untouched by his very tender appeal,
and treating him with indifference, he stopped, withdrew his hand, and departed. This roused her from
her lethargy, and brought her to her senses. She
had an ardent affection for the beloved, notwithstanding this exhibition of indifference. With the thought
of his tenderness and her own unkindness flashing on
her mind, the idea of losing his society, and having
him to remain longer under the chilling dews, touched
her heart, and roused into full vigour all her dormant
love.

In this state of apathy, Jesus makes attempts for

gaining admission to our hearts. The beloved did more than merely address the bride in endearing terms; he tried to open the door. Our Saviour not only "speaks to the heart of Jerusalem," but tries to unbar the entrance to the soul, that he may come in and sup with us, and take up there his abode. At times when, though the heart feels the value of Christ, faith and love, with their corresponding activity in his service, are slumbering, we find Jesus making efforts to arouse us by moving sweetly on the heart with his Holy Spirit, and by various gracious acts of his providence. Repeatedly may we have felt an influence on the heart, we could not tell how, or whence, surprising us in our coldness, coming even without our prayers, warming our affections, making us feel greater interest in spiritual things, and causing us to be sensible that it was indeed Jesus. He had truly come unsought. We were still in our slumbers, even yet hardly enough awake to feel the force of his whispers of love, so beautifully though inadequately shadowed forth by this touching language of the beloved. Circumstances of ease around us, gloom on the mind, drowsiness on the heart, made us reluctant to shake off our lethargy, and arise to give him a cordial welcome. We were precisely in the condition of a person partially aroused from sleep. His appeals failed to make a successful impression; and we were satisfied to quiet conscience with the most frivolous excuses. At length the influence felt moving on the heart began to subside; and the soul, instead of passing on to such full measures of the

Holy Spirit as had been enjoyed in the presence of Jesus, found the light of his countenance withdrawing, spiritual impressions growing fainter, and the affections settling down into deeper torpor and gloom. Symptoms of his withdrawal began first to bring us to our senses. The fear of losing one who had so loved us, and had just been speaking to us so tenderly, moved our hearts towards him, and made us rise to give him a welcome. The three following truths are therefore embodied in this verse:—when we are in a state of spiritual coldness and indifference, Jesus often takes steps for arousing us from our lethargy, and gaining admittance to our hearts; continued neglect on our part will lead him to stop these exertions and withdraw; then when he is withdrawing do we, frequently, first awake to a sense of the desirableness of his presence, and the value of his love.

VER. 5.—I rose up to open to my beloved; and my hands dropped with myrrh, and my fingers with sweet-smelling myrrh, upon the handles of the lock.

There is an interpretation of this verse which seems to us incorrect, and to have been suggested by a Roman custom:

> "With tears, the ling'ring lover at the door
> Hangs flowery wreaths, and with perfume bedews
> The threshold, and impresses many a kiss."*

With this the idea would be, that the beloved had poured liquid myrrh profusely on the handle of the bolt or lock, and this it was that perfumed the hand of the spouse. But the more reasonable view is, that

* Lucretius, iv. 1171.

in her room were standing, according to the custom
of the times, vases of perfumes as well as other presents, such as eastern ladies prepare for welcoming
their lovers: as in Hafiz,

> "For me the angel of my heart prepares
> Chaplets and unguents breathing fragrant airs."

With this compare Prov. vii. 17. In climates so warm
as to keep persons almost constantly in a state of
sensible perspiration, it is found a great comfort to
have the palms of the hands and the soles of the feet
in a comparatively dry state, particularly as to the
hands, which would otherwise moisten whatever they
handled. Perfumes, as mentioned by Pliny, were
placed on the back of the hand as the coolest part of
the body, and as causing their fragrance to exhale
with greatest richness.* The free use of odours by
oriental ladies in meeting their loved ones, is mentioned in Esther, chap. ii. 12. Now in rising to meet
her beloved, the spouse made use of these perfumes;
and according to the usual custom, poured of them
on the back of the hands, perhaps the more freely
from her anxiety and haste; this perfume, thus so
liberally used, bedewed the handles of the lock with
its precious drops. The word "sweet smelling,"
means liquid, or that which has wept drop by drop,
tear-like, from the tree, and is consequently most precious. To use such perfume, and thus liberally, was

---

* "He was making his toilet for the day; and his hands
were bedewed with the perfumes which his valets-de-chambre
had poured upon them."—*Lamartine's Restoration of Monar-
chy in France,* vol. ii. 195.

the most palpable proof a bride could give her lover, of welcoming his presence. Hence, after the indifference of the spouse, as she wished, on awaking to a sense of her unkindness, to make the beloved feel how cheerfully she received him, she naturally used her very best perfume, and that very freely, so much so that it dropped on the handle of the bolt. For showing her love, there came to Jesus a woman having an alabaster box of very precious ointment. The text does then represent the anxiety of the soul, when awaked to a sense of the unkindness and guilt of its spiritual sloth, to meet Jesus with every possible demonstration of welcome and affection. We wish to make amends for past ingratitude and indolence. In the case illustrated by the spouse, the believer has the influences of the Holy Spirit, the liquid myrrh, resting sometimes even richly on his heart. Without these, there can be no earnest seeking after Jesus. '

VER. 6.—I opened to my beloved; but my beloved had withdrawn himself, and was gone: my soul failed when he spake: I sought him, but I could not find him; I called him, but he gave me no answer.

At length, coming with a desire to give him a cordial welcome, the spouse opened the door for the beloved, but found that he had turned away, was gone. In the words, "my soul failed when he spake," we read the three latter, literally, 'because of his speaking,' or 'after his speaking.' Such may be the force of the preposition here used with the infinitive. The meaning would then be, not that her soul fainted, or she was overcome while he was speaking, but after, and in consequence of what he had said. Finding him gone, she called to mind his tender, affecting language, and was so overcome thereby as to be almost unmanned. Recovering herself, she began to seek him, but could not find him; she called, but got no answer.

It is dangerous for us to hesitate and delay when Jesus shows willingness to enter the soul again by his Holy Spirit. When he has been kind enough to seek us out in our decay, we should run with eagerness to meet him at the first intimation of his approach. Neglect to do so, leads to his withdrawal, and lays up for us periods of toil, sorrow, desertion, and humiliation. Grace in the heart may keep our affections vigorous; he will not gratify us with sensible proofs of his presence. The recollection of his kindness and his melting words of love during our period of sloth, affects us very deeply; causes our soul to fail; and arouses us to great exertions in seeking him for repairing the consequences of our neglect. By this carnal security and sloth, the believer has lost very many periods of delightful communion with Jesus, and been obliged to encounter painful difficulties, with seasons of darkness, reproach, and persecution.

Ver. 7.—The watchmen that went about the city found me, they smote me, they wounded me; the keepers of the walls took away my veil from me.

The spouse had before sought the beloved by night in the streets, but under different circumstances. See chap. iii. 2, 3. In the former case, there was no treating of the beloved with neglect; and as she sought him from the impulse of deep affection, she found him almost immediately, without difficulty; here as the result of her neglect she encounters much unpleasantness and trouble. The watchmen treated her in an unworthy manner. Watchmen were customarily employed in Jerusalem; and their post was at the gates; at night watchmen were accustomed to perambulate the city. These represent the ministers of the Church, with whom the believer is naturally brought in contact, when suffering under spiritual desertion, and seeking Jesus in times of darkness and trial.

The watchmen viewed the spouse as a bad woman; for females were not allowed to go about the streets in the night in common. They smote her, wounded her, and took away her veil: the last is the greatest indignity that can be offered to an oriental lady. The meaning is, they did not recognize her claims to respectability; and treated her as one positively vicious. Her conduct, though not morally wrong, was unusual. As it was not customary for them to see a respectable female under such circumstances, they supposed no one could be reputable while acting thus. Hers was a manifestation of female devotion they had never yet seen. Christians animated by a holy zeal, under intense influences of the Holy Spirit, have often met with ill-treatment from their brethren, and even from the ministry, the watchmen of Zion who should help them in their search for the object of their affection, rather than treat them as destitute of suitable claims to be considered real lovers of Jesus. This disposition has not been confined to any one sect; it belongs to human nature, and has shown itself in men of every creed. Every pious exercise differing in vigour and degree from the current feeling of nominal Christians and the imaginary standard of particular churches, is viewed with suspicion, as distempered and spurious, as the offspring of fanaticism, however unmistakenly it may bear the marks of the Holy Spirit. In their fear of what is called fanaticism, some persons shun what are genuine religious affections. Many a poor soul, with a heart aching and burning to know more of Christ, has had its honest inquiries met with reproach or indifference. Hence, in every age, when spiritual decay has been prevalent, persons taking the lead in reviving evangelical religion have had to encounter ill-treatment and persecution. "Your brethren that hated you, that cast you out for my name's sake, said, Let the Lord be glorified: but he shall appear to your joy, and they shall be ashamed." Jesus himself was cast out from the synagogue; and, at last, put to death. Shall we mention Chrysostom, Luther? nay, the whole history of the church is an illustration. Thus was Lady Guyon treated in France; Edwards at Northampton; and the evangelical brethren of the present day, in Scotland. Every Christian communion has a general type of piety peculiar to itself; and many look with incredulity on any manifestation of holy affections of a kind at all different.

VER. 8.—I charge you, O daughters of Jerusalem, if ye find my beloved, that ye tell him, that I am sick of love.

See remarks on chap. ii. 5—7. Leaving the

watchmen who had ill-treated her, the spouse turns
to the daughters of Jerusalem as more congenial
friends. To them she opens her feelings; their interest she seeks to enlist. Thus the humble believer,
received with coldness and repulse by those high in
authority, turns away to find kindred spirits and
sympathizing hearts among unknown brethren of a
deeper religious experience.

We see here that holy love and holy joy do not
always exist together in equal degree. There may
be very much of the former during an absence of the
latter. The soul may be sick of love to Jesus, while
mourning the withdrawal of his presence, and struggling amid the darkness of temptation, obloquy, and
sorrow. Want of joy is no proof of the absence of
grace. A beloved friend may be as devotedly loved
when we are separated from him by distance and
struggling with difficulties, as when we are peacefully
enjoying his society. It were certainly unreasonable to doubt our love to him, or his love to us,
because necessary duties of life often separated us.
And in these hours when Jesus has left us, even
though through our own neglect, we may still be
comforted with the assurance of loving him, if we
persevere in anxiously seeking him, even amid darkness, suspicion, and trial. We must assuredly love
him, when able to adopt the words of Augustin,
"What shall I say? what shall I do? whither shall
I go? where shall I seek him? or when shall I find
him? whom shall I ask? who will tell my beloved
that I am sick of love?"

VER. 9.—What is thy beloved more than another beloved, O thou fairest among women? what is thy beloved
more than another beloved, that thou dost so charge us?

The daughters of Jerusalem seeing the beauty of
the spouse, knowing her character, and noticing her
very fervent love, are naturally led to ask her what
there is so peculiarly attractive in her beloved, what
are his excellences more than those of any other.
This inquiry prepares the way very fitly for the
beautiful illustration that follows of the loveliness of
Jesus. On the words "O thou fairest, &c." see
chap. i. 8. This question was put, not by foreigners,
but by the daughters of Jerusalem. And when real
Christians sometimes meet with those who have had
brighter views than themselves of the loveliness of
our Lord, they are ready to make the same inquiry,
to ask what we see in Christ to make us speak of him
with such fervour. Every person has some leading
object of affection, on which the heart is devotedly
set. For instance, the soldiers of Napoleon found
this object in their emperor; and should they put
this question, what must be the answer? What is
Christ Jesus, the beloved of the saint, more than
the beloved of those soldiers? Others have the heart
set on a cherished husband, wife, or child: what is
Christ more than these? Again, some, like the fair
youth Narcissus, who became enamoured with the
beauty of his own form seen in a pellucid fountain,
make self the idol of their hearts; others fix their
hearts on a heap of dust, called gold; while others in
love with the beautiful, entwine around a work of

imagination, a picture, or a statue, the warm affections of the heart. What is the beloved of the saint, Jesus, more than the beloved of these?

VER. 10.—My beloved is white and ruddy, the chiefest among ten thousand.

The principles guiding the interpretation of this whole passage to the close of the chapter, have been already explained. The nature of this description, and of the others like it in the Song, is precisely such as is seen in the exhibition of a piece of fine statuary or a beautiful painting. Should a person wish to represent to another the impression made on his own mind by gazing on the Apollo Belvidere, he must proceed on the same general principles here adopted, though his comparisons and language must be necessarily different. Persons of cultivated taste feel it is not improper to study finished works of art; and even in the present advanced stage of civilization, statues with little or no drapery are placed among the choicest productions of genius, and gazed on by thousands of both sexes, in company, without a blush or thought of any thing indelicate. Does any one deem it an offence against good taste, to exhibit or te study the Apollo, the Venus de Medici, or the Greek Slave? Those who are willing to admire such undying productions, cannot with any consistency find fault with these portraits of the Song. The difference between the two cases is simply this—what statues do through marble, the Song does through words. These delineations in the Song give a picture of a noble human form, around which is thrown every drapery necessary to add to the beauty and gratify the most delicate taste. In defence of these exquisite delineations of the beautiful in the human form, we are not willing to plead, as might be justly done, that at the time the Song was written, its language was, in point of modesty, far ahead of the most refined nations; and that when our translation of the Bible was made, these passages were far above the general tone of English literature. We take rather the higher and stronger ground, that these representations are in perfect accordance with the constitution of the human mind, and with principles universally admitted in the fine arts. The sculptor wishing to represent the perfect beauty of the human form, portrays it by a resemblance of man wrought in marble. The custom of mankind is to set off the body with dress and ornaments drawn from different parts of the world, such as gold, gems, silks, plumes, &c. Why, therefore, should it be thought strange that the Holy Spirit should draw together beautiful objects from different quarters, for representing the beauty of the body. Beautiful attire invests the body according to a natural custom; why should not the same right be granted concerning an ideal body around which is thrown the drapery of the beautiful thoughts here grouped together. When it is said that such and such parts of the body are thus and thus beautiful, the meaning is, there is thrown over a human form a drapery and ornaments formed of the ideas suggested by these comparisons. These illustrations form a splendid drapery, the design of which is to set off with per-

fect grace, and heighten to the greatest possible degree, every beauty of the human form;—having done
this, the Holy Spirit points to such portraiture, to
such embodiment of beauty, and says, That may be
an illustration of the beauty there is in Jesus. Wishing to set forth to mortal eyes the beauty seen in
Christ, the wisdom of God, the Holy Spirit represents
these not in marble that may be mutilated, and may
perish, but in language that can never die; and
gathers in this language the most beautiful comparisons and richest expressions possible. Could no other
reason be given for inserting these passages in the
Scriptures, this would be sufficient—that Christians of
undoubted piety, deep experience, and great purity of
heart, have found these illustrations of the loveliness
of Christ, a source of instruction and unspeakable delight—not only not suggesting unhallowed thoughts,
but feeding the soul with meditations kindred with
those of heaven.

> "Ne from thenceforth doth any fleshy sense
> Or idle thought of earthly things remaine:
> So full their eyes are of that glorious sight,
> And senses fraught with such satietie,
> That in nought else on earth can they delight,
> But in th' aspec of that felicitie,
> Which they have written in their inward eye."*

Like pellucid rills from different springs, the trains of
beautiful thoughts flowing from the various illustrations here mentioned, combine into one full stream,
and inundate the soul with a flood of delight.

* Spenser's Hymn of Heavenly Beauty.

When it is said, the beloved is white and ruddy, the meaning is, that his complexion is the perfection of beauty and health. David was "ruddy, and withal of beautiful countenance, and goodly to look to." 1 Sam. xvi. 12. So beautiful is our beloved, that he is the chief among ten thousand; or literally, he is lifted up as a banner among an innumerable host; that is, in a countless host the eye would naturally rest on him conspicuous and pre-eminent above all others, as it distinguishes a banner amid tens of thousands of people. When Milton would represent Satan as distinguished above his compeers, his words are:

> "He, above the rest,
> In shape and gesture proudly eminent,
> Stood like a tower."

In the muster of the fallen angels in hell, the imperial ensign

> "Full high advanced,
> Shone like a meteor, streaming to the wind,
> With gems and golden lustre rich emblazed:"

thus, towers Jesus above all others, the centre of attraction to whom all eyes must ever be turned, even amid the innumerable company of angels. The believer feels most truly, that wherever he goes, under all circumstances, Jesus is, like the banner in an armed host, the centre of attraction to which his eyes are always anxiously turned, the rallying point of his soul, full high advanced above all others; the splendour of his divinity burning with a brilliancy of glory richer than a meteor streaming to the wind, brighter than the cloud that rested on the mount of transfiguration. That mount, with the crown-like glory of the bright cloud then resting there, was distinguished above all other mountains; and thus, amid the hosts of heaven, Jesus is pre-eminent by the crown of glory and honour, the radiance of the divinity encompassing him as a sun. He is even now the sun by whose light all the youth of "the sacramental host of God's elect" move to do the brave acts of their spiritual warfare. To him are we exhorted to look, him to imitate, him to follow. In this grandeur and glory of his divinity, does he loom up before the soul in the hour of repentance, in trouble, in the valley of the shadow of death. In heaven he will be the conspicuous object to angels, no less than to the redeemed; for who besides him is there like him, even in heaven? In him are combined the divine and human natures; and this union gives rise to a development of glory, splendid and remarkable, as it is singular and grand.

In this verse, therefore, as introducing the following description, there are two general statements: first, that he has the beauty springing from the clearness of complexion and ruddy glow, bespeaking perfect health; and that there is something in his general appearance which would draw attention to him above all others, even amid an innumerable host.*

* Kitto gives from the Persian, the following description of the patriarch Joseph, with which this description of the be-

Y

VER 11.—His head is as the most fine gold; his locks
are bushy, and black as a raven.

The words rendered "the most fine gold," seem,
from the original, to mean the choicest gold, such as
kings laid up among their peculiar treasures—gold
most carefully refined. Perhaps Rosenmüller's idea
may be correct, when he understands them to express
choice, pure, solid gold. Our apprehension of the
meaning is, that the head of the beloved was so exquisitely beautiful, and an object of such pleasure to
the contemplation of the bride, she could illustrate
her feelings in gazing on it, in no better way than by
saying, they were as delightful as they would be in
contemplating a statue or bust, a head, sculptured by
a finished artist from the finest solid gold. Beyond
the ordinary pleasure had in gazing on a finished
piece of sculpture from marble there is here added the

loved may be compared: "A beauteous youth, who eclipses
the charms and graces of the houris of Paradise. His form,
polished as the box-tree, erect as the cypress. His locks,
falling in ringlets, sealing the mouth of wisdom, and arresting
the feet of discretion. His forehead shining with immortal
beams, surpassing both the sun and the moon. His eyebrows
arched, and his eyelashes shading his sleepy eyes. His eyes
beaming mildness, his eyelashes darting arrows. His lips smil-
ing and shedding sweets, his lips dropping honey. His pearly
teeth between his ruby lips, like the lightning playing upon
a western sky. Laughing, he eclipses the Pleiades; smiles and
jests dance upon his lips. Pearly drops hang upon his double
chin; upon his rosy countenance a mole, as the dark ash in
the midst of a garden. His arms like silver, and well proportioned; but the waist, for want of silver, slender."

pleasure had from contemplating the same wrought from the finest gold.

The word "locks" expresses the forelocks about the temples; the word "bushy" has received different interpretations, varying in their shades of meaning, but conveying the same general idea. The Septuagint translate, "his hair is like the young leaves of the palm." Dopke renders "palm branches." "There is considerable uniformity in the shape of the leaves of the palms. They are generally feathery, or divided like the plume of a feather; sometimes the leaves are flag like, of a thin, flexible texture, and curl towards the extremities. The leaves of the Jaqua palm are sixteen or seventeen feet long, their extremities are curled like plumes; the ultimate divisions or leaflets flutter lightly and airily round the slowly balancing central leaf stalks."* The hair may be very aptly compared to the fine wavy young leaves of the palm on their first bursting forth from the sheaths in which they are contained. The idea is, that his locks were full, in flowing clusters, like waving pendulous branches, with curls rising above one another in profusion. They were black as a raven; that is, of the purest and jettiest black. So Ossian, "Her hair was the wing of the raven." And the Persian poet—

"Thy face is brighter than the cheek of day,
Blacker thy locks than midnight's deepest sway."

And again—

"Of black, e'en blackest hue, and unconfined,
Her shadowy tresses wantoned in the wind."

* Humboldt's Aspects, 318.

VER. 12.—His eyes are as the eyes of doves by the rivers of waters, washed with milk, and fitly set.

See note, chap. i. 15. Here the eyes of the beloved are compared to doves, rather than to the eyes of doves, on account of what follows. In Ps. lxviii. 13, "The wings of a dove covered with silver, and her feathers with yellow gold," there is reference to those brilliant and sometimes golden reflections which the lustrous plumage of some doves exhibits. All in their true wild plumage, have iridescent colours about the neck; and often reflect flashes of the same colours on the shoulders: this is expressed in the clearest light, by saying, that these doves were more beautiful than when washed in streams of the purest water, pure and brilliant as though washed in a limpid brook, combining with the transparency of water the whiteness of milk. The same picture occurs in the Gitagovinda: "His passion was inflamed by the glances of her eyes, which played like a pair of water-birds with azure plumage, that sport near a full-blown lotus, on a pool in the season of dew." And again, "She whose wanton eye resembles blue water-lilies agitated by the breeze." Doves by such streams, represent beautifully the pupil of the eye, surrounded by its clear, healthful white; and the brooks of water seem mentioned for illustrating the eye as the fountain of tears, and the eyes of the beloved as suffused with the tenderness flowing from a spring deep in the heart of sympathy and love. The whole comparison represents the eyes as sparkling with vivacity, purity, and love of the greatest tenderness. The last words, "fitly set," are referred by some interpreters to the beautiful setting of a gem in a ring, perhaps to the precious stones in the breast-plate of the high-priest. The idea would then be, that while his eyes amid his clustering, waving, raven locks, were beautiful as doves sporting by the transparent streams around which gathered trees of rich foliage, those eyes were brilliant and perfectly set in his head, as gems fitly set by the most skilful artist in the finest gold. We prefer, however, to render the whole verse—'His eyes as doves by valley-rills of water, washed in milk, reposing by the full fountain streams.' The idea would then be that of milk-white doves in a rural vale, reposing quietly by rich, full streams, flowing from pellucid fountains.

VER. 13.—His cheeks are as a bed of spices, as sweet flowers: his lips like lilies, dropping sweet-smelling myrrh.

Besides fragrant plants and flowers, the Jewish gardens were occupied, in a considerable degree, with the growth of medicinal shrubs and herbs. The word *bed* here means a bed raised throughout, or at least in the middle; such a plat, thickly covered with sweet-smelling flowers in full bloom, was a most delightful object; and the spouse laying under contribution every thing most beautiful in nature, says the pleasure felt by her in gazing on the cheeks of the beloved, could be best illustrated by the delight caused in viewing a bed filled with fragrant flowers.

She goes farther, however, and adds force to the idea. The next words, "as sweet flowers," rendered in the margin of our Bible, "towers of perfumes," do not seem to convey the idea intended by the original Hebrew. This word generally translated "tower," is used for an elevated stage or platform, in Neh. viii. 4, and ix. 4. It seems to mean trellises, and those of a towering height, covered with aromatic flowers. The whole verse would then read—'His cheeks are as banks or mounds of fragrant flowers, as towering trellises covered with aromatic blooms.' May this refer to the artificial terraces frequently covering the hills of Judea? In many places it is terraced continuously for miles. Steep hills are converted into numerous horizontal beds, rising successively till the top of the mountain forms the last. On ascending a mountain pass, a traveller counted sixty-seven terraces, which occupied the whole side of the hill; while considerably higher mountains were manifestly terraced all over by a proportionally greater number. These terraced sides formed hanging gardens, rising beautifully from the rich valleys, in the days of Israel's glory, when the scene must have been as fertile as now it is desolate, and as beauteous as now it is blasted. In this passage may the spouse therefore say, that the ruddy cheeks of the beloved excited a pleasure like that felt in gazing on beds of fragrant flowers, or contemplating those terraced hills covered with blooming aromatic herbs?

"His lips like lilies, dropping sweet-smelling myrrh." These words illustrate the beauty of his lips. There may be a reference here to a lily of deep red colour, mentioned by Pliny as much esteemed in

Syria. That the colour as well as sweetness and general beauty of these lilies is referred to, appears probable from the following allusions in oriental poets: "Him whose lips are like a red lotos in full bloom:" "How can tulip-coloured wine be compared to the rubies of thy lips:" "I meditate on the fragrant lotos of her mouth, on her nectar-dropping speech, on her lips ruddy as the berries of the bimba." See chap. v. 5, on "sweet-smelling myrrh." Sir Thomas Brown supposes this refers to "the roscid and honey-drops observable in the flowers of martagons and inverted flowered lilies; and is probably the standing sweet dew on the white eyes of the crown-imperial, now common among us." This whole comparison, then, means that his lips are beautiful as those roseate lilies, distilling drops precious as the most precious myrrh, limpid as the morning dew.

VER. 14.—His hands are as gold rings set with the beryl: his belly is as bright ivory overlaid with sapphires.

The idea here is, not that his fingers were covered with golden rings, but that the fingers were as gold rings, rollers, or cylinders, and the nails were as the beryl set in those rings. The original word *tarshish*, here rendered *beryl*, means a precious stone, so called because brought from Tarshish. According to the Septuagint and Josephus, it is the chrysolite—that is, the topaz of the moderns, which is still found in Spain. This is a precious stone having a strong glass lustre. Its prevailing colour is wine-yellow, of every degree of shade. The dark shade of this colour passes over into carnation red, and sometimes, though rarely, into lilac; the pale shade of the wine-yellow passes into greyish, and from yellowish white into greenish white and pale green. This stone was highly prized by the Hebrews. To them no illustration could be more beautifully appropriate for giving an idea of the most finely formed hands, with fingers and nails of extreme delicacy, than to say they were gold rollers set with the beryl.

"His body is as bright ivory overlaid with sapphires." The word body, rather than belly, is the proper one to be here used; it means the whole of the body from the shoulders downwards. The sapphire is a gem so called from its beauty and splendour. It is next in hardness and value to the diamond, and is mostly of a blue colour of various shades. In the choicest specimens it is of the deepest azure; and in others varies in shades of all degrees between that and the pure crystal brightness of water, without the least tinge of colour, but with a lustre much superior to crystal. The Hebrew word answering to "bright" in our version means something wrought, artificial work; and the idea intended therefore is, that his body excited feelings of beauty like those caused by gazing on a curious artificial work of ivory richly inlaid, even covered, with brilliant sapphires. For expressing the beauty of his body, the highly wrought finely polished ivory was not sufficient. It has a beauty combining with the whiteness and polish of ivory the splendour and glory of sapphires.

Ver. 15.—His legs are as pillars of marble set upon sockets of fine gold; his countenance is as Lebanon, excellent as the cedars.

The phrase "silver-legged" is common in Persia, to denote elegance of this limb. Thus Hafiz:

> "O thou whose polished legs like silver shine,
> My heart is ravished as thou bring'st me wine."

Ovid speaks of delicate marble feet. Aquila and Theodotion translate this, "his legs are pillars, or columns, of Parian marble." This was the whitest, purest, and best—that from which the Grecian statues generally were formed. "On sockets, or pedestals, of fine gold." These doubtless refer to the beauty of his sandals. From the many references to the beauty of sandals in the Latin and Greek poets, we take but one from Callimachus, in his hymn to Apollo:

> "A golden robe invests the glorious god;
> His shining feet with golden sandals shod;
> Gold are his harp, his quiver, and his bow."

Columns of fine marble, on bases of pure solid gold, were beautiful to the view; far more beautiful were his legs, with their costly, splendid sandals.

"His countenance is as Lebanon, excellent as the cedars." There are higher mountains than Lebanon, but none more truly deserving the epithet of Moses, "that goodly mountain, even Lebanon." Towering to a height of ten thousand feet above the sea, and deriving its name, not from the snow lying continually on its summits, but from the whiteness of its limestone rocks, "Lebanon presents us everywhere, with majestic mountains. At every step we meet with scenes in which nature displays either beauty or grandeur. When we land on the coast, the loftiness and steep ascent of this mountainous ridge, which seems to enclose the country, those gigantic masses which shoot into the clouds, inspire astonishment and awe."* "We were chiefly occupied with the view of majestic Lebanon. It is a noble range of mountains, well worthy of the fame it has so long maintained. It is cultivated in a wonderful manner, by the help of terraces, and is still very fertile. We saw on some of its eminences, more than two thousand feet high, villages and luxuriant vegetation; and on some of its peaks, six thousand feet high, we could discern tall pines against the clear sky beyond. At first the clouds were resting on the lofty summit of the range, but they cleared away, and we saw Sannin, which is generally regarded as the highest peak of Lebanon. The rays of the setting sun gave a splendid tint to the lofty brow of the mountain; and we did not wonder how the Church of old saw in its features of calm and immovable majesty, an emblem of the great Redeemer—'His countenance is as Lebanon.' The cedars of Lebanon excel those of all other lands. They are remarkable for the multiplicity and length of the branches, few trees dividing so many fair branches from the main stem, or spreading over so large a compass of the ground. No tree in the forest is more remarkable than the cedar for its closely woven, leafy canopy. Its mantling foliage—or overshadowing shroud, as Ezekiel calls it—is its great-

* Volney.

est beauty, which arises from the horizontal growth of its branches, forming a kind of sweeping irregular pent-house. And when to the idea of beauty, that of strength is added, by the pyramidal form of the stem and the robustness of the limbs, the tree is complete in all its majesty and beauty."* Besides their uncommon size and beauty of shape and foliage, they send forth a balsamic odour, which seems to be meant by "the smell of Lebanon." With perfect elegance and taste, the beloved is compared to Lebanon and the cedars for dignity and grandeur; and afterwards, the spouse is compared to Carmel and the palm-tree, for beauty and grace. Chap. vii. 5.

VER. 16.—His mouth is most sweet; yea, he is altogether lovely. This is my beloved, and this is my friend, O daughters of Jerusalem.

The mouth, or palate, together with the corresponding lower part of the mouth, is put for the voice. This may read, 'His voice is sweetnesses;'—that is, not merely pure sweetness, but so rich that its excellence cannot be better expressed than by saying, it is a combination of sweetnesses. Every possible beauty of sound and music is concentrated in the tones of his voice.

It will have been already noticed, that in this description there is a grouping together of objects and ideas of beauty and brilliancy, dazzling beyond expression, and beyond any power of conception by the unaided human mind. These different clusters of

* The Scotch Mission of Inquiry.

beautiful ideas are, like the various flowers brought
from different places for forming a boquet, drawn
together for giving us an idea of the cluster of glories
centring in Jesus. Yet they are, after all, further
from giving a perfect idea of his loveliness, than the
various flowers gathered as specimens into a cluster,
are from representing with any thing like faithfulness
the richness of the tropical landscape from which
they may have been gathered. All the things here
used for comparison are rich and radiant with splendour. The head is more beautiful than a finished
sculpture from the finest marble, it is a sculpture from
the purest solid gold; the eyes have, besides the live-
liness and tenderness of doves washing in a rural limpid stream, the brilliancy of gems elegantly set in gold;
the cheeks have the fresh hues of beds of blooming,
odoriferous flowers; the lips have the elegance of
lilies distilling dew-like myrrh; the hands and fingers
are cylinders of gold, the nails are precious stones;
the body combines the beauty of ivory united with
sapphires; the legs are pillars of the purest marble
set on bases of the finest gold; the countenance has
the grandeur and majesty of Lebanon, the nobleness
and excellence of the cedars. Were it possible for all
these splendours and beauties to be united in any
individual, how far would he transcend the fairest of
the sons of men. Combine into a focus at the heart
all the ideas and feelings of beauty gathered from all
these objects of splendour, and then you have something resembling the delight had by the believer in
contemplating the Lord Jesus. All these, however

infinitely more than these, are found in the person of him who is "fairer than the children of men." With this may be compared the language of Clytemnestra, on the return of Agamemnon:

> "Faithful—as dog, the lonely shepherd's pride;
> True—as the helm, the bark's protecting guide;
> Firm—as the shaft that props the towering dome;
> Sweet—as to shipwreck'd seamen land and home;
> Lovely—as child, a parent's sole delight;
> Radiant—as morn that breaks a stormy night;
> Grateful—as streams, that in some deep recess,
> With rills unhoped, the panting traveller bless;
> Is he that links with mine his chain of life,
> Names himself lord, and deigns to call me wife."*

How greatly was the beauty of the statues of Minerva and Jupiter, by Phidias, heightened by the fine carving, ornaments, and drapery of gold overlaying the figure formed with such majesty in ivory! The view of the Apollo Belvidere gives pleasure even in the simple marble; how much more thrilling must be the impression, could all the splendid ideas here grouped together, be superadded to the majesty of the simple, unadorned marble. Even then we must go farther, and add the idea of life. The whole would then be no more than an emblematical representation of the Lord Jesus, of him in whom dwelt all the fulness of the Godhead bodily. As the Shechinah was surpassed by the glory shown forth in him who spake as never man spake; who healed the sick; who raised the dead; who was transfigured on Tabor; so, infinitely

---

* Agamemnon of Æschylus, 828.

more is the glory of Jesus when on earth, transcended by the glory now investing him in heaven.

Hence, after all that had been said, the spouse adds, "Yea," or besides all these excellences, he has so many others, that we must say, "he is altogether lovely;" more literally, 'his wholeness is delights'—his very constitution and nature consist of pure delights. As God, considered as exercising kind feeling towards us, is said to be 'love;' so Jesus, viewed as the source of happiness in us, or as the author of pleasing sensations in us, is said to be 'delights.' These constitute his very being as thus contemplated; there is nothing in him which does not cause delights. There is nothing in him which is not lovely; and there is nothing delightful which is not centred in him. The whole creation is a manifestation of the glory of God. The Jewish tabernacle was a model on a small scale, fitted by the same Creator, for illustrating the excellence of Jesus Christ, the maker of all things, as the Redeemer of men; and showing forth characteristics of the divine nature not seen in creation, and rendered necessary by a state of things among men, which did not exist when the world was made. The ancient Shechinah assumed different appearances, according to the character of God at the time; sometimes exhibiting the terrors of his justice, as in the flaming sword at the east of Eden, and in the consuming fire on the top of Sinai; at others, manifesting the loveliness of his mercy, as in the cloud which dwelt between the cherubim, in the temple. Under the old dispensation, this mysterious cloud was the type of him who is the atoning Redeemer, and "the brightness of the Father's glory."

We come very far short of attaining full views of the blessedness of Jesus, by taking only one aspect or representation of him at a time, instead of combining in one view all that the Scriptures shadow forth of his glory. At one time, we view him as a King; then, as Almighty; again, as a Lamb leading his flock to living waters; then, as the light of that world of glory. This mode of unfolding his character is necessary and wise. But in studying his excellences, let us not detach any one of them from the rest; let us view them as a glorious combination forming together one whole. The King crowned with many crowns is Jesus, but not the full development of the glory of Jesus. The Shechinah of the Holy City is Jesus; but this, however magnificent, does not constitute our Lord as he appears in his glory. And these detached characteristics, however beautiful when viewed alone, are far more grand when seen amid the cluster to which they belong. In forming a conception of Jesus, let us bring together into one person or individual all the detached representations given of him in the Scriptures—the Son of God, the King of kings, the King crowned with many crowns, the Judge on the great white throne, the Godhead coming with clouds, the Lamb leading his flock to living fountains of waters, the Shechinah of the holy Jerusalem, the tender friend weeping with his people in sorrow at the grave of Lazarus, the first-born, the elder brother of the saints;—gather all these into one, so far as the

mind is able to do this, and then we have something
of what the Scriptures represent Jesus Christ as he
is in glory. Yes, add to these the splendour of the
burning bush, the grandeur of Sinai, the vision of
Isaiah with its overpowering majesty, (Isa. chap. vi.,)
the wondrous sight unfolded to Ezekiel, (chap. i.,) the
vision of Daniel, (chap. vii. 9,) the cloud of glory that
dwelt between the cherubim, the effulgence of the
transfiguration, the appearance to Paul on the road
to Damascus, the revelation to the beloved disciple at
Patmos, the ideas of beauty grouped together in the
Song, (v. 10—16,) the picture presented when he stood
on the mount of Olives and wept over Jerusalem;
when the mind can gather to its bosom all these ideas
at once, it can feel all that God has now opened of
the grandeur, glory, and loveliness of Christ. These
rays, small, very small part though they are of his excellence, when gathered to a focus are overpowering.
When thus attempting to comprehend even what is
revealed of our Lord, the mind feels its incapacity,
and sees the wisdom of having him revealed to us as
God has done it in the Scriptures, by unfolding a
part of his perfections at a time. We thus get a
better comprehension of those detached scenes, and
ultimately of the glory of Christ, by studying them
independently, than could be done by having them
all crowded into one. Yet, when the heart has
studied them separately, it is anxious to rise to the
highest conceptions possible of Jesus, by bringing
these clusters of glories together; but it finds its
powers to fail under the effort. These gems of truth

are as fitly set in the Scriptures, as were the stones
in Aaron's breast-plate; and with what effulgence do
they beam, when the Urim and Thummim of the Holy
Spirit kindles there his light; what a mellow radiance
do they throw over all the intermediate truths and
spaces of the word of God; the radiance poured
abroad by the Spirit through these representations of
the glory of Christ, lighting up all the other Scriptures with a more heavenly glow. And they light up
all nature with a beauty and splendour before unseen. The Holy Spirit causes us as it were to see
lamps of heavenly fire burning in every thing around
us, until all creation becomes to our view like the
golden candlestick in the view of the worshipper in
the sanctuary—every created thing, not only every
star, but every tree, every flower, becoming a lamp
more beauteous than gold, on which burns the richness
of the splendour of the divine glory. To the eye of
faith all this is reality. And to the soul whose vision
has been purified by grace, the works of God convey
sensations more delightful than could be experienced,
were every bud, every blossom, every blade of grass,
and every flower, a lamp burning with living fire.

> "The clouds that gather round the setting sun
> Do take a purer colouring from an eye
> Illumined with this inward purity:
> To such the humblest flower that blows can give
> Thoughts that do often lie too deep for tears."*

Substituting holy sensibility for mere literary taste,
and the inward illumination of the Spirit of grace for

* Wordsworth's Intimations of Immortality.

z

the love of the beautiful, we may use the words of Wordsworth for expressing nobler emotions than they seem to have been intended to embody:

> "I have seen
> A curious child who dwelt upon a tract
> Of inland ground, applying to his ear
> The convolutions of a smooth-lipped shell;
> To which, in silence hushed, his very soul
> Listened intensely; and his countenance soon
> Brightened with joy; for murmurings from within
> Were heard,—sonorous cadences! whereby
> To his belief, the monitor expressed
> Mysterous union with its native sea.
> Even such a shell the universe itself
> Is to the ear of faith; and doth impart
> Authentic tidings of invisible things;
> Of Him who formed and has redeemed them all.
> Thus by the Spirit led, whate'er we see,
> Whate'er we feel, by agency direct
> Or indirect, shall tend to feed and nurse
> Holy affections, fix in calmer seats
> Of moral strength, and raise to loftier heights
> Of love divine, our intellectual soul,
> And help the great Redeemer to adore."

In heaven we shall see that blessed one combining all these visions of beauty and glory in his one person, together with innumerable others of which the heart of man cannot now conceive.

> "Cease then, my tongue! and lend unto my mynd
> Leave to bethinke how great that beauty is,
> Whose utmost parts so beautifull I fynd;
> How much more those essentiall parts of his,
> His truth, his love, his wisedome, and his blis,
> His grace, his doome, his mercy, and his might,

By which he lendes us of himselfe a sight;
His goodnesse, which his beautie doth declare,
For all thats good is beautifull and faire."*

Thus contemplating our adorable Redeemer by a living faith, through the Holy Spirit, we say with humble exultation, in the language of the spouse, "This is my beloved, and this is my friend, my companion, O daughters of Jerusalem." So far from being ashamed of him, as in our unrenewed state, in him alone we now glory. He is the absorbing centre of our affections; his company is the desire and delight of our heart.

CHAPTER VI.

Ver. 1.—Whither is thy beloved gone, O thou fairest among women? whither is thy beloved turned aside? that we may seek him with thee.

Such a description of the beloved might well make the daughters of Jerusalem anxious to see him, and inquire where he might be found. A judicious holding forth of the character and loveliness of Christ, has ever been the leading means of drawing sinners to the cross. The salvation of souls is effected by preaching to them Christ crucified. Great multitudes of people followed Jesus, because his fame went throughout all Syria. Had those who saw his mighty works and were the subjects of his healing power, said nothing, his name could not have been known abroad, and many whose lives were spared must

* Spenser's Hymn of Heavenly Beauty.

have perished. "Ye are the light of the world. Neither do men light a candle, and put it under a bushel, but on a candlestick; and it giveth light to all that are in the house. Let your light so shine before men, that they may see your good works, and glorify your Father which is in heaven." Strange that there should be such backwardness among Christians in speaking to each other of their Lord, and in commending his grace to sinners. Love breaks through this icy restraint, even at the risk of being looked on with disfavour. While a relief to our own soul, this speaking of Jesus is often made a blessing to others. When the woman of Samaria "went her way into the city, and said unto the men, Come, see a man which told me all things that ever I did; is not this the Christ? Then they went out of the city and came unto him." John iv. 29. And what was the result of her so doing? "Many of the Samaritans of that city believed on him for the saying of the woman, which testified, He told me all that ever I did." Nor did the results of this conduct stop here. "They besought him that he would tarry with them; and he abode there two days. And many more believed because of his own word."

VER. 2.—My beloved is gone down into his garden, to the beds of spices, to feed in the gardens, and to gather lilies.

All the gardens mentioned in Scripture, like those in the East of the present day, were not in any way connected with the residence; but were outside the several towns, and were from half a mile to a mile

distant from the houses of the persons to whom they
belonged. Josephus relates that Solomon used to go
very early in the morning in great pomp to Etham,
about two miles from Jerusalem, a pleasant place
abounding with gardens and rills of water. In going
to Jerusalem, they spoke of going up; in going from
the city, they spoke of going down. The beloved
had gone out to his garden to enjoy the beauty and
fragrance of the beds of spices, "to feed,"—or as the
same idea is expressed in chap. v. 1—to eat its pleasant fruits; to have his various senses regaled with
the blooming flowers, the luscious fruits, the exhilarating fragrance, the beautiful scenes, the melody of
the nightingales, "and to gather lilies." Thus Moschus, describing the beautiful Europa,

> "And from the meads thy fragrant banks that bound,
> Plucked the sweet lilies gaily blooming round."

And Virgil,

> "Come, beauteous youth, the nymphs in baskets bring
> For thee the loveliest lilies of the spring."

Like the seven golden candlesticks, Rev. i. 20, the
gardens here mean the churches of Christ; and the
lilies his saints, the pure in heart who shall see God.
The spouse knew well the beloved's place of resort;
and felt that though withdrawn from her, he was still
among his churches and in the midst of his saints.
Thither must she go to find him. Jesus may withdraw from the soul of the believer; he never forsakes
his Church; and when our hearts are forsaken, we
may be comforted by knowing, that if diligently

sought, he will be found again in the spiritual garden of his Church, enjoying its delights and gathering to his bosom the lilies, his sanctified ones, that having their connection with earth broken off by death, they may lie nearer to his heart in glory, and adorn his heavenly home.

VER. 3.—I am my beloved's, and my beloved is mine: he feedeth among the lilies.

See chap. ii. 16. Throughout this whole scene we notice that after awaking from her sluggishness the spouse entertains ardent affection for the beloved, though his presence is withdrawn. Thus in times when we are without the sweet manifestations once had of the nearness of our Lord, love to him may remain ardent and unabated. The act of speaking concerning his loveliness and commending him to others, as in the close of the foregoing chapter, is attended with the happiest results to ourselves, and ends in our attaining again the full assurance of hope as here expressed.

VER. 4.—Thou art beautiful, O my love, as Tirzah, comely as Jerusalem, terrible as an army with banners.*

The very name of Tirzah, delight, bespeaks the beauty of its scenery. It is a city mentioned by

---

* The following description of a lady by her lover, is given by Kitto from an old Arabian romance: "The lovely virgin has struck my heart with the arrow of a glance, for which there is no cure. Sometimes she wishes for a feast in the sand-hills, like a gazelle, whose eyes are full of magic. She moves—I should say it was the branch of the tamarisk, that waves its branches to the southern breeze. She approaches—

Josh. xii. 24, remarkable for its elegance; and after
the revolt of Rehoboam, chosen as the royal city,
and preserving its pre-eminence till Omri founded
Samaria. Jerusalem was beautiful for situation, the
joy of the whole earth, called by Pliny the most
splendid city not of Judea only, but of the whole
East. To these capital cities of Judea, rising majes-
tically on its verdant hills, with towers, and walls,
and palaces of marble white and pure, does the beloved compare the spouse, as Jesus himself compares

I should say it was a frightened gazelle, when a calamity
alarms it in the waste. She walks away—I should say her
face was truly the sun, when its lustre dazzles the beholders.
She gazes—I should say it was the full moon of night, when
Orion girds it with stars. She smiles—and the pearls of her
teeth sparkle. The sun, as it sets, turns towards her, and
says: Darkness obscures the land; do thou rise in my absence.
And the brilliant moon calls unto her: Come forth, for thy
face is like me, when I am at the full, and in all my glory.
The tamarisk-trees complain of her in the morning and in the
evening, and cry: Away, thou waving beauty, thou form of the
laurel. She turns away abashed, and throws aside her veil,
and roses are scattered from her soft fresh cheek. She draws
her sword from the glances of her eyelashes, sharp as the
sword of her forefathers; and with it, though sheathed, her
eyes do slay. Graceful is every limb, slender her waist. Love-
bearing are her glances, waving is her form. The damsel
passes the night with musk under her veil, which draws inward fragrance from the fresher essence of her breath. The
lustre of day sparkles from her brow, and by the dark shade
of her curling ringlets night itself is driven away. When she
smiles, between her teeth is a moisture composed of wine, of
rain, and of honey. Her throat complains of the darkness of
her necklaces."

his people to a "city that is set on a hill." A hand-some Hindoo female is compared to the sacred city of Seedambaram. The words "terrible as an army with banners," mean terrible, or imposing and commanding, as a military host drawn up in battle-array under their several banners. According to Good, "In Persia, one of the most common epithets applied by a lover to his loved one, is synonymous with 'awe-striking,' or 'striking with fear.'" This expresses that characteristic of beauty and loveliness found pre-eminently in the bride, which so impresses the beholder with the sense of inherent dignity and majesty, as to strike with terror and repel bad men, while causing, even in the bosom of the beloved, feelings of respect and veneration. She possessed something more than beauty—beauty allied with majesty, dignity, and grace. Hence the strong language used in ver. 5, "Turn away thine eyes from me, for they have overcome me." See notes on chap. iv. 9.

On the last clause of ver. 5, see chap. iv. 1; on ver. 6, see chap. iv. 2; on ver. 7, see chap. iv. 3.

The same language, with little variation, is here repeated, that was used on a former occasion; as if for the purpose of assuring the believer that, notwithstanding our unfaithfulness and neglect, and the consequent withdrawal of Jesus from us for a season, the love of our Lord remains still unchanged.

VER. 8.—There are threescore queens, and fourscore concubines, and virgins without number.

There is no necessity for showing at large, that

among females of an oriental court there is one superior in rank to the rest, and like Vashti, distinguished
by wearing a royal crown, and by being called queen,
in a distinguished manner; nor does it throw the
least light on the significance of this passage, to point
out particularly the difference between the queen, the
lawful wife, and the concubines, and the daughters of
Jerusalem, here called virgins. The import of the
passage is clear. The beloved wishes to make the
spouse feel the greatness and fervour of his love. In
doing this he not only uses the illustrations of the
foregoing verses, but goes on to show, that while he
was surrounded by a numerous retinue of beautiful,
noble, and splendid women of all ranks, she stood
pre-eminent among them in his affections. The word
"threescore" is used in chap. iii. 7, for an indefinite
number; and he intends to say that he had around
him countless ones to love, noble and dazzling as
queens in their queenly attire, and other females of
great attractions and different ranks, calculated to
captivate the affections: amid such a company, could
there be any room left in the heart for love to her
who was dark as the tents of Kedar, who was lowly as
the rose of Sharon, who had so lately treated with neglect him who had so many others to love? The next
verse answers this inquiry.

VER. 9.—My dove, my undefiled, is but one; she is the
only one of her mother, she is the choice one of her that
bare her. The daughters saw her, and blessed her; yea,
the queens and the concubines, and they praised her.

The meaning is—notwithstanding the number and

personal attractions of the princesses and other splendid women of all ranks by whom I am surrounded, my
dove, my undefiled, my perfect one, she in whom I can
see no blemish, my angel, is the only one to me; the
one that stands out by pre-eminence above all others;
the favourite, the sole possessor of my heart. She is
as dear to me as an only child to her mother; as her
darling to her that bare her. While thus dear to the
king, she was no object of jealousy to others. They
all, with one consent, admired her beauty, and were
not backward in her praise.

Thus in Ps. xlv. "kings' daughters were among thy
honourable women;" or, as Horsley has it, "kings'
daughters are among the bright beauties of thy court:
at thy right hand the queen has her station in gold of
Ophir." Perhaps this might find an illustration in a
modern court, with the peers in their coronets and the
peeresses around the king; and she, the queen, the
most beautiful, and the favourite, among them all.
The object of the whole is to illustrate to the believer,
the place held by him in the love of Christ. Our Lord
is exalted far above all principality, and power, and
every name that is named even in heaven; around him
are an innumerable company that no man can number, of angels and spirits of just men made perfect,
cherubim and seraphim, holy and glorious beings of
every rank and grade; yet, among these, the soul of
the redeemed is to him what the spouse was to the beloved, his perfect one, his darling, his angel—as we
say of an object of special endearment—the one that
stands out by pre-eminence above all others in that

glorious host, loved with an affection such that human language can best express it by saying, such soul is *the* one, the sole possessor of the affections of his heart. See note on chap. iv. 5.

The glory of beings of a higher order is unfolded to us in the appearance of the angel at the sepulchre, whose countenance was like lightning, and his raiment white as snow; of the mighty angel who came down from heaven, clothed with a cloud, and a rainbow upon his head, and his face as it were the sun, and his feet as pillars of fire; of the angel who came down from heaven, having great power, and the earth was lighted with his glory; these are the noblest, highest, and most glorious order of creatures mentioned in the Scriptures; and hence the Apostle, in Heb. i., assuming the acknowledged principle that these are the most exalted rank of mere created beings, establishes the divinity of Christ by proving his superiority to angels. Yet to these shall the redeemed be superior in splendour, in rank, and in glory. We shall be glorious as she who appeared a great wonder in heaven, clothed with the sun, and the moon under her feet, and upon her head a crown of twelve stars. We shall be made like Christ as he is in glory, glorified with the glory he had with the Father before the world was. Who can know what was that eternal glory of God? Who, then, can know what is the glory now enjoyed by Jesus? Who, therefore, can tell what is the glory awaiting his saints in light? For "it doth not yet appear what we shall be; but we know that when he shall appear, we shall be like him, for we shall see him as he is." And when the Scriptures speak of him as the image of the invisible God, the first-born of every creature, the creator of all things, even of the different orders of angels, Col. i. 16, as having in all things the pre-eminence; they show that while Jesus, our Redeemer, is truly God, the human nature he has taken into union with this divine nature, shall be exalted to a degree of glory beyond that of angels; and to this rank and glory his redeemed ones shall with him be raised. Thus the humble virgin was raised from a retired rural condition to a rank in the court of Solomon, and to a place in his affections, beyond that even of the queens surrounding him; thus was the Jewish orphan, though a captive in a strange land, raised to a position beyond the queen and all the fair young virgins in the oriental palace of Shushan; thus was Joseph drawn from his dungeon to receive a ring from the royal hand, and be arrayed in vestures of fine linen, and have a gold chain put about his neck, and be invested with the pre-eminence over all the land of Egypt; thus was Daniel raised from the condition of a Hebrew captive to be clothed with scarlet, and have a chain of gold about his neck, and be preferred before the presidents and princes; thus, He who was made a little lower than the angels, for the suffering of death, and took upon him the form of a servant, has been crowned with glory and honour, raised far above all principalities, and power, and might, and dominion, and every name that is named, not only in this world, but also in that which is to come, crowned with many crowns.

Nor in that heavenly court of the King of kings, will there be the least jealousy felt towards the redeemed thus honoured. The disposition which led John the Baptist to say with real pleasure, "he must increase, but I must decrease," the love which seeketh not her own, will there be the ruling principle of every bosom; and such will be the admiration and devotion towards Jesus by those holy intelligences, that they will rejoice with him as he then sees of the travail of his soul; and will be satisfied in the advancement in glory and honour, of his ransomed ones, his spiritual body, even beyond themselves. This exaltation of the redeemed cannot diminish their happiness; it will add thereto by the new field opened for their love and adoration, in the display thus made of the character of God.

Ver. 10.—Who is she that looketh forth as the morning, fair as the moon, clear as the sun, and terrible as an army with banners?

Theocritus has a passage in the same spirit:

"As beams the beauteous face of dawning morn,
    When night retires; bright spring, when winter fades;
    Thus Helen golden moves among her peers."

In like manner Ferdusi:

"Born of Afrasiab, there Manizah shines
    Bright as the sun, o'er gardens, groves, and streams."

And the Gitagovinda: "My soul remembers him who disperses the gloom with beams from the jewels which decorate his bosom, his wrists, and his ankles: on whose forehead shines a circlet of sandal-wood, which makes even the moon contemptible, when she sails through irradiated clouds." Also Milton:

> "Eastward among those trees, what glorious shape
> Comes this way moving, seems another morn
> Risen on mid-noon."

Thus Spenser:

> "As far as doth the daughter of the day
>   All other lesser lights in light excell;
> So far doth she in beautifull array,
>   Above all other virgins beare the bell."

The beloved still continuing his commendations of the spouse, and showing her superiority even to the queenly beauties of his court, adopts the interrogative form in this comparison, for giving it a stronger affirmative force. Having said she surpassed those around her, he proceeds to say that among the spiritual host of heaven, she stands pre-eminent, as the morning, the moon, the sun, among the starry host of night. The angels are called morning stars, Job xxxviii. 7; the saint is compared to the sun, the brightness of the firmament, Dan. xii. 3; and Jesus himself is represented as more glorious than the sun, for in Rev. xxi. 23, it is said the Lamb is the light of the heavenly city, and so much more glorious than the sun is this light, that the city had no need of the sun, neither of the moon, to shine in it.

Believers are now in a process of change into this glory of Christ. 2 Cor. iii. 18. Hence in Job xi. 17, "Thine age shall be clearer than the noon-day; thou

shalt shine forth, thou shalt be as the morning."
She who was once as the lowly rose of Sharon and
lily of the valleys, who was black as the tents of
Kedar, is now glorious as the morning, the moon, the
mid-day sun. She is here compared to the morning
soon after day-break; then, to the moon as a yet
brighter light; then, to the full splendour of the sun.
When Diomedes went forth to battle, the goddess of
wisdom distinguished him amongst the hosts of combatants by making a flame

> "Blaze on his helmet and his shield, all pure
> And brilliant as the autumnal star fresh risen
> From mid the ocean waves."*

In the spiritual conflict of the present world, the
believer bearing the helmet of salvation and the
shield of faith, is distinguished by the light of the
Holy Spirit kindled there by Christ the wisdom of
God; but in heaven he will be invested with a splendour by which his present glory will be surpassed as
far as the flame on the crest of Diomedes is surpassed
by the light above the brightness of mid-day, in which
Jesus appeared to Paul on the road to Damascus, or
by the cloud which overshadowed him in the transfiguration. This outward glory of the saints in light
is a reality, and is a consequence of that inward
glory first wrought in the soul by the Holy Spirit.
Splendour is more inseparably connected with holiness than radiance is with light. Holiness is light-
like purity; and we may as soon conceive of a blazing

* Iliad, v. 5.

torch, or a sun without splendour, as a renovated soul of living holiness without that glory which shall be revealed in us, Rom. viii. 18, and with which Jesus our forerunner is already crowned.   In rearing a triumphal statue commemorating a victory, the artist forms his conceptions of what is beautiful, and then embodies it in marble, which can be at best a mere cold resemblance: God forms not an ideal but a real holiness, after his own image, in the sanctified souls of his saints; and then embodies this in their spiritual bodies, for being pillars in the temple of their God, living triumphal statues, purer than transparent marble; for what must such statues be, when the very streets of the city where they will be placed, shall be paved with something better than marble, with something beautiful as golden glass.

VER. 11.—I went down into the garden of nuts to see the fruits of the valley, and to see whether the vine flourished, and the pomegranates budded.

The nut here referred to is probably the walnut, which Josephus says, grows wild on the borders of the lake of Gennesaret.   This, the vines, and the pomegranates are put for the fruits of the garden in general.   Thus Captain Norden, in describing the gardens of Cairo, mentions only palm-trees and vine-arbours, possibly because these were the most flourishing and remarkable of their productions.   Their gardens were usually in low places, in valleys on the banks of brooks.   Say the Scotch Mission, "When we reached the bottom of the valley, it was one complete garden of fruit-trees.   The vines, the figs, pomegranates, peaches, citrons, quinces, and lemons were all budding or ripening in a most luxuriant manner. A clear brook flowing down the valley, gave freshness and beauty to every green thing."

The beloved gives, in the 11—13 verses, four statements showing the spouse what were his feelings during his withdrawal. He says, that when he left her, chap. v. 6, it was not in anger; but with kindly feeling and love unabated; only to withdraw to his favourite place of resort in the garden, and there amuse and occupy himself until such time as she might feel her unkindness, and seek again his presence; he was ready to welcome her return to his bosom at any moment. This language viewed as giving his feelings on leaving her, is of the same tender spirit with his words in chap. v. 2, and breathes the tenderest affection. Surely a love must be almost more than human, which could be thus calm and unabated under such a repulse. The love of Jesus, which this is designed to illustrate, is indeed more than human.

> "His love no end nor measure knows,
> No change can turn its course;
> Immutably the same it flows,
> From one eternal source."

This love is our life, the very spring of our being. Happy for us that its exercise towards us by our Lord, does not depend on our merit and watchfulness. Like the power which keeps the heart beating unconsciously without any act of our will, this **divine** love which began towards us while dead in sins, even

A A

before our being, continues to follow and bless us, even when unmindful of its source or its existence, and when unkindly forsaking the Redeemer. Even under neglect and repulse, Jesus turns away from us without anger; and leaves us until such time as we feel our unkindness, and seek again his presence and grace.

VER. 12.—Or ever I was aware, my soul made me like the chariots of Amminadib.

While a particular explanation of this passage is very difficult, perhaps impossible, the general meaning in its connection seems clear. We cannot undertake to give the various interpretations. Dᴼpke has stated and reviewed them at length. Amminadib is most probably the name of an individual, whose chariots were proverbial for swiftness; and the beloved means to say, that often thus withdrawing from the spouse without anger, with chastened affection— almost unconsciously, ere he was aware, his soul was filled with the desire of meeting her again, a desire so strong that it would have carried him to her arms with a swiftness that could be illustrated by nothing more appropriately than by the rapid, smooth-rolling chariots of Amminadib.

Such is the feeling of Jesus towards us, even when his presence is withdrawn, and the light of his countenance no longer felt. He changes not. When obliged by our neglect to turn away from us, he carries with him the same ardour of love that he manifested to us in our happiest hours of duty and affection; and when our love has grown cold, and our feet are wan-

dering on the dark mountains, or our souls slumbering in the indifference of carnal security, he still has
an affection which makes him ready to come and
meet us at any moment, with the swiftness of the
chariots of Amminadib? Yea, rather with the quick-
ness of the wings of the morning, or of that all-present Spirit who flies to the bosom of every repenting believer, with a swiftness outstripping infinitely
the wings of the morning or even the rapidity of
thought. Though seeing it necessary for our good
to hide his face, and even afflict us, he has all the
while this strong yearning toward us; and every act
however painful, has lying behind it, in his bosom,
this deep affection and tenderness.

VER. 13.—Return, return, O Shulamite; return, return,
that we may look upon thee. What will ye see in the Shulamite? As it were the company of two armies.

The word Shulamite, or Shulamith, is the feminine
of the name of Shelomoh, or Solomon, and means the
bride of Shelomoh, the prince of peace. The beloved
calls on her to return, or rather this was the language
expressing the feelings of his heart when separated
from her. We would translate, "Return, return, that
we may see in thee,—What shall you see in the Shulamith? A festive choir of rejoicing hosts." The interrogative form is thrown in for giving greater emphasis and beauty to the language. The beloved
would say, that she whose loveliness in his eyes he
had been illustrating by so many comparisons, was an
object of more delightful contemplation to him, than
bands beautifully attired, mingling in a sacred dance

on a day of public rejoicing; or was a source of pleasure like that derived from such a sight; far greater
than could be had from beholding any individual, however excellent; such as is felt from gazing on the combination of lovely forms, crowning with their elegance
of form, shape, beauty of dress, and grace of movement, some public festal scene;* more beautiful than
when on the shore of the Red Sea, Miriam took a tim-
brel in her hand, and all the women went out after

---

* In the scenes described by Homer as portrayed on the
shield of Achilles, none would have been introduced but those
deemed most attractive in his age, which could not have been
long after the time of Solomon. Now, he has given such a
scene as is noticed in the text, a place on that famous shield;
and thereby we may know such was an object of beauty to the
ancients, and proper to be used for illustrating any thing which
excited deep emotions of pleasure.

"To these the artist added next a dance
  Drawn with surpassing skill, such as of old
  In Crete's broad island Dædalus composed
  For bright-haired Ariadne. There the youths
  And youth-alluring maidens, hand in hand
  Danced jocund, every maiden, neat attired
  In finest linen, and the youths in vests
  Well woven, glossy as the glaze of oil.
  These all wore garlands, and bright falchions, those,
  Of burnished gold in silver trappings hung:
  They with well tutor'd step, now nimbly ran
  The circle, swift, as when, before his wheel
  Seated, the potter twirls it with both hands
  For trial of its speed, now, crossing quick
  They passed at once into each other's place.
  On either side spectators numerous stood
  Delighted."—*Iliad,* xviii. 590.

her with timbrels and with dances, Exod. xv. 20; than when David and all the house of Israel brought up the ark of the Lord, with shouting and with the sound of the trumpet, and with cymbals, making a noise with psalteries and harps, leaping and dancing before the Lord, 2 Sam. vi. 15; 1 Chron. xv. 26. As in chap. i. 9, the horse is the emblem of nobleness, energy, and activity in the believer; here, the reference is to elegance and grace of motion, as an element of beauty, while in the perfected saint perfect beauty is found. Thus, in something of a like train of thought, Byron says—

> "She walks in beauty like the night
> Of cloudless climes and starry skies;
> And all that's best of dark and bright,
> Meets in that aspect and those eyes."

As there is dignity, majesty, and grandeur in the calm movement of the evening sky, with its starry hosts, and therein is blended the beauty of darkness and of light; so this poet would say there was in her of whom he wrote, dignity, and majesty, and a blending of all that is beautiful. And in this passage the spouse is compared, if not to the starry hosts, to two hosts or companies rejoicing at a wedding, or on some festive occasion.

Poetry furnishes nothing of its kind more beautiful than the scene in the Fairie Queene, where, in a spot of singular loveliness, are espied, from the covert of a wood bordering "th' open greene,"

> "An hundred beauteous maidens lily white,
> All ranged in a ring and dancing with delight;"

and in their midst, was placed

> "Another damzell, as a precious gemme,
>   Amidst a ring most richly well enchased.
>   Look! how the crowne which Ariadne wore
>   Upon her ivory forehead that same day
>   That Theseus her unto his bridale bore,
>   Being now placed in the firmament,
>   Through the bright heaven doth her beams display,
>   And is unto the starres an ornament,
>   Which round about her move in order excellent:
>   Such was the beauty of this goodly band."

Now the spirit of the text implies, that the spouse was in the eyes of the beloved, an object causing more pleasure than such scenes as these. With a delight of which this is the best, though faint resemblance, does Jesus view the sanctified soul, and the innumerable multitude constituting his redeemed Church. All things are present to him; and even now he sees that rejoicing host which no man can number, redeemed from all kindreds, and tribes, and people, and tongues, standing before the throne, clothed in white robes and palms in their hands; of all his varied works of creation, this is to him the most glorious. Is it strange that on a day of public rejoicing, a kingly father should view a brave, gallant, and victorious son with more pleasure than that felt from the presence of all the host besides. While king Edward, beholding from his tower the battle of Crecy, had proper feelings towards all his valiant followers who surrounded his son, with what especial delight did he watch the progress of that son; and after the victory, amid the bonfires, and lighted

torches, and rejoicing of the soldiers, take the Black
Prince in his arms, and say, "You are my true son,
for loyally have you acquitted yourself this day, and
worthy are you of a crown." Thus, from his watch-
tower in the skies, the Captain of our salvation, our
friend, our beloved, has his eye on every one of his
saints; and when our conflict winds up with the victory over death, he will give us more than a father's
greeting, while bestowing the crown of righteousness
and glory which fadeth not away. Like the virgin
among the hundred lily-like maidens of Spenser,
"as a precious gemme amidst a ring most richly well
enchased," the glorified soul, the redeemed Church,
shall be in heaven an object of pre-eminent beauty to
Jesus, a brilliant gem amid the golden ring of innumerable angels encircling as a crown the throne of
the Lamb slain.

We may therefore be comforted by keeping in
mind the four things here stated concerning Jesus on
leaving us, when grieved away by our neglect: He
withdraws, not in anger, but in love; he feels without
ceasing, the strongest desire to return to us; he
earnestly invites us to return; he continues still to
view us with unabated love, with even greater pleasure than the angels, the hosts seen by Jacob at
Mahanaim.

CHAPTER VII.

VER. 1, 2.—How beautiful are thy feet with shoes, O prince's daughter! the joints of thy thighs are like jewels, the work of the hands of a cunning workman: thy navel is like a round goblet, which wanteth not liquor; thy belly is like an heap of wheat set about with lilies.

THE language of chap. vi. 4—10, is for encouraging the spouse to come on, and not hesitate on account of her recent neglect of him; in chap. vi. 11—13, he states his feelings of unabated tenderness during the time of his withdrawal; the object of chap. vii. 1—9, is to show his love towards her is still the same.

"Prince's daughter" seems to mean daughter of a noble, a word signifying generous, noble-minded; and in the thought of an oriental, is closely connected with liberality in giving; it is spoken of character and conduct, and according to a common Hebrew idiom, expresses one who is herself noble, the same with noble-woman. The whole of this description is a fitting portrait of a woman of noble character and majestic mien—the original words, "prince's daughter," referring to the nobleness of her disposition, and the following part of the passage setting forth the majesty and beauty of her appearance.* Having referred to grace of motion in the last verse of the

* With these descriptions of the spouse in the Song, we may compare the celebrated ivory and gold statue of Minerva in the Parthenon, which was an effort by Phidias to embody his imaginary conception of that goddess. "The statue stood in the foremost and larger chamber of the temple. It repre-

foregoing chapter, he naturally proceeds here to mention her feet and the elegance of her sandals. See chap. v. 15. Pindar speaks of "the silver-footed Venus;" and Milton of "Thetis' tinsel-slippered feet." Magnificent sandals constituted, in the East, a part of the dress of both males and females, who could afford to have them peculiarly costly; the oriental ladies were especially attentive to this fashionable ornament.

sented the goddess standing, clothed with a tunic reaching to the ankles, with her spear in her left hand, and an image of Victory four cubits high, in her right: she was girded with the ægis, and had a helmet on her head, and her shield rested on the ground by her side. The height of the statue was twenty-six cubits, or nearly forty feet including the base. From the manner in which Plato speaks of the statue, it seems clear that the gold predominated over the ivory, the latter being used for the face, hands, and feet, and the former for the drapery and ornaments. The eyes, according to Plato, were of a kind of marble, nearly resembling ivory, perhaps painted to imitate the iris and pupil; there is no sufficient authority for the statement which is frequently made that they were of precious stones. It is doubtful whether the core of the statue was of wood or of stone. The various portions of the statue were most elaborately ornamented. A sphinx formed the crest of her helmet, and on either side of it were gryphons, all, no doubt, of gold. The ægis was fringed with golden serpents, and in its centre was a golden head of Medusa. Even the edges of the sandals, which were four *dactyli* high, were seen, on close inspection, to be engraved with the battle of the Lapithæ and Centaurs. The shield was ornamented on both sides with embossed work, representing, on the inner side, the battle of the giants against the gods, and on the outer, the battle of the Amazons against the Athenians."—*Smith's Dictionary*, art. *Phidias*.

The sandals of Judith were so brilliant that, notwithstanding the general splendour of her bracelets, rings, and necklace, these principally succeeded in captivating the ferocious Holofernes; for we are expressly told that "her sandals ravished his eyes." Judith xvi. 9. Lady Montague, describing her eastern dress, says her shoes were of white kid leather embroidered with gold. According to Pausanias, in the statue of Olympian Jupiter, the sandals of the god, as also his robe, were of gold—the latter wrought over with all sorts of animals and flowers, particularly lilies.

Our translation of these verses is, "How beautiful are thy feet in sandals, O noble woman. The contour of thy person is like the rounding of a necklace, wrought by the hands of a finished artist: thy waist is a round goblet that is full of rich spiced wine: thy body is a heap of wheat enclosed with lilies." The principles regulating the interpretation of this passage have been already explained. Introduction, p. 40, and notes on chap. iv. 1—7, and chap. v. 9—16. The great misapprehension that prevails concerning these verses, has arisen from a misunderstanding of the spirit of the original. That seems to be expressed in this translation. We have shown, that as ancient statues of the gods were attempts to represent to human comprehension, certain ideas entertained concerning particular deities, so these descriptions of the Song are attempts to represent to the human mind the loveliness of Christ, and of the redeemed, by illustrations embodied in language, rather than in marble and gold. The statues of Olympian Jupiter and of Minerva by Phidias, were highly adorned, and among other things, with drapery of gold; and Cornelius Nepos states that it was customary in the statues raised to conquerors in the Olympic games, to represent them in the habits in which they had gained the crown.

The "joints of the thighs," did the original words mean what these express, would convey a finished idea of beauty and perfection; as the joints would then be compared to such work as the jewelled wheels of a watch. The word "joint" means, however, rounding, curvature; and the two words express the beautiful symmetry of that part of the person. There is now in existence a famous statue of Venus at Naples, to which the Grecian epithet "beautiful hipped" was applied.* The word "jewels" means necklaces, things on which great art was bestowed by the ancients. As Wilkinson remarks, "handsome and richly ornamented necklaces were a principal part of the dress of both men and women;"† and some idea may be got of the beauty of this allusion, by examining the illustrations of them he has given. The necklace was made sometimes to resemble a serpent coiled about the neck of the wearer, as was the case with that given as a nuptial present by Venus to Harmonia, which was ornamented in so elaborate a manner, that Nonnus devotes fifty lines of his Dionysiaca to its description. This same necklace afterwards appears in the mythology, as the bribe by which Eriphyle

* Καλλίπυγος.
† Ancient Egyptians, vol. iii. 375.

was tempted to betray her husband. The beauty and splendour, as well as the value of necklaces, were enhanced by the insertion of pearls and precious stones, which were strung together by means of linen thread, silk, or wires and links of gold. Smith gives patterns of three splendid gold necklaces in the British Museum, that were found in Etruscan tombs; also a wood-cut exhibiting the central portion of a very ancient and exquisitely wrought necklace, which was found near Naples, in the sepulchre of a Greek lady. It has seventy-one pendants. Above them, is a band consisting of several rows of close chain-work, which we now call Venetian. The specimens of ancient chains which we have in ornaments for the person, especially necklaces, show a great variety of elegant and ingenious patterns, whose name expresses their fineness and delicacy as well as their minuteness. These valuable chains were commonly worn by women, either on the neck, or round the waist, according to a statement of Pliny. In a head of Minerva engraved from an antique gem, we see a necklace with a row of drops on the under side, which, when worn, arrange themselves upon the neck, like rays proceeding from the centre.* These facts enable us to see why the necklace should be mentioned in this connection, and with what delicacy of taste it is used for illustrating the graceful outline of the lower part of the body.

The original word rendered " navel," in the Eng-

* Smith's Dictionary. Articles—Monile and Catena.

lish version, expresses what we mean by the waist; and the roundness of the waist is compared to a goblet or bowl filled with spiced wine made of myrrh and fragrant cane. The Hebrew word seems here to express what was known among the Latins and Greeks, as the crater. This was a vessel in which the wine, according to the custom of the ancients, who very seldom drank it pure, was mixed, and from which the cups were filled. In the Homeric age, the crater was generally of silver, sometimes with a gold edge, and sometimes all gold or gilt. It stood upon a tripod, and its ordinary place in the dining-hall, was in the most honourable part of the room, at the farthest end from the entrance, and near the seat of the most distinguished among the guests. Craters were among the first things on the embellishment of which the ancient artists exercised their skill. Homer mentions among the prizes proposed by Achilles at the funeral games for Patroclus, a beautifully wrought silver crater, the work of the ingenious Sidonians, which, by the elegance of its workmanship excelled all others on the earth. According to Wilkinson, "Many of the ornamental vases of the Egyptians, as well as those in common use, were of alabaster, glass, ivory, porcelain, bronze, silver, or gold, and present the most elegant forms; and so strong a resemblance do they bear, both in shape and in the fancy devices which adorn them, to the productions of the best epochs of ancient Greece, that some might even imagine them borrowed from Greek patterns. We admire not only their forms, but the

richness of the materials of which they were made—
the colours and the hieroglyphics themselves, showing them to have been of gold and silver, or of this
last inlaid with the more precious metal. Gold and
silver cups were often beautifully engraved and studded with precious stones." We know the direct
intercourse there was between the region of Sidon
and Judea, and of Egypt and Judea; and hence we
may know the goblets used by Solomon would be no
less splendid. In oriental poetry, there are allusions
entirely similar: "Graceful is every limb, slender her
waist. Place a circlet of music on this breast, which
resembles a vase of sacred water, crowned with fresh
leaves, and fixed near a vernal bower."

The beauty of the waist expanding upwards into
the fulness of the bosom, is therefore most aptly illustrated by such a goblet, to the natural beauty of which
is added the beauty of the richest spiced wine. The
beauty of the form below the waist, what we often express by the word body, is set forth by "a heap of
wheat enclosed with lilies"—a heap of wheat in a bed
of full-blown lilies rising around and drooping over it.
Putting together these illustrations, the costly goblet
filled with choice wine and covered with rich devices,
and the heap of wheat in the midst of a bed of lilies,
we have in the mind a cluster of ideas of great beauty:
thus beautiful was the impression made by gazing on
the person of the spouse. Our view of this passage
might receive confirmation by noticing the manner in
which one part of the body is mentioned after another; first, the feet more beautiful in the elegant san-

dals; then the contour, the folds of the bridal dress falling around the hips, graceful as the curvature of a rich necklace wrought by a finished hand; next, the body like a heap of wheat encompassed with lilies; then, the waist expanding into the bosom, elegant as a goblet rounded gracefully upwards, and filled with the richest spiced wine.

VER. 3.—Thy two breasts are like two young roes that are twins.

See note on chap. iv. 5.

VER. 4.—Thy neck is as a tower of ivory.

See note on chap. iv. 4. In his Illustrated Commentary on 2 Kings ix. 17, Kitto gives a drawing of a group of modern oriental towers, which adds to the elegance of the illustration here used. He remarks: "So far as we have examined the Hebrew word, it is always used wherever it is possible to understand that a tower of ornamental character is intended. The great beauty of many of the forms here given will not be disputed." Josephus mentions the numerous towers of Jerusalem, that "were for largeness, beauty, and strength, beyond all that were in the habitable earth; they were of white marble, each stone was twenty-five feet in length, ten in breadth, and five in depth; these stones were so exactly united to one another, that each tower looked like one entire rock of white marble, so growing naturally and afterwards cut by the hands of the artificers into their present shape."* To such a structure, is the neck of the

* Jewish War, book v. 4. 4.—"Here and there, the clustering

spouse compared, with the additional elegance that would be imparted by substituting in the materials ivory for marble.

Thine eyes like the fish-pools in Heshbon, by the gate of Bath-rabbim.

So Philostratus says, "Thou seemest to carry water as it were from the fountain of thine eyes, and therefore to be one of the nymphs." Heshbon was a town about twenty miles east of the point where the Jordan enters the Dead Sea. The ruins of a considerable town still exist at Heshbon, covering the side of an insulated hill, but not a single edifice is left entire. The view from the summit is very extensive, embracing the ruins of a vast number of cities. There are reservoirs here, which may be those mentioned in this verse. It was in the tribe of Gad, who desired this country because it abounded with pasturage, and with rivulets and brooks from which the pools of Heshbon were supplied. The pools of a place situated in such a country as that around Heshbon, would be likely to be supplied with water purer and fresher than those of Jerusalem. Bath-rabbim was probably some neighbouring city to which the gate here mentioned led. These pools were remarkable for their purity and quietness—therefore a most fitting emblem of the clear, limpid eyes of those who

blossoms of the orange or the nectarine, lay like foam upon that verdant sea. Minarets, as white as ivory, shot up their fairy towers among the groves; and purple mosque-domes, tipped with the golden crescent, gave the only sign that a city lay bowered beneath those rich plantations."—*Crescent and the Cross*, vol. ii. 154.

are pure in heart. "Some varieties of gold and silver fishes," says a traveller in China, "were seen playing in ponds of pellucid water, upon a bottom studded with pebbles of agate, jasper, and other precious stones."

Thy nose is as the tower of Lebanon, which looketh toward Damascus.

Warburton says, "In the magnificent array of the mountains of Lebanon, with their various hills, glens, and crag-perched villages, each of those acclivities has a little tract of richly coloured vegetation hanging from its shoulders like a tartan cloak, and wears a fortress for its crown." This tower of Lebanon was probably a tower built on some part of that range of mountains in the frontiers of Israel, on an eminence overlooking the beautiful valley of Damascus, where "the vast and fruitful plain, with the seven branches of the blue stream which irrigates it, the city embosomed in gardens of surpassing richness, and overshadowed with the deepest verdure and richest luxuriance of oriental foliage, amid which rise towers and a forest of minarets of every form, the glittering lakes which reflect the heaven upon the earth, the majestic frame-work of the mountains—all combine to render this a terrestrial paradise." In such a landscape, a tower of white marble on one of the cliffs of Lebanon, would be an imposing feature—more so, from being on a commanding eminence overlooking such a landscape as that of Damascus. While the neck of the spouse is compared to the tower of David adorned with a circlet of the costly shields of heroes, and to a

B B

tower of ivory, her nose is compared to a tower rising in majesty on a noble eminence of Lebanon, and having associated with the grandeur of its position, the luxuriant beauty of the plain of Damascus. A fine, well-proportioned nose is most essential to beauty; and to this tower is compared the nose of the spouse.

VER. 5.—Thine head upon thee is like Carmel, and the hair of thine head like purple: the king is held in the galleries.

Philostratus has a similar comparison, though far less rich: "Thy head is a large meadow full of flowers, which are never wanting in the summer, and disappear not in the winter." Carmel is of beautiful shape, about twelve hundred feet high, and was in former days fruitful to a proverb. Hence its name Carmel, signifying a "fruitful field." "And when covered over with vineyards, olive-groves, and orchards of figs and almond-trees, not on the sides alone, but also along the table-land of its summit, would not Carmel, worthy of the name, appear an immense hanging garden in the midst of the land? And would not the beholder in other days at once understand the meaning of the beautiful description given in the Song— "Thine head upon thee is like Carmel,"* "And the hair of thine head like purple."

The ancients used the word *purple* for expressing what was most beautiful in colour; and when it is said her hair, or tresses, is like purple, the meaning is, it was of the most beautiful colour. As Porphyry says, "the poets are accustomed to use purple for beautiful."

* Mission of Inquiry, 235.

Thus Horace speaks of "purple swans;" Pindar of "purple wings," and Virgil of "purple hair." And Spenser has, "the morrow next appeared with purple hair." Speaking of oriental females, Lady Montague says, " I never saw in my life so many fine heads of hair. In one lady's I have counted one hundred and ten tresses, all natural; but it must be owned that every kind of beauty is more common here than with us."

The word here translated "galleries," means full, flowing ringlets, or tresses, so called from their falling down or flowing; and in the words "the king is held in the galleries," the import is, the king is captivated with the beauty of her full-flowing tresses. Thus an oriental poet—

"A thousand secret snares, like links entwined,
    Lurk in those ringlets waving to the wind."

The meaning of the whole verse is, her head of hair in its fulness had the beauty of Carmel, was of the richest colour, and with its full-flowing tresses, captivated the heart of the king.

VER. 6.—How fair and how pleasant art thou, O love, for delights!

Thus captivated, he exclaims—"How beautiful art thou, O love, and how fascinating in attractions." The beloved had enumerated numerous beauties of the spouse: the feet more beautiful in rich sandals, the outline of the hips graceful as the curvature of a most finished necklace, the waist elegant as a costly goblet filled with the finest wine, the body like a heap of wheat encompassed with lilies, her bosom like two

young gazelles feeding among the lilies, her neck as a
tower of ivory, her eyes pellucid and calm as the pools
of Heshbon, her nose as a tower on a cliff of Lebanon
rising over the landscape of Damascus, her head like
Carmel in its richness and flowers, her hair full, flowing, and of the richest colour, and entrancing the king
with the beauty of her tresses; having thus illustrated
these several features of loveliness, he gives further
utterance to his admiration by saying, as in this verse,
that to all these was added the attractiveness arising
from manners inexpressibly fascinating: how beautiful
and how fascinating in attractions. Her general beauty
of form and elegance of movement was lighted up by a
living spirit within, which enabled her to know in-
stinctively how to please and hold the beloved entranced with her attractive grace. She is represented
as something more than an amiable nonentity, more
than a mere Grecian statue, however perfectly finished.
With more than mortal elegance of bodily form, she
combined more than the fascinations which in an
Aspasia could enthral the towering intellect of Peri-
cles. The word "delights" expresses the characteristic
which enabled the daughter of Herodias so to bewilder
Herod by her accomplished graces, as to make him
promise, under the spell, to give her even the half of
his kingdom. It is recorded of Wilkes, that though
the most homely man in the United Kingdom, no one
could listen for a few moments to his conversation,
without forgetting his ugliness in the attractiveness of
his address. In the female character, this is far more
powerful than mere inanimate beauty. Without it,

beauty soon grows insipid and loses its charm; with this, homeliness is forgotten, and the individual becomes more attractive, the character more beautiful, even amid the decay of declining age. Hence, how greatly is our impression of the splendid character of the spouse heightened, when in addition to such grace of movement and beauty of form, she is said to possess manners so fascinating and attractive.

VER. 7.—This thy stature is like to a palm-tree, and thy breasts to clusters of grapes.

In this and almost all other Asiatic poems, the true eastern beauty is represented as being light as a fawn, tall as a cypress or cedar, slender as an arrow, erect as a palm-tree. The elegant slenderness of the beauful Kadha is particularly mentioned, and repeated in frequent choruses:—"Surely thou descendest from heaven, O slender damsel, attended by a company of youthful goddesses; and all their beauties are collected in thee." The cedar, the cypress, the pine, and the palm-tree, from their general beauty, and more especially their erect and stately growth, offer a common source of imagery for elegance and dignity of person among oriental poets. Thus Hafiz—"Like the reed, my heart trembles to possess that soft waving pine-tree:" and another, "The graceful cypress yields to thee in grace." Homer compares the beautiful Nausicaa to a palm:

"Thus seems the palm with stately honours crown'd
By Phœbus' altars; thus o'erlooks the ground,
The pride of Delos."*

* Odyssey, vi. 162.

Humboldt says, "Palms are the loftiest and noblest of all vegetable forms, that to which the prize of beauty has been assigned by the concurrent voice of all ages. Smooth and polished stems of palms, carefully measured by me, had attained one hundred and ninety-two English feet in height. The port and physiognomy of palms have a grandeur of character very difficult to convey by words. Their lofty, slender, ringed stems, terminate in aspiring and shining either fan-like or pinnated foliage. The leaves are sometimes of a dark and shining green, at others of a silvery white on the under side; sometimes the middle of the fan or palmate leaf is ornamented with concentric yellowish or bluish stripes, like a peacock's tail, and the leaves are flag-like, of a thinner and more flexible texture, and curl towards the extremities, while there is a fine play of light from the sun-beams falling on the upper surface of the leaves. The peculiarly majestic character of palms is given, not only by their lofty stems, but also in a very high degree, by the direction of the leaves. The more upright the direction of the leaves, or, in other words, the more acute the angles which they form with the upper part of the stem, the grander and more imposing is the general appearance of the tree. The fruits are large, egg-shaped, and beautifully coloured, resembling peaches, and tinged with a golden yellow, mingled with a roseate crimson. Seventy or eighty of them form enormous pendulous branches, of which each tree annually ripens three. This fine tree, the Piriguao palm, might be called the peach-palm. The fleshy fruits are, from the luxuriance of vegetation, most often devoid of seeds, and offer to the natives a farinaceous food, as yellow as the yolk of an egg, slightly saccharine, and extremely nutritious."*

The original word means simply clusters, and refers to the palm instead of the vine. When therefore the beloved compares the stature of the spouse to a palm-tree, and her breast to its clusters, he gives the strongest possible illustration of her beauty. Now, the Holy Spirit has grouped these things together for enabling us to get some idea of the beauty which shall be revealed in the saints, and is already seen in them by Jesus. He does not merely say, we are beautiful in his eyes, as is the highest development of female beauty to us; but taking the most beautiful human form, cluster around it all the ideas of splendour drawn from feet with magnificent sandals, the splendid curvature of the most finished necklaces, the golden goblet filled with fragrant wine, the heap of newly harvested wheat set about with lilies, the two young twin roes feeding among the lilies, the tower of ivory, the pools in Heshbon, the marble tower on a cliff of Lebanon, looking towards Damascus, Carmel covered with flowers, the palm-tree with its golden clusters, to these, add the delights springing from the attractions of most accomplished manners and a loving heart; when we can form an idea of the ecstasy thrilling the soul, as all these different objects pour their star-like radiance of beauty bright upon

* Humboldt's Aspects, 209.

the heart—then and then only, can we have some conception of the beauty, attractiveness, and loveliness, seen in his redeemed and sanctified people by our adored Lord. As the eye turned towards the sun is dazzled, and cannot take in the radiance; so the mind is dazzled with this beauty, and unable fully to comprehend it. For the love of Christ passeth knowledge. Of that love these brilliant comparisons are the illustration and nothing more.

Yet, if the saint is the bride of the Lamb, it must be expected he would thus view us, and thus love us. And as we naturally desire and try to remove every thing unpleasant and like a failing in one thus loved —Jesus is doing even this for us in sanctification. The diamond, though exceeding in value more than a hundred thousand times its mass in gold, the most cherished treasure of kings and the most brilliant ornament of their crown, is of all precious stones "the meanest in its elements, the weakest in its structure, and the most perishable in its nature, a lump of coal, which it reduces to a cinder and dissipates into that insalubrious gas, which ascends from the most putrid marsh;" its native bed is among rough valleys, barren rocks, and desolate regions. He who can take such elements, so valueless, and perishable in themselves, and form them into a brilliant so dazzling, so precious, and so enduring, can take such elements as those found in the nature of fallen man, an offcast in this world of pollution, and form them into a gem which shall be the brightest ornament of heaven, and a peculiar treasure of the

King of kings, set in the very front of his crown, worn on his heart.

VER. 8, 9.—I said I will go up to the palm-tree, I will take hold of the boughs thereof: now also thy breasts shall be as clusters of the vine, and the smell of thy nose like apples;* and the roof of thy mouth like the best wine for my beloved, that goeth down sweetly, causing the lips of those that are asleep to speak.

Having thus spoken of the loveliness of the spouse, the beloved here expresses the wish to gather her to his bosom, and assures her how agreeable her presence must be to him. These verses are but a statement of these ideas, in the highly figurative language of the orientals. The smell of the fruit of the citron-tree, for that is here meant by apples, was delightfully fragrant. The "roof of the mouth" is the same Hebrew word with that translated "mouth" in chap. v. 16, and means the palate, put by a common figure for the voice itself. The remainder of the ninth verse is not obscure in the general meaning, though it is difficult to explain satisfactorily some peculi-

---

* "Formerly it was usual to anoint the nostrils, which was reckoned very healthful and refreshing to the head; as well as was done, that they might give the more agreeable smell: and some sort of ointments, it seems, gave a smell like that of apples, which in some is very grateful and delightful; and Cicero observes, that the plenty and variety of apples, their pleasant taste and smell, show that they were only made for man: and indeed there was an ointment made of them, called *melinum;* so that the nostrils, being anointed with it, might well be said to smell apples; and which was accounted one of the best."—*Gill.*

arities here found in the original. We translate, 'like that best wine for my best loved friend, which flows pure, and causes even the lips of those who are asleep to move gently.' The meaning seems to be, that the voice of the spouse was pleasant as the best wine, such as Solomon kept for some special friend, and which was so mild and rich as to go down sweetly, producing effects that continued long, and were so pleasant as to make the lips move and gently murmur in sleep.* "A dream cometh through the multitude of business." Eccl. v. 3. As the thoughts and things which have engaged our attention during the day, give a colouring to the mind during sleep, and a direction to our dreams; so this wine was so

---

* Interpreters are divided concerning this passage; and though the general meaning is perfectly clear, there can hardly be an exposition given against which there may not be brought some objection. This word, "beloved," is indeed never applied to the spouse, but always to the bridegroom; and hence, even in this connection, designates a cherished friend. The ordinary import of the Hebrew word is one beloved, an acquaintance, a friend, a friend of the family, an intimate friend. The speaker wishing to illustrate the pleasantness of the voice of the spouse, does therefore say, that it is like the delicious wine which he kept for a most cherished friend—referring not to the spouse, but to some well-loved associate in the circle of his acquaintances. This seems to remove the difficulty, and set aside the necessity for dividing the passage so abruptly as is done by Rossenmüller, Delitzsch, and Dopke, who suppose the beloved to speak until the words, "like the best wine," and then the spouse to interrupt him by taking the sentence unfinished from his mouth, and saying, "that goeth sweetly to my beloved, &c."

mildly fitted to the tone of the system, was so delicious as to produce effects that continued during sleep, and caused pleasant dreams, and murmurs to steal over the lips of the slumbering, expressive of a pleasantness yet diffused by that good wine through our whole constitution. In accordance with this, is the representation of Mercy's dream by Bunyan, in the Pilgrim's Progress. The comparison is that of a delightful voice and its effects on the heart, to such wine. As the beloved says in chap. ii. 14, "Sweet is thy voice," and as his love is said to be better than wine, the most delightful of the pleasures of sense— these words show that nothing can be more pleasant to Jesus than the voice of his redeemed. See chap. ii. 14.

And will our Lord thus take us to his bosom? "He shall gather the lambs with his arm, and carry them in his bosom," Isa. xl. 11; and every saint shall be treated with affection great as that shown to the beloved disciple who leaned on Jesus' bosom at the first sacramental supper. At the marriage supper of the Lamb, when the beloved drinks with us the new wine in his Father's kingdom, to that bosom shall we all be gathered; and if oppressed with a sense of unworthiness, we would know how agreeable our presence will be to him, we find the answer here given with a fulness leaving nothing more to be desired. In the state of heart here represented, is fulfilled the prayer of the Apostle, "That Christ may dwell in your hearts by faith; that ye being rooted and grounded in love, may know the love of Christ which passeth knowledge, that

ye might be filled with all the fulness of God." Eph.
iii. 17.

With this verse ends the general division of the
Song, embracing the motives addressed to the soul for
winning it away from earth, and particularly those
drawn from the greatness of the love of Christ. In
how full and glorious a manner does it conclude. The
spouse had in the first verse earnestly longed for the
kisses of his mouth; here that desire is gratified to the
fullest possible extent, by the strongest assurances of
love given from time to time, in various ways, and at
last by the beloved's taking her to his bosom with the
tenderest and deepest exhibition of affection. So
true are the words, "Whatsoever ye shall ask in my
name, that will I do, that the Father may be glorified
in the Son. If ye shall ask any thing in my name, I
will do it." John xiv. 13.

VER. 10.—I am my beloved's, and his desire is toward
me.

Here begins the third part of the Song, which shows
the effects produced on the heart by these manifestations of Jesus' love. How naturally does the first follow from what has been mentioned. Thus cheered by
our Lord, and lying in his bosom, well may the believer
feel the full assurance of hope, and thus adopt the
language of this verse. See notes on chap. ii. 16.

VER. 11 —Come, my beloved, let us go forth into the
field; let us lodge in the villages.

A second effect of this love, is the desire to be much
alone with Jesus in retirement. When we feel the

loveliness of Christ, as here set forth, and realize the greatness of his affection towards us, we naturally desire to be with him apart from all things interfering with these communications of his love.

One most essential difference between the gardens of the Hebrews and our own, is that they are not in any way connected with the residence, but are situated in the suburbs, sometimes a mile distant from the house of the person to whom they belonged. See notes, chap. i. 16. To such a retreat did the spouse wish her beloved to withdraw, where there might be nothing to interrupt their love.

The heart naturally desires retirement with those sincerely loved. And shall not this be especially true of affection towards Jesus? The pleasures of solitude have ever been eagerly sought by multitudes; they are found only by the believer. He is never less alone, than when to the world he seems most alone, for there is he most uninterruptedly in the society of Jesus, his friend. All this he has in addition, while enjoying equally with the impious man of refined taste, the sweets of solitude and delights of meditation. How does the presence of an agreeable friend draw away our attention from the discomforts of an unpleasant scene, and throw richer beauties over one in itself attractive. So, with our beloved Lord, solitude is delightful; doubly so, for there we can commune with him of all that is in our heart.

> "O solitude, come thou and with me climb
> Nature's observatory, whence the dell,
> Its flowery slopes, its river's crystal swell,

> May seem a span; let me thy vigils keep
> 'Mongst boughs pavilion'd, where the deer's swift leap
> Startles the wild bee from the foxglove bell.
> But though I'll gladly trace these scenes with thee,
> Yet the sweet converse of an innocent mind,
> Whose words are images of thoughts refined,
> Is my soul's pleasure; and it sure must be
> Almost the highest bliss of human kind,
> When to thy haunts two kindred spirits flee."

It is not only almost, but altogether the highest bliss, when to those haunts two kindred spirits flee, and one of those is Jesus, gathering the humble soul of the believer more closely to his loving heart. There we are away from the distractions of the world; there we may have time for meditation, for study of the Scriptures, for contrition, for prayer, for praise. And while thus withdrawn from the world, even in sadness, like the disciples journeying to Emmaus, Luke xxi. 37, how often does he join himself unto us, and cause our hearts to burn within us, while unfolding to us the Scriptures by his Holy Spirit.

VER. 12.—Let us get up early to the vineyards; let us see if the vine flourish, whether the tender grape appear, and the pomegranates bud forth: there will I give thee my loves.

In this verse is mentioned the third effect of the love of Jesus on the heart;—we engage spontaneously in duties of holiness and love, such as are enjoined by our Lord, and in which we may consequently hope for his presence. "Early rising is, indeed, constantly indicated in Scripture, in conformity with the universal custom of the East. The orientals generally rise very early in the morning. To be 'up with the sun,'

is not in the East regarded as early rising. Every one
who is not prevented by infirmity or sickness, from
the ruler to the meanest of his subjects, is usually up
and dressed by the morning dawn; and even in royal
courts, the most important public business is transact-
ed at a very early hour, before, in this country, even
the workman rises to his labour. The women almost
invariably rise even sooner than the men, often a
good while before day."* Thus early did man in
Eden awake to his duties, and converse with God.
Thus Adam to our first mother—

> "Awake: the morning shines, and the fresh field
> Calls us; we lose the prime, to mark how spring
> Our tended plants, how blows the citron grove,
> What drops the myrrh, and what the balmy reed,
> How nature paints her colours, how the bee
> Sits on the bloom extracting liquid sweet."†

Jesus himself, in the morning, rising up a great while
before day, went out and departed into a solitary
place, and there prayed. Mark i. 35. Such was his
activity; and this would he have us imitate. Indolence is no part of the Christian character; it had no
place in man before the fall; it can have no place in
heaven, where they rest not day nor night. Indolence
is imperfection, and must therefore be crowded out
from the soul as we advance towards perfection by
sanctification. Love knows no weariness in serving
its cherished object; and that love to Christ only can
be genuine, which leads to activity in his service.

* Kitto's Bible Readings, 345.
† Paradise Lost, book v. 20.

> "Thyself and thy belongings
> Are not thine own so proper, as to waste
> Thyself upon thy virtues, them on thee.
> Heaven doth with us, as we with torches do;
> Not light them for themselves: for if our virtues
> Did not go forth of us, 'twere all alike
> As if we had them not.   Spirits are not finely touched,
> But for high purposes : nor nature lends
> The smallest scruple of her excellence,
> But, like a thrifty goddess, she determines
> Herself the glory of a creditor,
> Both thanks and use."*

Pre-eminently is this true of the grace granted to the saint.   Not he who hoarded his talent in the earth, but those who improved their several gifts, received commendation and reward.   The degree of our activity will be proportioned to the vigour of our love. Love to Christ was the constraining principle of the holy Apostle, who was in labours more abundant; and he says, "the grace of God which was bestowed upon me, was not in vain; but I laboured more abundantly than they all; yet not I, but the grace of God which was with me." 1 Cor. xv. 10.   Activity without love is a spurious thing; equally so is love without activity.   Hence, says Leighton, "Assurance is no enemy to holy diligence, nor friend of carnal security; on the contrary, it is the only thing that doth eminently ennoble and embolden the soul for all adventures and services.   This confidence of love is the great secret of comfort, and of ability to do good service.   Nothing makes so strong and healthful con-

---

* Shakspeare, Measure for Measure, act i. sc. 1.

stitution of soul as pure love. A heart thus composed
goes readily and cheerfully unto all services, to do,
to suffer, to live, to die, at his pleasure." While,
therefore, love to Jesus makes us crave retirement
with him, it animates us to untiring diligence in
works of activity and self-denial, no less than of
meditation and prayer. Thus did man give the
Creator his love in Eden. In such ways must we
give him our loves.

VER. 13.—The mandrakes give a smell, and at our gates
are all manner of pleasant fruits, new and old, which I have
laid up for thee, O my beloved.

This love prompts us to lay up for Jesus and con-
secrate to him our best gifts, as well as our diligent
services. Kitto says, the Hebrew word here rendered
mandrakes, has occasioned so much discussion as to
evince clearly enough that we know nothing about it.
Sir Thomas Browne has a curious dissertation on it
in his quaint style.* The Abbe Mariti thus describes
the mandrake: "At the village of St. John, in the
mountains, about six miles southwest from Jerusalem,
this plant is found at present, as well as in Tuscany.
It grows low like lettuce, to which its leaves have a
great resemblance, except that they have a dark green
colour. The flowers are purple, and the root is for
the most part forked. The fruit, when ripe, in the
beginning of May, is of the size and colour of a small
apple, exceeding ruddy, and of a most agreeable
odour. It is generally valued by the inhabitants
as exhilarating their spirits when eaten." Perhaps

* Bohn's Edition, vol. i. 192.

Junius and Tremellius are not far wrong, when, looking to the etymology of the word, they render it
"lovely flowers." By "gates" is probably meant the
entrance to the kiosk or summer-house; and "pleasant
fruits" means, as in chap. iv. 16, every delicacy the
garden could afford. The meaning of the passage then
is, that the spouse had already laid up in the summer-
house every variety of fragrant flowers and luscious
fruits, so that they could be had without the trouble
of going to gather them, and would be to him an
evidence of her forethought prompted by love.

Love ever hoards up for the object of affection
the very best of every thing that exertion can enable
it to procure, without waiting to be asked. It seeks
to anticipate every want, and takes delight in bestowing unexpected gratification. This feeling enters
into the very essence of love, and is to it what vital
warmth is to the body. Without it the affection
cannot exist. Hence, love to Christ ever prompts us
to hoard up spontaneously our choicest gifts for him.
Whatever we possess, we wish him to have the first
and the best of it. We feel hurt at the idea of his
taking any secondary share. This was the principle
sought to be inculcated on the Jews, when required
to offer the first fruits. This made Gregory Nazi-
anzen say, "If I have any possessions, health, credit,
learning, this is all the contentment I have of them,
that I have somewhat I may despise for Christ, who
is altogether lovely and alone to be desired." This
made a nobler than he exclaim, "I count all things
but loss for the excellency of the knowledge of Christ
Jesus my Lord."

CHAPTER VIII.

V ER. 1, 2.—Oh that thou wert as my brother, that sucked the breasts of my mother! when I should find thee without, I would kiss thee; yea, I should not be despised. I would lead thee, and bring thee into my mother's house, who would instruct me: I would cause thee to drink of spiced wine of the juice of my pomegranate.

WE would translate these verses, 'Oh that thou wert as a brother to me, nourished in the bosom of my mother; should I find thee abroad, then would I kiss thee, nor would it be imputed to me as an impropriety. I would lead thee, I would bring thee to the house of my mother; thou shalt teach me how to gratify thy wishes; I will make thee drink of the spiced wine, of my fresh juice of the pomegranate.' These verses carry out the desire expressed in the last verse of chap. vii. Having spoken of manifestations of love she was able to make, in giving him her most delicious fruits and her choicest flowers, she is here carried away by the ardour of affection, and wishes it were possible to do towards him as she would desire. Were her relation to him different from what it was, she might give him demonstrations of love that would not be viewed by the world as improprieties. Hence she is led to wish he sustained to her the relation of a brother, for then, however ardent and multiplied her attentions, they could never be regarded as improper. On the words "my mother's house," see notes, chap. iv. 4. In that retirement she would learn from him what might be most agreeable, and with the alacrity of love manifest her affection by every possible attention.

The wines produced in the vineyards of Lebanon had a fragrant odour: "The scent thereof shall be as the wine of Lebanon." Hos. xiv. 7. The orientals frequently put spices into their wines to increase their flavour. Savary, in his Letters on Greece, states that various kinds of naturally-perfumed wines are produced in Crete and some of the neighbouring islands. Spiced wines were not peculiar to the Jews. The celebrated Persian poet, Hafiz, speaks of wine, "richly bitter, richly sweet." The Romans lined their vessels with odorous gums, to give the wine a warm, bitter flavour; and it is said that the Poles and Spaniards adopt a similar method, in order to impart to their wines a favourite relish. The juice of the pomegranate is often employed in the East, to give a pleasant sub-acid flavour to a variety of beverages; and where the laws of the Koran are not allowed to interpose, or their prohibitions are disregarded, a delicious wine is frequently manufactured from this juice alone. The spouse, therefore, means to say she would offer him the richest and most refreshing drink, her greatest delicacies.

The import of this verse is a desire that every thing hindering the full and perfect interchange of affection between Jesus and our soul, might be removed, and it were possible to enjoy his love to us and express our love to him, as we shall be able to do in heaven. Much as we may now long for stronger displays of his love, and to give stronger evidence of our love to him,

we acquiesce in the present state of things, because
we feel there would be an impropriety, no less than
impossibility, in those overpowering exhibitions of love
that belong to heaven. But this does not preclude us
from feeling that, were it seen best by him, we would
rejoice even now in those raptures which belong to
heaven, where we shall be able to speak of his love in
the strongest language, and give expression to it in
the most exalted praise, without danger of exposing
ourselves to the contempt of the world. There, shall
our fellowship and communion with him be far more
intimate and endearing than was possible on earth.
The language of these verses expresses the real feeling of the pious heart. How often do even nominal
Christians charge on brethren as an impropriety, or
as a species of excess, exercises which are perfectly
free from fanaticism, and spring from overflowing influences of the Holy Spirit on the heart. In the present world, we are not able to feel as we would wish
to feel towards our Lord; we cannot speak of him as
we would wish to speak of him; we cannot do as we
would wish to do towards him. We are prevented by
our position among those who are unable to understand these things; by the remaining corruptions of
the heart; by the peculiar duties now resting on us;
and by the relation Jesus must necessarily bear to us
in the present world. Well may the wearied heart,
with so many obstructions between us and the object
of our love, desire that they may be removed, and that
our relations to him may be made such as to give us
the power to gratify perfectly our affection.

Ver. 3, 4.—His left hand should be under my head, and his right hand should embrace me. I charge you, O daughters of Jerusalem, that ye stir not up, nor awake my love, until he please.

See notes on chap. ii. 6, 7. These verses seem here mentioned, as though the happy state expressed by them was viewed by the soul as a blessed and satisfying foretaste of what may be expected hereafter, and as much as is best or possible for us in this world.

Ver. 5.—(Who is this that cometh up from the wilderness, leaning upon her beloved?) I raised thee up under the apple tree: there thy mother brought thee forth: there she brought thee forth that bare thee.

According to our reading of this passage, the daughters of Jerusalem say, 'Who is this coming up from the wilderness, leaning on the beloved?' Answering this question, the beloved says to the spouse, as though for the purpose of reassuring her, by calling to mind that she was truly his rightful wife, 'Under the citron-tree I gained thine affection; there thy mother pledged thee; there she that bare thee betrothed thee.' This is one of the verses which cannot be explained but on the supposition that this poem is an allegory. We do not know that it throws any light on this passage to remark, that among many nations the Cydonian apple was sacred to love; or to notice the golden apple which Paris adjudged to Venus, who is sometimes represented in her statues with an apple in her hand. Theocritus has the following:

"First I beheld thy beauties, blooming maid,
When o'er the hills, in every charm arrayed,

> Thy mother led thee, and thy fingers fair
> Plucked the wild hyacinths that blossomed there.
> And I was guide to thee along thy way."

This verse gives the seventn result flowing from the divine love. Though we cannot now enjoy what we could desire, and what shall be enjoyed in heaven; though the delightful scenes now had must be interrupted, yet we are permitted to go up from this wilderness leaning on the beloved; we feel that underneath us are the everlasting arms; in all circumstances he sustains us; and throughout our pilgrimage we are thus upheld by him who first found us, raised us up, and took us into covenant relation, "under the apple tree," as in chap. ii. 3, under the shadow of Christ. Here is, 1. The blessed privilege enjoyed by the believer, of going up from this world towards heaven, leaning on the beloved; 2. The soul who enjoys this privilege, is the soul that has been found by the beloved under the shadow of Christ; 3. There he first awaked and won our love; 4. There we were given to him by the one who had the right to dispose of us. What force do the last three considerations give to the first. Had she who was leaning on the beloved the right to lean there as his espoused wife? Yes, as is clearly shown. Have the believers that go up to heaven, the right to lean on Jesus, as his bride, the wife of the Lamb? Hence we see why the language changes so abruptly from the daughters of Jerusalem to the beloved; as though he would say, She has this right, because under such and such circumstances, and in such a place, she was betrothed to me by her mother's hand.

He on whom we are leaning, found us under the citron-tree, Jesus Christ. See notes, chap. ii. 3. There did he awaken us first to his love. This love is shed abroad in our hearts by the Holy Spirit, who is given unto us. The awaking of this love within us is the giving unto us of a new life. It introduces us into a new world, leads us to lean on new objects for comfort and support, and fits us for enjoying even the presence of God. Could the intellect of a man be imparted to an inferior creature, it would not more exalt his nature, than does the love of God elevate degraded and imbruted man. Before Jesus found us, our condition was truly forlorn. Like a poor, way-worn pilgrim in an oriental desert, under the withering heat, we had with Hagar sat down to die, Gen. xxi. 16; but we saw one who was as the shadow of a great rock in a weary land; to him we turned, and under his shadow we sat down with great delight; there one touched us, greater than the angel who was sent to the disheartened prophet, 1 Kings xix. 5; there God called on us to arise from our despondency; there he opened our eyes, and caused us to see a well of living water, and made us go in the strength of that food onward to the mount of God, where he had appeared, not in the terrible darkness of Sinai, but in the mercy of Calvary and gentleness of Zion. There, beneath the dropping of his blood, were we given away to him in covenant relation, by one who had the right to dispose of us, even God the Father—given to him as the purchase of his blood; and with a ten-derness infinitely surpassing that with which the beloved disciple fostered the mother of Jesus, committed to his care by the dying Saviour on the cross, did our precious Redeemer from that hour take us into his own fortune, his own bosom, his own home.

Thus found by Jesus, quickened by him to his love, and given to him by the Father, we are led away from our disconsolate condition, up from this wilderness, to the city of the living God. The wife looks to the husband for wisdom, for protection, for support; she leans on him in confidence and love. Thus lean we on our blessed Lord. He gives us support, wisdom, protection. With Israel, we feel there is none like unto the God of Jeshurun, who rideth upon the heaven in our help; and underneath us are the everlasting arms. Deut. xxxiii. 26. On him we lean in repentance, in temptation, in trial, in sorrow, in times of desertion by the light of God's countenance, or of persecution by the world, in sickness, in death, in the judgment, in our entrance into the heavenly city, and in our presentation, amid the splendours of his court, to the king of glory.

VER. 6.—Set me as a seal upon thine heart, as a seal upon thine arm.

This alludes to jewels having the name or portrait of the beloved person engraved on them, and worn next the heart, or on the arm. In the pictures of the eastern princesses and heroines, there is sometimes a large square jewel on the fore-part of the arm, a little below the shoulder. "When all the persons had assembled in the divan, every one remained sitting or standing in his place without moving, till in about half an hour came two kapudschis, one of whom carried the imperial signet-ring, and presented it to the grand vizier, who arose from his sofa, and received the signet-ring with a kind of bow, kissed it, put it on his hand, took it off again, and put it in the bag in which it had been before, and placed both in a pocket at the left side of his kaftan, as it were upon his heart."* According to Roberts, "When a husband is going to a distant country, the wife says to him, 'Ah! place me as a seal upon thy heart;' that is, let me be impressed on thy affections, as the seal leaves its impression upon the wax. Let not your arms embrace another; let me only be sealed there." There may possibly be a reference here to the stones in the breast-plate of the high-priest, and those worn on his shoulders.

These words do therefore give as the eighth result of the divine love, the desire to lie continually near the heart of Jesus, and be perpetually in his remembrance. Feeling thus the love of Christ, and the privilege of leaning on him, we pray to have ever a part in his intercession. How comforting to know that we have one in heaven to intercede for us. This is often overlooked; but as we grow in love we feel more and more the preciousness of this truth. How glorious a position is that of the gem on the finger of the king, how inseparable from his presence. "Thou shalt be a crown of glory in the hand of the Lord, and a royal diadem in the hand of thy God," Isa. lxii. 3; "They

* Rosenmüller.

shall be as the gems of a crown." Zech. ix. 16.
Here the saint desires to be a seal so precious as to
be borne on the heart. A believer writes thus, concerning his experience at a certain time: "I never
felt so strongly and sensibly that I had a place in his
loving heart. It seemed to my spiritual perception,
as though my soul had passed not only into his bosom,
but far away into his very heart, and my sensations
were such as they would be, were the thing possible,
were I lodged in the centre of his heart with love,
such love as belongs to Jesus only, above, below,
around, within me, the air, the light, all, the very
richness of love, my heart buried thus in the fountain
of life and love, and feeling tenderly, exquisitely, the
beating of the heart of Jesus in the outgushings of
that love in the Holy Spirit springing up within me
as a fountain of water unto eternal life. Never may
I forget these sensations. They seemed the delicious
perfection of union with Jesus, my soul like a spark
of light, a star of flame, broken off from the sun of
righteousness and wandered afar, but returning towards its centre, till passing into the depths of this
fountain of light, it reposes at the very centre, lost to
all things else, and calm amid the quiet splendour of
eternal peace. This coalescing of our soul with the
spirit of Jesus, this oneness with him, is the perfection of sanctification, the end to which the death and
intercession of our Saviour lead: 'That they all may
be one, as thou, Father, art in me, and I in thee,'
John xvii. 21; 'I in them, and thou in me.' Ver. 23.
Faith gives such a substance to these truths as to

make me feel just as I must feel, if my heart were lodged in the very centre of the heart of Jesus. It is something more than being gathered in his arms and carried in his bosom, than being set as a seal on his heart. It is the consciousness of being one with Jesus, of resting in Jesus, heart in heart. Here is the full meaning of the words, 'His soul shall dwell in goodness.' Ps. xxv. 13. 'Shall lodge in goodness,' in that fountain of life, the streams issuing from which are, according to the condition of those they reach, goodness, mercy, compassion, or love."*

The seal has generally engraved on it some device commemorating something which is most valued by the possessor: the soul of the saint is such a seal; on

---

* "The love of God, and of God alone, was my soul's great business. I seemed so entirely lost in God, as to have no sight of myself at all. It seemed as if my heart never came out of that divine ocean. Oh! loss, which is the consummation of happiness, though operated through crosses and deaths! I could say with the Apostle Paul, that Christ lived in me; and that I lived no more. Every inward motion, originating from self, seemed to be taken away and lost; so much so, that all the soul's movements and actions were now in God, under the dominion of his will, and entirely in union with him; the soul living in and of God, as the body lives in and of the air it breathes. Human language cannot well describe this state. God only knows perfectly what it is. Souls, who are in this state, are very precious in the sight of God, though outwardly there is nothing which especially attracts notice. They are the little ones of the earth;—meek, humble, quiet. Their humility, however, does not wholly protect them from the world's opposition, they are not unfrequently the objects of the world's scorn and rage."—*Madame Guyon.*

it is traced that which is a commemoration of the glorious mercy of the King of kings; and so peculiar is the engraving, that whoever sees it will know to whom the soul belongs. Rev. ii. 17. The seal is set in gold; and our spiritual body is the golden setting for the precious seal of the renewed heart, on which the Holy Spirit is now engraving by sanctification the lineament of our Lord. It is not only allowable, but the duty of the saint to pray, that we may be with Jesus where he is, to behold his glory. John xvii. 24. And in what way can we more clearly and comprehensively offer this prayer, than in the language of this verse.

For love is strong as death; jealousy is cruel as the grave: the coals thereof are coals of fire, which hath a most vehement flame.

Rather translate—'Devoted affection is unrelaxing as the realms of the dead; its flames have the energy of lightning-flames, which have the fiercest blaze.' These words illustrate the devotion of this love to the object of affection, the Lord Jesus. The privilege, the glory, the happiness of being thus set as a seal, appears such, that the believer is ready to sacrifice every thing for its attainment. While the various endowments of the soul are representations of the excellences of God, every affection of a pure and exalted cast is the image of what our devotion should be to him; and then this devotion is the image in return of what God's love is towards us. All other loves were intended as subsidiary to this love to God, and streams for feeding its strength. Of this love pre-

eminently may be said what Coleridge has sung of a
subordinate passion:

> "All thoughts, all passions, all delights,
> Whatever stirs this mortal frame,
> Are all but ministers of love,
> And feed his sacred flame."

There is a law in nature that the attractive power
of bodies is proportioned to their size or quantity of
matter; and the attractive power of lovely objects
depends on the amount of loveliness centred in them.
Now, what is the loveliness centred in Christ. In him
is not only every thing actually, but every thing possibly lovely. He is the citron-tree, as it were continually putting forth fresh successions of buds, blossoms,
and fruits of beauty; the fountain of life and loveliness. What must, therefore, be the attractive power
with which he draws holy souls towards him and binds
them to him? This nothing can withstand. The devotion will be in proportion to the degree of the love.
Love is devotion. So lovely does Jesus seem, so great
his attractiveness, so numerous our obligations to him,
that we rejoice to "count all things but loss" for him.
The inquiry on every point of duty, is not whether
the performance of it is difficult, dangerous, or even
seemingly possible; but simply, "Lord, what wilt thou
have me to do?" The practicability of a duty is felt,
to be properly judged of, not by the appearance it
presents to our judgment, but by the command of our
Lord. If he has commanded, we go forward, fearing
nothing that may seem to lie in the way. The true

principle was stated by the Duke of Wellington, when in reply to a person who asked whether his knowledge of things in India would not lead him to recommend the friends of missions to drop their work as hopeless, he said, "Your business is to look only to your marching orders—Go ye into all the world, and preach the gospel to every creature."

True, the amount of our contributions may seem small and swallowed up like a rain-drop in the ocean; our efforts may seem unimportant, hardly felt if put forth, or missed if withheld; yet we hesitate not, but go forward, feeling that whatever result may attend our labours, we are grateful for opportunities of showing our love to Jesus, even though the exertions be unattended with any further results. Truly, as Leighton says, "This love makes the soul delight in the hardest tasks and greatest difficulties, where it may perform God service either in doing or suffering for him. The greater the task, the more real is the testimony and expression of love, and therefore the more acceptable to God. If times be for suffering, love will make the soul not only bear, but welcome the bitterest afflictions of life, and the hardest kinds of death, for his sake. In a word, there is in love a sweet constraint, or tying of the heart to all obedience and duty."

VER. 7.—Many waters cannot quench love, neither can the floods drown it: if a man would give all the substance of his house for love, it would utterly be contemned.'

These words set forth the tenth effect flowing from the love of Christ—the power thereby imparted to the soul of withstanding every thing that would draw us away from the Saviour. The ninth effect, mentioned under the second division of verse sixth, shows the devotion of this affection; this verse illustrates its power. The power of anything must be determined by looking at the resistance which it may be able to overcome. And what does this love in the heart overcome? Against it are combined mighty influences, the world, the flesh, and the devil. Cherishing for the blessed Saviour a devotion strong as death, the saint finds himself surrounded by enemies who would crush or uproot this love, and bar the way effectually against our ever becoming able to attain the enjoyment of the divine glory in heaven. This host of foes avail themselves of our every instinct, impulse, passion, and feeling, taking advantage of every weakness and every opportunity for injury to us that can be conceived. But, "in all these things we are more than conquerors through him that loved us;" for the love of Christ constraineth us; and we can do all things through Christ who strengthens us. Our position is now very different from what it was in Eden, where there was but a single propensity on which the tempter could work, and every facility was offered for resistance. But had we never fallen, the energy and power of this love could not have been so fully seen. Its power does not appear so great in keeping holy beings in their sphere, as in taking hold of the fallen, and carrying them up through all these opposing influences, to their proper place beside the throne of God, and reinstating these lost stars in their orbits, never again to wander, never to fall or grow dim. The excellence of a vessel, the power of its machinery, is shown by the angry tempests amid which it can live, and the stormy waves through which it urges its way. Devotion in the pilot to his duty cannot avail, unless the vessel be sea-worthy, its engine perfect and strong. This divine love is the motive power of the soul in its passage over the angry waters of life's tempestuous sea. The force of the elements combining for its destruction may be seen in the fiery persecutions which marked the course of Jesus through this life, and have marked the track of his people in every age. Yet has this love ever proved sufficient to carry even the frailest bark of humanity in which it has been lodged, safe through all surges into the haven, where the wicked cease from troubling and the weary are at rest. Never, in a single instance, has one foundered in the depths of that sea which shall never give up its dead. Sometimes amid sorrow and temptation, like the disciples in the storm on the sea of Galilee, we may be sore afraid, and cry, "Lord, save us; we are perishing;" yet shall we ever find Jesus is with us: and when in jeopardy, like the Apostle, we beseech the Lord even thrice that the peril may depart from us, if he does not say unto the wind and the waves, "Peace, be still;" he will at least say, "My grace is sufficient for thee." Herein lies the power of this love. While this grace with its attending love continues in vigorous operation in the soul, we are safe, however heavy the surges and violent the storm; if

DD

its power be diminished, our peril proportionally increases; were it withdrawn, we must inevitably perish. This has been happily illustrated by Bunyan, when "the interpreter took Christian by the hand, and led him into a place where was a fire burning against a wall, and one standing by it, always casting much water upon it to quench it; yet did the fire burn higher and hotter; at the back of the wall was a man with a vessel of oil in his hand, of the which he did also continually cast, but secretly, into the fire." Hence we say with the Apostle, "I am persuaded, that neither death, nor life, nor angels, nor principalities, nor powers, nor things present, nor things to come; nor height, nor depth, nor any other creature, shall be able to separate us from the love of God, which is in Christ Jesus our Lord."

VER. 8.—We have a little sister, and she hath no breasts: what shall we do for our sister in the day when she shall be spoken for?

Rather read, 'We have a young sister, and she hath not yet reached womanhood: what shall we do for our sister with reference to the day when she shall be spoken for in marriage.' These are understood by us as words of the spouse to the beloved. In her exalted position as the spouse of Solomon, she does not forget those allied to her, who are yet in their natural, humble position. This represents the interest felt and manifested by the believer, in prayer to the Lord Jesus, for those who are yet in their native impenitent state. From Matt. xii. 50, we see that all are here meant who may be brought to do the will of God;

and hence all impenitent persons in general, no less than those of our own household. An interest for the salvation of the souls of others is a characteristic of genuine grace. The evidence of right feeling is right action. Right action will show itself in prayer and efforts for the good of souls. He who is crucified to the world, and he only, estimates the world aright; and truly enjoys it. He feels for the miseries of others, not from the promptings of natural benevolence, but from the impulse of love to Christ. It is delightful to pray and labour in the cause of benevolence; especially to pray and labour for those we love. The believer will seek the salvation of his impenitent friends, by going to Jesus, and making interest for them in prayer; if they are young, not yet arrived at years of discretion, he will be training them up and attending them with his prayers, that when they do reach proper years, they may be ready to receive the divine blessing. In such labours, we should not be discouraged because our efforts may be small, and apparently promise little reward. Duty is ours; results are with God. Trifling acts are often the cause of much happiness, and issue in most important consequences.

> "The blessings which the weak and poor can scatter
> Have their own season. 'Tis a little thing
> To give a cup of water; yet its draught
> Of cool refreshment, drained by fevered lips,
> May give a shock of pleasure to the frame
> More exquisite than when Nectarian juice
> Renews the life of joy in happiest hours.
> It is a little thing to speak a phrase

Of common comfort, which by daily use
Has almost lost its sense; yet on the ear
Of him who thought to die unmourned, 'twill fall
Like choicest music."*

In Chrysostom's introduction to his homilies on the rich man and Lazarus, are the following admirable sentences. "As the springs run when no one uses their waters; as the fountains pour forth when none draws from them; as the rivers flow on although no one drinks from their waves; so must the believer discharge his whole duty, though no one gives attention. Though by our efforts none may be converted, yet thereby are the impenitent kept from going on as freely in sin. I have not raised the sick, but I have rendered stronger the healthful; my discourse may not have recalled any from vice, but it has made the virtuous more careful. Moreover, he who hears to-day and resists, may to-morrow hear and obey; he also who despises this message to-day and to-morrow, may, after a longer time, attend carefully to these instructions; for the fisherman may often draw an empty net through the whole day, but in the evening, when about to depart, take the fish that had till then escaped. Were we to suspend business and sit down in idleness, when unsuccessful in our undertakings, our whole life would be lost, its spiritual as well as temporal advantages. Were the husbandman to suspend all labour on account of one, or two, or many disasters from unfavourable weather, we should all perish from famine; and did the mariner abandon

---

* Talfourd's Ion, act i. sc. 2.

the sea even on account of many tempests, the business of navigation would cease, and all the conveniences thence derived to society be excluded; and were men to act in reference to the various employments of life as too many Christians act in reference to the interests of religion, all things would go to ruin. When the husbandman has repeatedly sown the same field without a successful harvest, he returns again to the tillage of the same ground, and in a single year reaps a full reward for all his labours; and the merchant, though he has suffered many wrecks, again fits out his vessels, and embarks in the same enterprise, with no better prospects of success than the former. It is so with men in every calling. Since they exercise so much diligence and perseverance in temporal things, the issue of which is uncertain, shall we, when our exhortations are unheeded, be at once discouraged? When his vessel is wrecked, the mariner finds none to relieve his poverty; and when the tempest, deluging his grounds, destroys the harvest, the husbandman must bear his wants. It is not so with us. Although the hearer may not receive the seed of the word, nor bring forth the fruit of obedience, you shall receive from God a recompense as great when he disobeys, as you would have received had he been obedient. You did what you could. We are not responsible for our hearers being persuaded, but only for their being properly exhorted: to admonish is our duty, to be persuaded is theirs. Let the limit of your exhortation be the obedience of him who is exhorted. The devil is constantly opposing our salvation, though gaining nothing thereby, and injuring himself by his zeal. So great is his phrenzy, that he often undertakes impossibilities, and assaults not only those whom he may hope to supplant and overthrow, but those who are probably superior to his devices. When he heard that Job was commended by the omniscient God, he hoped to be able to overthrow him; nor did the deceiver cease his various efforts and devices for destroying this just man, even though God had commended so highly the integrity of his saint. Tell me then, shall we not be ashamed, shall we not blush, if, when the devil never despairs of our destruction, but constantly expects it, we despair of the salvation of our brethren? The devil does not retire from his assault against us, even when God forbids. Will you then abandon your brethren, when God is encouraging and urging to their aid?"

VER. 9.—If she be a wall, we will build upon her a palace of silver: and if she be a door, we will inclose her with boards of cedar.

The spouse having thus interceded with the beloved for her sister, receives from him the encouraging answer contained in this verse. It is the usual parabolic mode of speaking in the East. The imagery here used was probably drawn from the walls of Jerusalem and from the temple. The spouse had been compared to a city such as Tirzah; illustrations drawn from turrets and doors is here applied to her sister. Josephus states, that on the walls of Jerusalem, thirty feet high and built of stones fifteen feet broad and thirty feet long, there were one hundred

and ninety towers, "solid as the wall itself, wherein
the niceness of the joints and the beauty of the stones
were no way inferior to the holy house itself."* Such
towers added very much to the strength and beauty
of the city; and formed as they were of white marble, must, together with the temple, make the holy
city "the beauty of the whole earth." The Hebrew
word means a battlement or turret. There were on
the walls battlements three feet high. The reference
may be to these, though more probably to something
in the time of Solomon, like the turrets here mentioned. Nothing could be more elegant than such
turrets made of silver. The other allusion here seems
to refer to the peculiar beauty of some doors, possibly to those of the temple. 1 Kings vi. 31—35.

---

* Jewish War, book v. 4. 3. According to Diodorus Sicu-
lus, the walls of Nineveh were one hundred feet high, and so
broad that three chariots might be driven abreast on them.
They were furnished with fifteen hundred towers, each two
hundred feet in height. The gates of ancient cities were often
of great size, sometimes of brass, and flanked by towers adorned with sculptures, as at Koyunjik. May this have something
to do with associating a door with a turret in the text?

Speaking of the emperor Akber's efforts to adorn the city of
Agra, Maurice remarks, "The castle itself, the largest ever
erected in India, was built in the form of a crescent along the
banks of the Jumna; its lofty walls were composed of stones of
enormous size, hard as marble, and of a reddish colour,
resembling jasper, which at a distance, in the rays of the sun,
gave it a shining and beautiful appearance. It was adorned
with many stately porticoes, galleries, and turrets, all richly
painted and gilded, and some even overlaid with plates of
gold."—*Indian Antiquities*, vol. i. 208.

"For the entering of the oracle he made doors of olive-tree; the lintel and side-posts were a fifth part of the wall. The two doors also were of olive-tree; and he carved upon them carvings of cherubims, and palm-trees, and open flowers, and overlaid them with gold, and spread gold upon the cherubims, and upon the palm-trees. So also made he for the door of the temple posts of olive-tree, a fourth part of the wall. And the two doors were of fir-tree: the two leaves of the one door were folding, and the two leaves of the other door were folding. And he carved thereon cherubims, and palm-trees, and open flowers; and covered them with gold fitted upon the carved work. And he built the inner court with three rows of hewed stone, and a row of cedar beams." Such doors would certainly supply materials for a very suitable comparison. The meaning of the whole verse would then be, that to fit this sister for her new position, a glorious change should be wrought in her character, great as that in a wall like the walls around Jerusalem, on which should be raised turrets of silver; or as that in an ordinary door, which should be so overlaid with cedar, and finished as to be beautiful as the doors made by Solomon for the temple. Her nature should be adorned with ornaments, giving more beauty and strength than turrets of silver, or a richly carved door of the most elegant cedar.

Believers shall be made pillars in the temple of God, Rev. iii. 12; here, such are compared to towers of silver built on a wall of white marble, and to the richly wrought door of the temple, of carved cedar

and olive adorned with gold. The Holy Spirit, at work
on the soul in sanctification, is developing graces of
holiness, which are rising over the heart, like towers
of silver on the holy city's walls. The spouse is said
to be beautiful as Tirzah, elegant as Jerusalem: these
were lovely, indeed, when the morning sun fell on their
towers, even though of white marble; how much more
so would they have been, had those towers been of
silver. Who, then, can tell what will be the glory of
the soul, when beautiful as these imperial cities with
walls and towers of marble, it shall have the virtues
developed by sanctification, rising there purer than
turrets of silver, lighted up by the splendour of heaven, and over it shall be spread the holiness which is
the carved work of the Holy Spirit, richer, more elegant, than the carving of cherubim and palm-trees, and
open flowers on the olive, and cedar, and gold of the
doors of the temple.

Ver. 10.—I am a wall, and my breasts like towers: then
was I in his eyes as one that found favour.

The meaning of this verse is, that the change promised by the beloved to the younger sister, had already
been wrought in the condition of the spouse; and the
consciousness of this furnished her with grounds for
indulging the assurance of continuing to enjoy his
favour. In the eighth, ninth, and tenth verses, these
four considerations are distinctly stated: 1. Those
truly actuated by the love of Christ, show an interest,
by effort and prayer to Jesus, for the souls of the impenitent, ver. 8; 2. Two grounds of encouragement

are then noticed—the promise of God to work the necessary change in the unrenewed; and 3. Our experience of his gracious power in having wrought such change in ourselves, ver. 9, 10; 4. Then, by reference to our own state, finding that God has shown favour to us, we are encouraged to pray and labour for the salvation of others. There can be no stronger ground of encouragement than the declaration of God, yet our faith may receive confirmation by seeing that word fulfilled. This confirmation becomes the strongest possible, when that confirmation takes place, not only under our eye, but in the very experience of our heart. We should consider effort for the salvation of souls a hopeless thing, were it not for the two considerations here presented—the promise of God, and the experience of his regenerating and sanctifying power in our own sinful hearts.

VER. 11, 12.—Solomon had a vineyard at Baal-hamon; he let out the vineyard unto keepers; every one for the fruit thereof was to bring a thousand pieces of silver. My vineyard, which is mine, is before me: thou, O Solomon, must have a thousand, and those that keep the fruit thereof two hundred.

There have been many conjectures concerning the locality of Baal-hamon. Some have supposed it situated near Baalbec; others, probably with more reason, in Palestine, at no great distance from Jerusalem. A knowledge of its exact situation is perfectly immaterial, and can throw no light on the truth here embodied in the allegory. These pieces of silver were doubtless shekels, each in value about fifty-six cents of our money. It seems probable that the vineyard consisted

of a thousand vines, each required to afford a shekel
to the owner; for we see that Solomon received a
thousand shekels from this vineyard, and we learn
from Isa. vii. 23, that a thousand silverlings, or shekels, was the profit of a thousand vines. The vines
of Johannisberg are valued at a ducat—about an American dollar—each, according to Michaelis, who thinks
that, with allowance for the change in the value of
money, this price was high even for a valuable vineyard. The whole income of this vineyard would then
have been worth between five and six hundred dollars
to Solomon. While those who were tenants were
obliged to pay this rent, the spouse speaks of a vineyard which was her own, but which she would nevertheless so keep under her own control and manage, as
to be able, while paying the keepers equitable wages,
to offer yearly to the king a thousand pieces of silver
as a testimonial of her love.

Viewed in connection with the parable of the la-
bourers in the vineyard, Matt. xx. 1, and xxi. 33,
these verses illustrate the truth, that we are all the
stewards of God, and that all our property, intellectual endowments, and influence, are things intrusted
to us by God, who will require of us an account of our
stewardship; they furthermore show that were we,
like the spouse in reference to her vineyard, under no
requirement or command to give to Jesus, yet would
we, under the impulse of this love, give him of our
possessions every thing that could be spared from the
necessary demands made on us by justice to others.
The spirit of Jesus, our example, is a spirit of liberali-

ty.* In 2 Cor. viii. 9, the word grace means liberality; "Ye know the liberality of our Lord Jesus Christ, that, though he was rich, yet for your sakes he became poor, that ye through his poverty might be rich." There is an error among men concerning the nature of the title by which they hold their property. When any man has such a claim on a property as to remove at will, under the just sanction of the law, one tenant after another, and place others in their stead, we consider him the legal owner, whatever the ejected tenants may think of their claims; and we feel that the law would not justify him in doing so, unless the possessions were righteously his. Now, God is daily giving us proof of this very kind, that all we have and hold belongs not to ourselves, but to him. At will, he

---

* "An improper use must be called an abuse. Were we pilgrims in a distant land, unable to live happily save in our native country, being miserable in our wanderings, and desiring to end our wretchedness, did we wish to return to our country, we should be obliged to use conveyances by land or by sea, for reaching and enjoying our home; but did the pleasures of the journey and the conveyance of the vehicles delight us so that we might fall into the enjoyment of what we ought only to use, we would grow unwilling to hasten the journey, and becoming involved with those dangerous comforts, would grow alienated from the land whose pleasures could make us blest: thus, in this mortal life, aliens from the Lord, would we return to heaven, our home where we may be truly blest, we must use this world, not enjoy it; that the invisible things of God may be seen, being understood by those things which have been made, that is, that we may understand eternal and spiritual things by things sensible and temporal."—*Augustin. De Doct. Christ.*, book i. 4.

makes one rich and another poor; causes riches to take wings and flee away; removes men from their possessions by death, and causes their wealth to pass into the hands of others; nor does any person think of questioning the justice of these proceedings, or his right to dispose of us at his will. Every thing we have, belonging thus to him, and being held in trust, we cannot repress a liberal spirit and refuse contributions to his cause, without committing a breach of trust and incurring a responsibility fearful to be met in the judgment.*

---

* "Be charitable before wealth make thee covetous, and lose not the glory of the mite. If riches increase, let thy mind hold pace with them; and think it not enough to be liberal, but munificent. Diffuse thy beneficence early, and while thy treasures call thee master. Give not only unto seven, but also unto eight—that is, unto more than many. Though to give unto every one that asketh may seem severe advice, yet give thou also before asking; that is, where want is silently clamorous, and men's necessities, not their tongues, do loudly call for thy mercies. For though sometimes necessitousness be dumb, or misery speak not out, yet true charity is sagacious, and will find out hints for beneficence. Acquaint thyself with the physiognomy of want, and let the dead colours and first lines of necessity suffice to tell thee there is an object for thy bounty. Spare not where thou canst not easily be prodigal, and fear not to be undone by mercy; for since he who hath pity on the poor lendeth unto the Almighty Rewarder, who observes no ides but every day for his payments, charity becomes pious usury, Christian liberality the most thriving industry; and what we adventure in a cock-boat may return in a carrack unto us. He who thus casts his bread upon the water shall surely find it again; for though it falleth to the bottom, it sinks but like the axe of the prophet, to rise again unto him. If avarice be thy

But were there no divine command, and no obliga-
tion thus resting upon us, love would seek to pour its
riches, its all, at the feet of Jesus, and feel such consecration the highest privilege. With such a spirit,
the richest blessings are connected. "Honour the
Lord with thy substance, and with the first fruit of all
thine increase; so shall thy barns be filled with plenty, and thy presses shall burst out with new wine."
Prov. iii. 9. "For this thing the Lord thy God
shall bless thee in all thy works, and in all that thou
puttest thine hand unto." Deut. xv. 10. "He that
soweth bountifully shall reap also bountifully." 2 Cor.
ix. 6. On whom is the blessing pronounced by the
Judge in the last day, "Come, ye blessed of my
Father, inherit the kingdom prepared for you from
the foundation of the world?" On those who fed the
hungry, who gave drink to the thirsty, who sheltered
the stranger, who clothed the naked, who visited the
sick, who sought out the prisoner. While the Mag-
dalen may then rejoice in having followed him from
Galilee to Calvary, to minister unto him; and Mary
in having broken the box of alabaster at the feet of

vice, yet make it not thy punishment. A slave unto mammon
makes no servant unto God. Covetousness cracks the sinews of
faith, numbs the apprehension of any thing above sense, and,
only affected with the certainty of things present, makes a per-
adventure of things to come; lives but unto one world, nor
hopes but fears another; makes their own death sweet unto
others, bitter unto themselves; brings formal sadness, scenical
mourning, and no wet eyes at the grave."—*Sir Thomas Brown's
Works*, vol. iii. 90.

Jesus; and Joseph of Arimathea in having given to the outcast corpse of him who through life had not where to lay his head, a peaceful resting-place in his own new tomb; we may equally rejoice, as he says, "Inasmuch as ye have done it unto one of the least of these my brethren, ye have done it unto me."

VER. 13.—Thou that dwellest in the gardens, the companions hearken to thy voice: cause me to hear it.

The Hebrew puts it beyond doubt that these words are addressed to the spouse, as we suppose by the beloved. "Our first parents had for their residence a beautiful garden, which may have had some influence upon their immediate descendants, in giving them a predilection for such situations. People in England will scarcely be able to appreciate the value which the orientals place on a garden. The food of many of them consists of vegetables, roots, and fruits; their medicines, also, being indigenous, are most of them produced in their gardens. Here they have their fine fruit-trees, and the constant shade; and here they have their wells and places for bathing. See the proprietor, in his undress, walking around his little domain; his fence or wall is so high no one can overlook him: he strolls about to smoke his shroot, to pick up the fruit, and cull the flowers; he cares not for the world; his soul is satisfied with the scenes around him."* See notes on chap. i. 16. Before the fall, "the Lord God took the man and put him in the garden of Eden, to dress it and keep it." Gen. ii. 15.

* Roberts.

The Church is now his spiritual Eden; and the saint is placed in this spiritual garden, to enjoy it and feed on its healing fruits, but not, therefore, to lead an idle life. It is his privilege to enjoy it; his duty, to be engaged in dressing and keeping it. Then do we find the presence of our Lord pleasant to us, and him ready to receive us into communion with himself. Those actuated by the love of Christ feel an interest for the impenitent, and show liberality in the cause of our Lord; and those thus acting are encouraged by Jesus to prayer. The words "vineyard" and "garden" were often used interchangeably by the Jews; the expression, "thou that dwellest in the gardens," is probably applied to the spouse in consequence of her care of the vineyard mentioned in the foregoing verse; and hence this faithfulness on her part is connected with delight and readiness on the part of the beloved to hear her voice in praise and prayer. Those animated by this love, while showing its genuineness by effort and liberality in the cause of Christ, have a lowly opinion of themselves, and need encouragement to come to their Lord. And how sweetly does the beloved address this language to the heart. See notes on chap. ii. 14. Not only has he given us exceedingly great and precious promises; he sends his Holy Spirit into our hearts for constraining us sweetly to the mercy-seat. And in times of trouble, when we feel the insufficiency of the world, and are driven to the necessity of going to the throne of grace, he is but using such dispensations for saying unto us, "Let me hear thy voice." To him no less pleasing is the voice of praise. And that we may never fear he will grow weary with us, he addresses to us these cheering words.

VER. 14.—Make haste, my beloved, and be thou like to a roe, or to a young hart upon the mountains of spices.

See notes, chap. ii. 17. The Song concludes with the same sentiment expressed in different words, and repeated with emphasis, in Rev. xxii. 7, 12, 20. "Behold, I come quickly:" and "Surely I come quickly." These words are properly the answer to the desire of the spouse in the text, sent by the beloved from his dwelling-place on the mountain of myrrh and hill of frankincense, where he abides till the day breaks and the shadows flee away. Thus encouraged to dwell at the mercy-seat, in confidential and constant communion with our Lord on earth, we are becoming fitted for being with him in heaven; and this fitness, combined with the displays of his love before mentioned, carries with it a stronger and stronger desire for the enjoyment of his glory, as it shall be revealed when the Lord perfects that which concerneth us, at his second coming. To this, as the ultimate, absorbing desire of the soul, do all these assurances of the love of Jesus lead. As the book begins with a burst of desire for the love of Christ, as that love can be enjoyed only by his intimate friends, chap. i. 2, it ends with a prayer for the hastening of the time when we shall no longer see him through a glass darkly, but face to face; when there shall be nothing to interfere with the manifestation of his love to us, and the expression of our love to him:

E E

this desire is expressed, and its intenseness shown, by the prayer that he would hasten that happy day, and come with the celerity of a roe, or a young hart bounding over the mountains of spices, and at every step shaking fragrance from the dewy boughs. When Jesus came forth from the ivory palaces, all his garments smell of myrrh, aloes, and cassia: how fragrant will they be when the sacred perfume of his divine nature shall, at his second coming, flow forth around him more boundless, more life-giving, than the atmosphere which encompassed him when in human form on earth. Truly his presence will be more delightful than that of a gazelle through mountains of spices. To the sentiments of chap. ii. 17, is added, "mountains of spices," for associating with the second coming of the beloved every possible idea of delight; and well may he be said to come as a gazelle or fleeting fawn, for his words are, "I come quickly." Rev. xxii. 20. And, "As the lightning cometh out of the east, and shineth even unto the west, so shall also the coming of the Son of man be." Matt. xxiv. 27. To this promise the Holy Spirit has taught us to pray, "Even so, come, Lord Jesus."

To this period, it would be strange if the believer did not look forward with the greatest interest. In regeneration, we were betrothed to the beloved; that day is to be the day of our espousals with "Him who loved us, and gave himself for us." Jesus himself has taught us to view it as the time of our redemption, of the full, glorious, and eternal completion of our salvation. Taught by this blessed Redeemer, the Apostle was comforted in the midst of his chains, by being able to say, "Our citizenship is in heaven: from whence also we look for the Saviour, the Lord Jesus Christ; who shall change our vile body, that it may be fashioned like unto his glorious body." Phil. iii. 20. Were Sir John Franklin, with his companions, yet living, and aware of the efforts made for his deliverance, with what earnestness would he long for the appearance of those sent to rescue him from the desolation of the polar regions, and for the day when he could see again the long lost friends awaiting him in his native country: Amid the wintry desolations of the curse in this world of sin, we know that Jesus our beloved has gone away into heaven, to receive a kingdom unto himself, and return the second time without sin, for the salvation of his saints; and insensible indeed must we be to his love, could we cease to anticipate that period with emotions of unspeakable delight. Æschylus draws an affecting picture of the sad consequences of war, when speaking of the siege of Troy, he says, Mars sends back to friends at home from the so-called field of glory, sad relics burned in the funeral fire, wept with bitter tears, urns filled with ashes, all that remains of what was once men in the vigour of youth.*   But when

> "The day shall come, the great avenging day
> When sins proud glories in the dust shall lay,
> And Satan's power and Satan's self shall fall,
> And one eternal ruin swallow all;"†

and the Captain of our salvation, the King "crowned

---

* Agamemnon of Æschylus, 402.   † See Iliad, iv. 164.

with many crowns," shall come for our final deliverance, he will bring to us—what?—the sad relics of mortality, gathered from the tomb where they had been so long mouldering, formed by his creative power into a body flushed with perennial youth, like the glorious body of him who is glorified with the glory he had with the Father before the foundation of the world.   To that period of deliverance from the bondage of corruption into the liberty of the glory of the sons of God, of release from our warfare with sin, the period that puts an end to the separation from him whom our soul loveth—we may well look forward with earnest longings; and as much as the glory of that unending day, and the splendour of that resurrection morning, surpass the brightness of any day on earth, so much more earnestly "our soul waiteth for the Lord than they that watch for the morning: I say, more than they that watch for the morning." Ps. cxxx. 6.

Animated by these cheering assurances given us by Jesus, the creator of all things, the soul contemplates the world and the heavens, under the light of the great deductions of modern philosophy, and sees amid these ruins, traces of magnificence and grandeur big with the promise of future glory. "If the man of clay has been honoured with such magnificent apartments, and fed at such a luxurious table, may not his undying and reasoning soul count upon a spiritual palace, and sigh for that intellectual repast at which the Master of the feast is to disclose his secrets.   In its rapid and continued expansion, the mind, conscious of its capacity for a higher sphere, feels, even now, that it is advancing to a goal more distant and more cheering than the tomb. Its energies increase and multiply under the encumbrances of age; and even when man's heart is turning into bone, and his joints into marble, his mind can soar to its highest flight, and seize with its firmest grasp. Nor do the affections plead less eloquently for a future home. Age is their season of warm and genial emotion. The objects long and fondly clasped to our bosom have been removed by him who gives, and who takes what he gives; and lingering in the valley of bleeding and of broken hearts, we yearn for that break of day which is to usher in the eternal morn— for that home in the house of many mansions which is already prepared for us—for the promised welcome to the threshold of the blest, where we shall meet again the loved and the lost, and devote the eternity of our being to the service of its almighty Author."*

"He which testifieth these things, saith, Surely I come quickly. Amen. Even so, come, Lord Jesus." "Make haste, my Beloved, and be thou like to a roe or to a young hart, upon the mountains of spices."

* North British Review, No. 11, art. 8. "The Revelations of Astronomy."

THE END.